A SAMPLING OF REVIEWS

"The author of this r_____ a chaplain at the Univer_____ of Pope John Paul II, _____ view has the feel of an _____ that Father Malinski _____ Polish Church as well as_____ now spiritual leader from the_____ days, so we are able to enter with him the early life of the charismatic Pope."
—*The New York Times Book Review*

". . . this biography gives the reader unique insight not only into the personality of the Pope, but also into the history of the Polish nation . . . It makes for engaging reading."
—*Catholic Library World*

"Malinski's style is often rhapsodic, and the book, which moves back and forth between past and present, is easy reading. It offers much interesting information not otherwise available."
—*Religious Studies Review*

"This intimate biography is more than fond reminiscences: it also gives the reader an understanding of the Pope's philosophy and spirituality."
—*Library Journal*

". . . well worth reading. It is a volume one can use for reference, having a handy index, surprising in a book of so few pages . . . it will appeal to all who are interested in knowing about the Pope."
—*Review for Religious*

". . . a thoughtful, sensitive study."
—*Bestsellers*

". . . a warm, anecdotal book . . . should be read by anyone fascinated by the kind of man who comes out of a humble background and rises to the heights of his profession."
—*The New Review of Books and Religion*

"A uniquely intimate picture of John Paul II that will make this book valuable even after more formal biographies are written."

—*The Wall Street Journal*

"A biography of great charm and warmth . . . will be warmly received by a world that wants to know so much more about the amazing man who sits on the throne of Peter."

—*Emmanuel*

"The author intersperses material from the early days of his acquaintance with Karol Wojtyla and the more recent days of his rise in the church to the highest office of the church. But with reasonable care the reader will find this method makes the picture all the more vivid and memorable."

—*Denver Post*

MIECZYSLAW MALINSKI

Pope John Paul II

THE LIFE OF KAROL WOJTYLA

TEXT COMPLETE AND UNABRIDGED

Translated by P.S. Falla

IMAGE BOOKS
A Division of Doubleday & Company, Inc.
Garden City, New York
1982

Image Book edition published September 1982 by special arrangement with The Crossroad Publishing Company, 575 Lexington Avenue, New York, N.Y. 10022

Printed in the United States of America

Library of Congress Cataloging in Publication Data

Maliński, Mieczysław.
    Pope John Paul II.

    "Text complete and unabridged."
    Includes index.
    1. John Paul II, Pope, 1920–   . 2. Popes—Biography. I.
Title. II. Title: Pope John Paul Second. III. Title: Pope John
Paul 2.
BX1378.5.M35 1982   282'.092'4 [B]
ISBN 0-385-18218-X   AACR2
Library of Congress Catalog Card Number: 82-45205

Acknowledgments: All photographs unless otherwise noted © by M. Malinski. The rights in all photographs are reserved. For rights in those © by M. Malinski, contact The Crossroad Publishing Company. All footnotes in this book were supplied by the translator.

Contents

I

A Polish Pope

I had come out of my room to watch the evening news on television when a foolish-faced nun rushed along the corridor exclaiming, "It says on the radio that they've elected a Polish Pope—Wyszynski or some such name!"

Suddenly everything and everybody seemed to me unreal—the long-faced sister and the convent at Münster where I had been staying for the past four days.

"If it's a Polish cardinal, it must be Wojtyla," I replied without pausing to think.

"Yes, maybe that was it."

I felt astounded and overwhelmed. With a tiny part of my mind I managed to doubt the news, to tell myself that it might be a mistake—either the nun had heard wrong or it simply wasn't true.

We went along to the television room. I pretended to be composed and even made jokes, but it felt as though somebody else were speaking, as though I were listening to my own voice from a distance. I reminded the sister that I had been saying for a long time that something like this was a real possibility—but I realized now that although I had known this intellectually, I had not in the least believed it.

Suddenly my fellow students, who had also heard the radio news, burst into the room. The Korean who was doing a thesis on the Old Testament congratulated me with his usual exuberance, and the Argentinian, who could not stand Italians, embraced me warmly, shouting and waving his arms. Only the Portuguese, calm as ever, walked over to turn on the TV set and then take a bottle of wine out of the cupboard. The Swiss was not there— on the previous evening he and I had been arguing about the Polish cardinals and Wojtyla's chance of being elected. . . . I laughed and replied to the congratulations as best I could, but I still felt half paralyzed—I could not take in the news or believe that it had really happened.

At last the television rescued me from having to say anything more or answer the barrage of questions. The announcer declared that Cardinal Wojtyla had been elected in a surprise vote, and added that a month ago he had accompanied the Primate of Poland, Cardinal Wyszynski, on a visit to the Federal Republic of Germany. A moment or two later the screen showed St. Peter's Square crowded with 200,000 people, the famous chimney illuminated by searchlights and Cardinal Felici on the balcony announcing to the City and the world: *"Habemus papam Carlum"*—instead of "Carolum"; then he pronounced very clearly, indeed overclearly, the name "Wojtyla."

The silence that followed alarmed me, accustomed as I was to the piazza and the reactions of the crowd on such occasions. There should have been an outburst of applause, and the silence seemed to me a disaster, as though the crowd had refused to acknowledge the election. By this time, however, the reporter was explaining that the people had not understood the name pronounced by Cardinal Felici and were frantically asking one another who it could be. Some thought it must be a Negro. It was only after ten or twenty seconds that the crowd, who had been perplexed by the foreign name, began to realize that it was a Pole. When they did so, the news traveled around the square with the speed of lightning, and the frozen silence gave place to an outburst of joy.

Next there was a pause during which a huge colored carpet was hung over the balcony. A small procession emerged, preceded by the cross, and—I had waited tensely for this moment, still unable to believe it—the new Pope appeared on the balcony, with cardinals on either side of him. The Pope—but I could not yet think of him as Pope; to me he was Karol. All the same, I hardly recognized him—whether because of the unfamiliar vestments, or the broad stole protruding above his head, or just because of the bad light. He made stiff gestures in response to the frenzied acclamation of the crowd. In a moment, however, I realized that it was nothing to do with the light or the vestments, but that he himself looked quite different. "He must have been crying," I thought.

The cheers died down, and I wondered what the Pope would do next. His predecessor, John Paul I, had left the balcony without a word. I was in an agony of fear lest Karol would do the same. If only he would say just one word, just something in Italian like "Blessed be Jesus Christ"—not simply leave the balcony without speaking. Then, as I looked and listened, I heard his voice:

"Dilettissimi fratelli e sorelle!"

At once there was an outburst of delight all over the square. The Pope stood for a long time watching the crowd, and it seemed to me that his face gradually resumed its normal appearance. At first I could not understand why those few words had caused such an explosion of joy. Then I understood the reason: when the crowd heard that the new Pope was a Pole they feared that he would not be able to speak Italian, and they were overjoyed to hear his greeting, spoken in a strong voice and with a perfect accent. At last the applause died down, and the Pope continued:

"We are all still plunged in grief at the death of our beloved father, Pope John Paul I."

More applause, more cheering. I may have been mistaken, but it seemed to me that this time it was not only because of the tribute to his predecessor but because his words showed that he could speak Italian fluently and had not just memorized a phrase of greeting in that language.

"And now the Most Eminent Cardinals have chosen a new Bishop of Rome."

Another wave of applause. I felt as if I were at last hearing Karol's voice, which I had been unble to recognize before. I had blamed this on the positioning of the microphone, the noise from the square, the distortion due to the loudspeaker. But no, at first it had not been his real voice. Now I could hear his own speech-tune once again, though he was not yet speaking quite naturally.

"They have called him from a faraway country, but one which has always been close to the community of Christian faith and tradition."

More applause. How glad I am that he is talking, how very glad. If only he would go on, if only he would speak a little more.

"I was afraid to accept this choice, but I did so in a spirit of humility and obedience to our Lord and complete trust in his most holy mother, the Madonna."

Another outburst of joy. This time it came as no surprise to me—it was due to the magic word "Madonna," the quintessence of Italian religious feeling. In the last few years since the Council, various mistaken ideas have tended to eliminate it from the vocabulary of Christians and Italians; hence the crowd's gratitude at hearing it uttered in such circumstances and restored to its proper dignity.

"I do not know whether I can express myself properly in your"—here the Pope hesitated and corrected himself—"in *our* Italian language."

Another burst of applause. The crowd, listening keenly to every accent and every syllable, at once understood the reason for his hesitation.

"If I make mistakes, please correct me."

This time the response took the form not only of cheers but of shouts: "Yes, we will!" The Pope continued:

"Today I stand before you to make a profession of our common faith, our hope and trust in the mother of Christ and the mother of the Church, and to set out on a fresh stage of the history of the Church, with God's help and that of men and women."

The address was over. As people were still clapping and shouting for joy the prelates on the balcony brought a book and opened it before the Pope, who chanted from it in a strong, melodious voice and blessed the City and the world in the name of the Father, Son and Holy Spirit. The cheers and applause continued, and the Pope continued to wave for a long time before withdrawing from the balcony.

That was the end of the broadcast from the Vatican, and the announcer proceeded to other news. I went back to my room. So it was true—I knew now that it was true, I had seen it with my own eyes. Yet even now there was something unreal about it—I had not assimilated the news, I could not yet think of it as just one fact among others.

The telephone rang—a call from abroad. A friend of mine, a reader in a publishing house who had recently published two of my books, offered congratulations. I was pleased, but somewhat taken aback. Suddenly he said, "Couldn't you write a biography of the new Pope?"

"A biography?" I said in amazement.

"Well, you said you had known him for some time."

"For some time—my goodness, yes, you could call it that."

"For quite a long time, in fact. How many years exactly?"

"How many years? Since 1940. When you say I know him, that isn't really the right word; we were friends."

"Why do you say 'were friends,' Father? Did anything happen to put an end to your friendship?"

"Well, if I said 'the Pope is a friend of mine' it would sound absurd or at least conceited, don't you think?"

"So you wouldn't call him a friend nowadays?"

"Well, now you put it like that—to answer as honestly as I can, I do regard him as my friend in the deepest sense of the word, and there is nothing I can add to that statement."

"All the same, Father, I would like you to write a life of the present Pope."

"I have never dreamed of doing such a thing. It seems to me that there is something wrong about it, a lack of delicacy anyway. It's one thing to write about imaginary people, or even someone who has lived and died. But to write about a man who is still alive and, please God, has many years before him—I must say I don't like the idea at all, not in the very least."

"It needn't be long, just your own recollections."

"I'll think about it," I replied.

Less than half an hour later the telephone rang again. This time it was a director of a publishing firm in yet another country.

"You must write the Pope's biography. You knew him, didn't you?"

"I've just been talking to a publisher. I made a kind of promise to him."

"Well, you could do a selection of his pastoral letters."

"That's an excellent idea. All right, I'll try and do something about it."

I went on thinking about the idea of a biography—but what would it mean, and was I capable of doing it? In any case it could not be more than my own memories of things we had done and experienced together, of what I had heard and seen for myself. Put like that, it didn't sound so absurd. To understand the Pope as he was today one would have to describe the past, the time when his personality was developing most intensively— that is to say, the war years.

Dr. Gunther Mees telephoned—a friend of many years' standing, editor of the weekly *Kirche und Leben*, to which I have contributed a column for some years past.

"Congratulations—you know what about! Listen, I've held up our latest number for the result of the conclave. Can you write something on the new Pope? A short piece, for the time being?"

"All right."

Mees came and called for me, we went to his office and I helped him choose pictures for publication. I started to write, but my notes developed into a long article. We agreed that I would finish work by the morning, and he drove me home.

The KNA (Catholic News Agency) rang up from

Bonn, asking for a long article on the Pope for next day. This I agreed to do.

I telephoned to Cracow. For a long time I got no answer—everybody was engaged or out. When I finally got through to someone, he replied: "Why are you surprised? They're all talking about it to one another, or else they're out on the streets. The whole town has gone mad. The churches are crammed, there are Masses of thanksgiving everywhere, and the market square, the streets and parks are full of people with flags and banners, playing guitars and singing for all they're worth."

"That's incredible."

"You're right, it is. Complete strangers are embracing, kissing and crying."

"It sounds crazy."

"Crazy's the word. It's like the day the war ended—a different feeling, of course, but the same excitement. But I must stop now, I'm going to Mass at St. Anne's [the university church]. What a shame you're not here!"

"Yes, it is."

I went on writing, but it was a slow business. I could not choose among the memories that crowded in on me. I would have liked to include everything, but I had to stop somewhere. The hours sped by, and I was afraid the noise of my typewriter would wake up my sleeping colleagues. When I finished it was four in the morning. I had only written eight pages, but it would be too long for the KNA—they'd have to cut it themselves. I went to bed, but I could not sleep. Everything I had been writing about was as clear in my memory as though it had happened the day before, instead of nearly forty years ago. What had it been like—my goodness, what had it been like? . . .

2

The Occupation

I had just been to early Mass at my parish church, St. Stanislaw Kostka's in the Debnicki quarter of Cracow. How old was I?—sixteen, maybe seventeen. Just outside the door was a slim, smiling man of about forty in a dark trench coat, his fair hair combed back. He was looking at me, and was evidently waiting for me. I have never liked surprises. I looked closely in case I might have met him somewhere before—but no, I had never seen him in my life. I started to walk past him, but he stopped me.

"Good morning. Do you mind if I talk to you?"

I bristled at this approach—it reminded me of the police.

"No, what about?" I replied in a cool, not to say hostile tone. What could he be—a spy, an informer, a Gestapo man, somebody from the underground?

"I have noticed you for a long time now. You nearly always come to early Mass."

This puzzled me even more. He went on:

"And so I wondered whether you would care to join our 'Living Rosary' circle."

So that was all! I still felt reluctant, but replied as politely as I could, "Yes, of course why not?"

The stranger was still irksome to me, despite his smile and tactful manner. I wanted to shake him off, but he continued:

"Do you mind if I come with you? I expect you're going home, and if I am not mistaken we go the same way. I beg your pardon, I forgot to introduce myself. My name is Jan Tyranowski; I live in Rozana Street, and I believe you live in Madalinski Street."

Still feeling irritated, I mumbled my own name, "Malinski."

"I expect you're still at school?"

I did not like talking about myself. The first years of the German occupation had taught me a lot, young as I was. Above all they had taught me not to talk about myself or other people—certainly not to give names or addresses, or any personal details.

"Yes, I am."

"What school do you go to?"

I liked the conversation less and less, but replied, "The School of Engineering."

"Then we're both in the same line—I'm concerned with machines too."

I looked at him skeptically. With his slight build, slim figure and delicate features, he was not at all my idea of an engineer.

"That surprises you? Well, I have a sewing machine—three, in fact. I'm a tailor by profession."

I felt more and more disillusioned. He went on talking cheerfully in a soft voice, almost a whisper, and seemed to have no idea what I was thinking. We turned into Rozana Street. I did not like it either, and usually avoided going that way even if it was a short cut. It was a narrow lane between ancient buildings, and I had often thought what a convenient place it would be for a police roundup.

We stopped at No. 11. "This is where I live," said my companion. "Why don't you come in for a minute or two? I'd like to chat for a bit longer, and it's not a good idea to stand about in the street."

I still don't know why I said "Yes"—perhaps it was because I agreed with him that the street was always unsafe. He pushed open the front door and we climbed up a dark, narrow stairway to his flat. A narrow hall led to a dark sitting room full of ancient furniture.

"Do sit down. Will you have some tea?"

I looked around. My first impression had been of untidiness, but that was a mistake: despite the clutter of furniture, the flat was well looked after. There were pictures, some old portraits, and quantities of books on the shelves. It was not, I thought, the sort of flat where you'd expect a tailor to live, and he himself was an unusual type. . . . He brought in the tea and said:

"As you see, I have quite a few books. I'd be glad to lend them to you."

I didn't want his books. Although in good condition, they were old and had a used look, and in my eyes this was a disqualification.

"What subject are you interested in?" he asked.

"Cars," I replied somewhat defiantly.

"But I'm sure you are also interested in people's characters and how they are formed, in types of behavior and the workings of the mind."

He could not have known that he had hit the nail on the head—or could he?

"Yes," I said eagerly. "And not only myself, but I have a friend with whom I have discussed such things for a long time past, and not only discussed them, but tried to do something about them." To my own surprise, I was now talking freely. Suddenly there was a knock at the door.

"Excuse me, that must be Karol. He should have arrived before, but something must have held him up. I'd like you to meet each other."

Tyranowski went to the door and returned with his friend, a youth whom I had not seen before. He was of middle height, two or three years older than myself, with broad shoulders, but somewhat stooped. Our host introduced us: "This is Karol, and this is Mieczyslaw."

As we shook hands, the newcomer added in a clear voice that his surname was Wojtyla. Again I mumbled my own name indistinctly, as was customary under the Occupation—unless one gave a different name, to be on the safe side. Meanwhile Tyranowski went on talking cheerfully.

"Well, this is a meeting of two worlds—science and the humanities. Mieczyslaw wants to be an engineer, and Karol here is an actor. So far he's studied philology, but what he'll study in the future remains to be seen."

This was said in a significant tone that did not appeal to me either.

I glanced at Karol suspiciously. He did not look like an actor, at any rate not of the handsome type. He had a good-natured face with a strong lower jaw, deep-set eyes and a broad forehead; his dark brown hair was disheveled, his clothes neat but rather shabby-looking.

"I'm sorry, Mieczyslaw, but we must say good-bye for the present; Karol and I have an appointment. But I expect we'll meet again soon."

I still did not care for this way of taking our acquaintance for granted, but Tyranowski continued: "What about next week?" He took out his diary and suggested a day and hour. "And before that, no doubt we'll meet to say the rosary after evening service, won't we?"

I made no reply, saying to myself that this was by no means as certain as he imagined. And that is how it all began.

"Out of pure curiosity"—as I told myself—I did go next Sunday to join the group of young people saying the rosary after evening service. Apart from Tyranowski and Karol I knew nobody there. The devotions were led by a parish priest of the Salesian order whom I knew by sight, wearing a surplice and stole. He conducted the prayers in a rather impersonal manner and did not add any words of his own: I was given a white card with a text relating to the Mystery I was to recite, and that was all. I waited for a few minutes on leaving the church, and noticed that Karol, after a short conversation, was also alone. I went up to him, and asked where he lived.

"At 10 Tyniec Street."

This was in my own quarter of Debnicki. I thought I knew all the boys of my own age living there, but could not remember having seen him.

"Strange that we haven't met," I remarked. "I live in Madalinski Street, quite close by."

"Yes, but we only moved to Cracow a year before the war."

"Oh, I see. Where from?"

"Wadowice. I graduated from school there. My father brought me to Cracow in 1938 so that I could study Polish philology."

"Is your mother not alive?"

"No, she died in 1929."

"Have you any brothers and sisters?"

"No, none."

"What does your father do?"

"He was in the army, but now he's retired."

We parted at the gate in front of his house.

Some days later I happened to meet Karol in the street. He was dressed in dark blue worker's overalls and clogs, and I barely recognized him except for his stooping figure. I was curious to know if he was really an actor. To my question he replied:

"That's an exaggeration, though I did act in school plays at Wadowice. At present, some friends and I have got up something a bit different. We call it the 'rhapsodic theater.'"

This was a new word to me. I asked what it meant.

"It's a long story. But you might say we are trying to carry on an old Polish tradition, the artistic recitation of poetry or poetic prose."

"You mean like the old-time storytellers?"

"Not exactly. The main idea is to pronounce every vowel and every word with the greatest possible precision, not slurring or swallowing anything but at the same time not exaggerating, so that the general effect is attractive and natural."

This sounded to me rather funny and unimportant. "Is that all?" I asked disappointedly.

"We also try to read whole sentences giving full weight to the punctuation—commas, full stops, exclamation marks—so as to convey everything that the text contains and make it fully intelligible."

I still could not quite see the point of all this.

"Is that all you mean by the 'rhapsodic theater'?"

"Yes. We generally say our lines in front of a dark curtain, and we may do a bit of dressing up or use a prop or two, some kind of symbol to enrich the text."

"But you don't have scenery or perform the actions?"

"No, not as a rule."

This seemed to me a poor kind of theater. Before the war I myself had played in amateur theatricals, the real kind. However, I said politely:

"I'd like to see it sometime. Where do you perform?"

"In private houses, of course."

"So it's really an underground theater?"

"Yes, it is."

"And who's in charge?"

"Mieczyslaw Kotlarczyk, master of the word."

A pompous expression, I thought. Karol noticed my re-action and added, "He's an old friend of mine from Wadowice. He taught Polish there at a private school for girls."

I met Kotlarczyk on another occasion, when Karol and I were walking in town. He was a rather short man with black hair and a bristly face, but what chiefly surprised me was his voice—it was hoarse and dull, quite the oppo-site to what I expected, in fact little more than a loud whisper. I told Karol of my disappointment.

"Yes, but you'd be amazed how well he can recite in spite of his weak voice. He's a marvelous teacher too—he can really draw you into the spirit of great literature." Karol was full of admiration and enthusiasm.

"Whose works do you perform?"

"Just now we're up the ears in Norwid. Do you know him?"*

"A bit, but rather from hearsay," I replied shame-facedly.

"You should read him—it's worthwhile. I think he's our greatest poet. I'll lend him to you. You might start with *Promethidion*—but take it quietly. Would you like to hear some?"

"Yes, please."

Karol began to recite, and I listened with growing ad-

* Cyprian Norwid (1821–83), Polish poet and dramatist. *Promethidion* (1851) is a colloquy in verse about the philosophy of labor and art.

miration. He really spoke beautifully—I had no idea poetry could sound like that. After finishing the passage he
said, "Do you like it?"

"Yes."

"Then I'll bring you the book. Where exactly do you
live?—because I'm rather hard to get hold of."

I gave him my address, and told everybody at home
that a new friend would be coming to see me, so that
they should not be alarmed. He turned up one evening
and we persuaded him to stay for supper, though he was
in a hurry. There was not much to eat in those days, but
my sisters produced scrambled eggs, which he enjoyed.
We all talked for a long time, and the girls managed to
find out all they wanted to know about my new friend.
It turned out that he was employed by the Solvay chemi-
cal company.

"What do you do there?"

"I'm a workman. My first job was to look after the cars
carrying limestone to the factory."

"You mean the ones that travel by an overhead line?"

"Yes. But that was only for a short time. What I do
now is to make sure the water for the boilers is free from
minerals, because otherwise they form a deposit on the
boiler plates and lessen the heating capacity."

I knew about this: steam boilers were one of the subjects we learned about at the technical college.

"I prefer the night shift, because there's less going on
in the factory, and once the right quantity of lime and
other substances has been delivered, I can spend the time
reading."

It turned out that the house in Tyniec Street where
he lived had belonged to his mother's family.

"Were you an only child?"

"No, I had a brother, twelve years older than I. He

died in 1938, of scarlet fever. He was a doctor, and was assistant physician at a hospital in Bielsko."

"Were there just the two of you?"

"No, I had a sister, but she died as a child. She was older than I, but younger than my brother."

My sisters kept plying Karol with questions, to which he replied freely. He spoke of a public performance of Slowacki's *Balladyna*,* directed by Kotlarczyk at Wadowice, in which he had played the part of the magnate Kirkor. This, it appeared, had been a tremendous success. He had also played the leading role in Wyspianski's *Sigismund Augustus*,† and had helped to stage-manage the production.

We talked for so long that I became anxious, as it was nearly curfew time. I said, "You'd better go now, Karol, it's getting late."

I went down with him and opened the front door. It was dark outside and at first we could see nothing whatever, as usually happens when one has just come out of a lighted room. We could hear the rapid steps of a belated pedestrian; then a car came slowly by, lighting up the cat's eyes in the roadway with its dimmed headlights. The stillness was broken by a distant burst of fire from a submachine gun.

"Hold on a minute," I said; then, after straining my ears for further sounds, "You'd better make a run for it now, it's really late."

I shut the front door and went back upstairs. My sisters and brother were delighted with my new friend.

* Juliusz Slowacki (1809–49), romantic poet and playwright. *Balladyna* (1834) is a dramatized fairy tale.

† Stanislaw Wyspianski (1869–1907): poet, dramatist, painter and draftsman. Sigismund II Augustus, King of Poland, 1520–72.

"He's a splendid chap. You must ask him again. What fun he is to talk to! Where did you meet him?"

After that Karol came to see us several times, generally in the evening, for a chat over his favorite dish of scrambled eggs.

I also saw more of Tyranowski. His world and that of his friends was one of thorough discipline and self-control; every moment of the day was organized for either activity or relaxation, and time was regularly made for spiritual exercises: reading of scripture and devotional works, Mass if possible, and in any case a few minutes' prayer in church. This program went on for a period of months, with weekly meetings at Tyranowski's flat where we would compare notes on our activities. For this purpose we kept a notebook in which, every evening, we recorded the day's doings under such headings as "reading scripture," "morning prayer," "evening prayer," "afternoon recreation" etc., with a tick or a cross according to whether they had taken place or not; we would also note how many hours we had spent on homework.

I once asked Karol how he had gotten to know Tyranowski. He replied:

"It's rather a long story. In February 1940 the Salesian fathers organized a Lenten retreat for young men at our church in Debnicki. Did you go to it?"

"No, I used to take part in a lot of parish activities, but as you may remember, at the very beginning of the Occupation the Germans deported the priests to Auschwitz—about seven altogether, including Father Swierc, our parish priest, and Fr. Walenty Waloszek, who taught me religion at primary school."

"Yes, I've heard about it."

"So after that a new lot of priests came along, and I got rather out of touch with the parish."

"Well, after the retreat, people wanted to continue it in some way, and Fr. Jan Mazarski, a biblical scholar and a lecturer at Cracow University, organized weekly meetings to discuss theology."

"Yes, I remember going to them once or twice."

"That was when the 'Living Rosary' was started, and Tyranowski was put in charge of it because Father Matlak, who was then parish priest, said he simply hadn't time."

"I see. But what else do you know about Tyranowski?"

"The last time I went to see him, an old lady brought us tea from the kitchen. That turned out to be his mother. He also has a younger brother Edward."

"But what about himself? How old is he, anyway?"

"He was born in 1900, and the family have lived at 11 Rozana Street for a long time. His father was a tailor; he himself first worked as an accountant after leaving high school, but afterward he gave that up and worked with his father and brother—evidently he wanted a quieter life in which he would have more time for prayer and meditation. Before the war he worked as a secretary for Catholic Action, but he says himself that in those days he was more of an organizer than a truly religious man. Apparently he underwent a major conversion of some kind later on—he doesn't like talking about it, or talking about himself in any way."

"Is it true that he once had psychiatric treatment?"

"I've heard it said, but I don't know if it is so. In any case ever since I've known him I've found him the most normal person in the world."

I observed with close attention, not to say suspicion,

Tyranowski's method of "taking me in hand." He began by talking of matters that interested me most, such as self-education and the formation of one's own character. He explained to me the ideas of modern psychologists and teachers about human types and temperaments, and I realized that he knew these thoroughly. But as time went on he turned to more religious and even theological subjects, and I came to enjoy our meetings and conversations less and less. There was something importunate, even bossy about his manner, and I kept wondering what he really wanted of me. Besides, there was an old-fashioned air about his talk—the vocabulary and the advice to make excerpts, or "notes" as he called them, from ancient religious tomes.

"I ask you, Tanquerey on morals and theology—could anything be more boring?" I once said to Karol.

Karol, as was his manner, listened patiently and at length to my complaints and objections. Finally he said, "Yes, I agree, Tyranowski's language is formal and old-fashioned, but you mustn't mind that. What is really important is the man behind the language, and the truth he tries to express in his awkward vocabulary. He really is a person who lives close to God, or rather with God."

This, I found, was indeed the key to Tyranowski's personality. Although his "fusty" language, as I called it, still got on my nerves, I listened attentively and realized that everything he said was directed to a single object, the truth of God dwelling within us. All his efforts, instructions, advice and methods of teaching were designed to show us, and me in particular, how to remain in the presence of God, both in our prayers and in our daily lives.

After a time I discovered that my first opinion had been too hasty: his religious mentors were not theologians such as Tanquerey, but St. John of the Cross and

St. Teresa of Avila. He did not introduce us to their works at the beginning, but at a later stage he lent them to me.

Reviewing his system objectively, I realized that it followed a coherent plan. He did not unsettle us by saying at the beginning what he thought ought to be left till the end, but took us through each stage calmly and methodically, almost with a bookkeeper's precision, until we reached the essential core of his teaching—namely what he called the plenitude of inner life, or, in different language, fellowship with God.

He taught us, patiently and at length, what he understood by meditation. The reader may be put off by this term, as I was; but as Tyranowski explained, it does not denote merely an activity of the mind, but the fact of experiencing with one's whole being the presence of God within us. It is not the intellect but the will and feelings that have to be trained, so that with the help of grace, we may perfect ourselves in the theological virtues of faith, hope and charity, and be capable of receiving the gifts of the Holy Spirit.

I began to visit the parish church more often. Sometimes I would see Karol there, generally kneeling on the bare floor or at the railing in front of the high altar, his head bowed and resting on his hands.

3

The Pope's Message

When my alarm clock rang I awoke feeling fully refreshed, as though I had slept eight hours and not two. I began the day by concelebrating Mass with my fellow priests in the nuns' chapel, for the intention of Pope John Paul II. Despite all my efforts I could not really take in the fact that I was praying for the Pope and that the Pope was also Karol. Every now and then I felt a kind of sob or whimper of joy, a reaction I could neither control nor understand.

At breakfast almost the whole community was present, including our director, a German priest named Willy. Everyone was still in a state of amazement over the election, and to my relief they were so full of their own ideas and interpretations that I was able to remain silent. Someone finally asked me what I thought, but before I could open my mouth the others had started up again. Breakfast went on for an unconscionable time; at last we got up from table, but the corridor was still alive with discussion.

I looked through the papers. The *Münstersche* and *Westfälische*, the *Süddeutsche* and *Frankfurter Zeitung* all carried full front-page stories emphasizing the surprise (or "shock," as some reporters called it) and accounting for it in various ways. Some advanced the rather vague theory of a "compromise Pope"; others thought the decision represented a positive choice, but they knew too little about Karol Wojtyla to make any useful comment. Others again spoke of him as conservative, pious, devoted to Our Lady—in short, the conventional idea of a Polish cleric. The first predictions as to the new reign followed the same lines: "It will mean a shift to the right, a more conservative, almost pre-Conciliar trend. Nothing very outstanding, however: a pious man, but not especially intelligent. No doubt he took the name John Paul II because he intends to be like his predecessor, only in a Polish version. He even laughs in the same way."

Then the publisher on the telephone once again: "Have you made up your mind, Father?"

"I suppose so—what can I do with people like you?" I replied jokingly. The memories of bygone years were crowding in on me, and I was a little vexed by some of the things that others were writing. . . .

"Incidentally, have you seen some of the gossip that the press have already dragged up?"

"No, not yet."

"One story is that the Pope was engaged and even married, and that it was after the Germans shot the girl at Wadowice that he decided to be a priest. Is that true, by any chance?"

I was taken aback until I remembered something that had happened to an older friend of Karol's. Then I replied, laughing: "Yes, it's true—in much the same way as the Radio Erivan joke.* You remember, a listener asks if

* An imaginary station from which mildly satirical jokes were broadcast in the Soviet Union. Erivan is the capital of Soviet Armenia.

it's true that they are giving away bicycles on the Red Square in Moscow. Yes, the reply goes—except that they're not giving them away, only one citizen has had his bicycle stolen. . . . It's the same thing in this case: there was a man at Wadowice whose fiancée died and who then decided to be a priest, but his name, as it happens, wasn't Wojtyla. I could tell you his real name if necessary."

"No, you needn't. But it only shows that you must write something to counter the avalanche of gossip, guesswork, suspicion and misunderstanding that has already begun and will go on for a long time. The more true facts you can give, the better—things you know about at first hand, things you shared with him."

"All right, I will."

An hour later he rang up once more: "I've talked to my director. He would like about three hundred pages, with photographs—but we must have it quickly, in four weeks' time."

"Four weeks? But it takes me longer than that to write an article."

"Yes, but all you have to do this time is to remember things just as they were."

"Great heavens—if only it were as easy as that!"

The radio this morning says that, after early Mass and before the conclave dispersed, the Pope read to the cardinals a *messaggio* setting out the guiding principles of his pontificate. John Paul I had done the same, but, as the commentator observed, that message was clearly drafted by the Curia, whereas the present Pope's was the work of his own hand.

As I waited to hear the text I remembered how, at table in the Collegio in Rome, Karol Wojtyla had expressed the view that John Paul I's message might really

be his own work, while I maintained that it could not be
. . . I now listened to the new Pope's message with all
the attention that its importance deserved.

To begin with, the Pope declared that he intended to
be faithful to the Second Vatican Council and that his
first task would be to carry out its principles and to create
a new mentality in the Church in accordance with its
teaching. He directed particular attention to the Constitution *Lumen gentium,* which he called the Council's
Magna Carta. He went on to say that he wished to give
a fuller meaning to the collegiality of bishops and that it
was the task of the synod to guarantee a uniform spirit
in the Church. Then he appealed to all the faithful to
remain loyal to the Church by adhering to the magis-
terium of St. Peter, especially in doctrinal matters. The
objective of doctrine must be intimately realized, and
must be defended against the threats that beset it on
every hand. There must also be loyalty to the liturgical
norms prescribed by church authority: this ruled out various uncontrolled innovations in different rites. Finally,
loyalty meant respect for church discipline, which was a
guarantee of the order of the Mystical Body. For the
multitude of members of the Church, loyalty meant
readiness to obey its teaching authority and those who
are responsible for the Church.

Turning to non-Catholic Christians, the Pope said that
he could not forget other churches and denominations
and that he attached great importance to ecumenism.

He also addressed himself to the peoples of the whole
world, and declared that it was his wish to serve them.
By virtue of his mission he desired to contribute to all
causes involving peace, development and justice, while
making clear that his motives were purely religious and
he had no intention of intervening in politics. The
Church, he emphasized, was not concerned with catego-

ries of the secular order, and the duty of rapprochement with peoples was exclusively a religious one. It was the Church's task to strengthen the spiritual basis of human society so as to do away with the inequalities and misunderstandings that threatened the whole world. The Pope therefore wished to open his arms to all who suffered injustice or discrimination or were restricted in their freedom of conscience or religion, for he wanted all forms of injustice to cease in order that human beings might live as their dignity required. Finally, he said of himself, "Our own person must disappear in the fullness of the dignity of the functions we desire to perform." He asked for prayers to support him in the work he was about to undertake.

The radio commentator attempted, with great delicacy, to evaluate this document. He emphasized the declaration of fidelity to Vatican II, but seemed surprised by the stress laid on the collegiality of papal power. He took a favorable view of the assessment of the Church's place in the world and its concern not only with religion but with spiritual matters in general, such as concerned every state and the whole of mankind in its efforts to build a new order.

Having heard the message and the commentary, I thought it remarkable that a man who had been appraised in somewhat patronizing terms should have been able to produce a document of such high quality.

That evening a further sensational piece of news came from the Vatican. On the first day of his pontificate, at 5 P.M., the Pope had gone to the Gemelli Clinic to visit an invalid friend of his, Bishop Andrzej Deskur.

Who would have thought it! . . . I had read in the papers that Andrzej had been taken ill: on the previous Friday he had suffered an embolism of the artery leading to the brain; he had been paralyzed and was taken to the clinic in an unconscious state. He was a friend of mine too, and I knew how close he was to the present Pope. I remembered how, in 1946, he had entered the seminary in the Podzamcze district of Cracow, as a student of civil law. Karol and Andrzej, Staszek Starowieyski and I were linked in those days by our work for Bratniak, a students' self-governing organization. Later Andrzej left the seminary to study in Rome, and remained there. He worked closely with Karol during Vatican II, where his knowledge of the Vatican was specially useful, and later when Karol stayed in Rome for sessions of the Episcopal Synod.

The Pope drove to the clinic in an open car, acclaimed by crowds of the faithful who were as surprised by his trip as were the Vatican officials and the world at large. When he arrived he greeted the doctors and staff, went to the Bishop's room and stayed there for a quarter of an hour. Unfortunately the patient was unconscious the whole time.

The Holy Father then spoke briefly to the other patients and the hospital staff. Characteristically, his address was partly humorous and partly solemn and dignified. He began by thanking his escort for protecting him from the enthusiasm of the citizens of Rome, which, he said, was so exuberant that he himself might have ended up in the hospital. Then he said he had come to visit not only his old friend, but also all the other patients. Finally he told them, "You have within you the great strength and power of the suffering Christ. I thank God for this meeting between us."

Before leaving he thanked the doctors and staff for looking after Bishop Deskur and all the other patients. As he was about to go, his secretary reminded him that he should confer his pastoral blessing on those present.

At this the Pope remarked jokingly, "Ah yes, Monsignor Caprio has just reminded me how the Pope ought to behave—I forgot to give you my blessing."

When Gunther rang me that evening he observed admiringly that for a man from a "faraway country" the Pope certainly seemed to feel at home in the City. Indeed, it was probably the only time on record that a Pope had gone to visit sick people in Rome on the very day after the conclave. The radio commentators, at any rate, described it as an unprecedented event. But perhaps the world, and the journalists in particular, were not so impressed by the visit itself as by the manner of it: the Pope's completely free, natural and simple behavior, the cheerful friendliness with which he treated everyone, and the way in which he made jokes about himself and the situation.

To judge from all I had seen on television and newsstands, on the first day after the conclave the world press was already publishing a huge amount about the Pope, both text and pictures. Most magazines had made it their chief news and devoted several pages to it. The Italian radio had been broadcasting long talks on the Pope since early morning, interviewing both eminent and simple people in Italy and in foreign countries. Television news bulletins in Italy were almost entirely concerned with the new Pope. Everyone emphasized the surprise of the election itself and its enthusiastic reception by the Italian people, even though they had been so used to having a Pope of their own nationality.

The papers pointed out that the Pope was not a stranger to Rome—he had studied there thirty years ago, he had taken an active part throughout Vatican II and in every session of the Synod of Bishops. Two years earlier he had conducted a retreat for the Holy Father Paul VI, which testifies to his theological and pastoral qualifications. At the same time it was unanimously pointed out that his election marked a turning point for the Church. In a long interview on Italian television the Polish Bishop Rubin, secretary to the synod and a friend of John Paul II, pointed out that as Cardinal Wojtyla and Metropolitan of Cracow he was also prorector of the Polish church of St. Stanislaw and of the Polish hospice in Rome. Bishop Rubin recalled his many contacts with the Cardinal during the Council and sessions of the synod, and spoke from personal experience of his knowledge and wisdom.

German television programs were in similar vein. The surprise was already of a somewhat different kind from what it was immediately after the election. The West European public evidently expected that a Polish Pope would answer to their idea of a Pope by being full of piety and devotion to Our Lady, and by displaying this piety and devotion in a somewhat uncritical and sentimental form. Instead they were confronted by a man no less Western than themselves, in fact far superior to many of them in what they like to regard as their own special qualities of openness, frankness and sincerity. Yet, at the same time, they knew that he was truly a man from Eastern Europe, and that was an additional point in his favor.

4

The "Living Rosary"

In the terrible years of the Occupation, when I left for school in the morning and my brother and sisters went off to work we never knew whether we would see one another at supper that evening. For breakfast we had a thin slice of black bread, in which wood shavings could often be detected, spread with beet conserve and accompanied by ersatz coffee with saccharin. Each day, for all we knew, might be our last. Police roundups, deportation to camps and forced labor in Germany or some other place unknown, beating up by SS men, death by shooting in the street—all these things were part of daily life, and at home we were not free from fear either. Any night the police or the Gestapo might turn up, batter down the apartment door and drag one off to prison or straight to Auschwitz. Shots were frequently heard at night after curfew hours, when the police arrested people caught walking the streets without passes, and fired at any who did not stop when challenged. The whole town was in a state of constant terror and intimidation.

During that fearful time Karol's father suddenly died. A friend of mine burst in one evening to tell me the news. I did not go at once to Karol, knowing I would see him at early Mass next day.

"What happened to him?"

"A heart attack."

"Were you there?"

"No, I had just gone out shopping. He was quite all right then, but of course he wasn't a young man and his health wasn't good. When I got back it was all over."

There was a simple funeral at Rakowicki cemetery. I felt sorry that I had not seen more of that modest, unassuming man who had kept in the background and devoted his whole life to his son.

The atmosphere of hatred and vengefulness toward the German enemy became more and more intense. It was especially strong among young people and even children. Small boys dreamed of armed retaliation for the wrongs and humiliation of their country and the murder of their parents, brothers and sisters. Members of the resistance movement would come by night and execute death sentences on informers and traitors.

Our "Living Rosary" group became more and more popular in the neighborhood, and boys kept coming and asking to join it. Since the membership was limited to fifteen—one for each Mystery—we decided to form additional groups, each led by a member of the original fifteen. We ourselves met regularly once a week with Tyranowski, and held similar meetings with our respective groups. We discussed with them the problems of modeling oneself on Jesus Christ in the light of one's own temperament and one's good and bad qualities. We tried to instill in each person a sense of responsibility for his thoughts, words and actions, and encouraged them to review their progress day by day. We tried to convey to them our ideas and experience of prayer and the Mass and to train them in religious practices which would help them in the imitation of Christ. Tyranowski considered this a right and proper development of the training he had himself given us, on the principle *"contemplata aliis tradere."*

Youths who had been our schoolfellows and were now in the resistance movement used to come and urge us to join clandestine military organizations. It was the duty of every Pole, they declared, to take part in the armed struggle, to shed his blood and, if need be, to die for the sake of freedom. When we replied that we wanted to train young people to serve their country in peacetime, and that in any case those under our care were too young to fight, the partisans accused us of stupidity, cowardice and bourgeois narrow-mindedness. Unfortunately we could not prevent all our boys from going with them. Some disappeared "into the woods"; occasionally they would return afterward for a brief spell, and then be heard of no more.

I used to talk to Karol about these matters, as we felt the ring of danger tightening around us. We realized that at any moment the Gestapo might get wind of our meetings and pack us all off to Auschwitz—they would never believe that we met for purely religious purposes and not for military or illegal ones. We decided that we must warn our juniors of the danger, since it was literally a matter of life and death.

"You talk to your boys and I'll talk to mine. Wouldn't it be better to call off our meetings and disband the groups, for a time at least, as the situation is getting more threatening day by day?"

We talked to them, but all without exception were unwilling to give up meeting either in groups at church or individually. Maybe it was overoptimism or lack of imagination, but in any case we decided to go on taking the risk. At any rate, we said to ourselves, we are doing something useful in trying to prevent their being infected by the attitude of hate.

Unexpectedly, however—and Tyranowski had not foreseen this either—the subject matter of our meetings altered to some extent. Basically they were still concerned with modeling one's character on that of Christ and behaving responsibly before God, but in addition we talked more and more about the future and about preparing ourselves for the work of rebuilding our country. This led to the discussion of Polish history and culture—prose and poetry, painting and sculpture—and of political and social questions.

One day Karol said to me, "The Germans are throwing the Szkockis out of their house, and I'm trying to find a place for them to live. I offered them a share of mine, but it's too small."

I had known Mrs. Irena Szkocka and her daughter since about the autumn of 1940; the latter, Zofia, was married to the musicologist Jan Pozniak. Karol had taken me to see them, saying, "You must meet these friends of mine. She's a wonderful old woman, I look on her practically as my grandmother." They lived at 55A Poniatowski Street, in a fine house called Linden Tree Villa. It had a terrace with a parapet and a splendid view across the Vistula to the Salesian seminary nestling in a clump of trees on the other side. But the chief attraction was Mrs. Szkocka herself, a delightful old lady whom I too immediately thought of as "Granny." I asked her how Karol had come to know them.

"Oh, it was some time ago, in 1938. I was a schoolteacher before the war, and one day a pupil of mine, Juliusz Kydrynski, brought Karol along and said, 'Here's my new friend.' Afterward Karol came to see us regularly, and sometimes we were his guests as well. He invited us to a performance of *The Moonlight Cavalier*, which he and his friends staged in the courtyard of the University library. If there's one thing I'm thankful for about that time, it's that Karol brought Osterwa to see us.* You mustn't think the war has broken everything up, though. We still go on reading together and learning things."

"What do you read?"

"Poetry, and especially our greatest poet, or so I think."

"Who is that?"

"Norwid, of course. Everyone says the three great Polish poets are Mickiewicz, Slowacki and Krasinski, but I find Norwid more inspiring than any of them. Karol, too, is starting to put him on a level with the others."

Mrs. Szkocka brought out an elegant tea service and served us fine tea and cakes. We had a delightful afternoon, during which her daughter Zofia played the piano. It was hard to believe in the war and the Occupation as we listened to the strains of Chopin and looked out on the slow-moving river and the park beyond.

When the Germans commandeered their home Mrs. Szkocka was over sixty, but this made no difference to her: although advanced in years she was perpetually young in spirit. Undaunted and full of energy, she managed to find a handsome apartment close to Karol's home, on the first floor of 12 Szwedska Street. Although not to be compared with Linden Tree Villa it was a large, quiet place overlooking some trees and with a view of her beloved Vistula.

Not long afterward Karol told me that he was sharing his flat with his teacher, Mieczyslaw Kotlarczyk, who

* Juliusz Osterwa (1885–1947), celebrated actor and stage manager.

had been trying desperately to find a home. "It's not the most comfortable place in the world," Karol remarked, "but as things are now, it's not too bad."

It was indeed ideal for Karol to have his teacher under the same roof and Mrs. Szkocka two or three doors away. Their theatrical and literary activity was soon in full swing. The group of young enthusiasts included Tadeusz Kwiatkowski, whose wife came from Wadowice; the Olszewskis—a sculptor married to an actress; the rising star Danuta Michalowska; and Juliusz Kydrynski, who helped to organize performances although he did not take part. Mrs. Szkocka kept open house for the whole company and placed her biggest room at their disposal. There they rehearsed Fredro's comedies, Zeromski's *Little Quail* and Slowacki's *Samuel Zborowski*.* Mrs. Szkocka helped in the rehearsals and always offered a modest snack afterward—the best one could provide during the Occupation—and, if time allowed, her daughter would end the proceedings with a short piano concert.

This description, however, gives a false idea of the atmosphere of those occasions. It was not just a group of actors and amateurs getting up private theatricals—there was a sense of mission, of aesthetic and patriotic inspiration. The performers were like a priesthood, guarding and imparting the deepest truths of life; it was their task and their opportunity to regenerate the world by a display of artistic beauty. Such was the ideology of the "arch-priest" Kotlarczyk.

Listening to Kotlarczyk's views and to what Karol said about them, I realized how profoundly my friend was torn and how difficult it would be for him to take the

* Aleksander Fredro (1793–1876), Poland's chief comic dramatist. Stefan Zeromski (1864–1925), novelist and playwright. *Samuel Zborowski*, a philosophical drama about a sixteenth-century rebel.

basic decision of his life. For he had also introduced Tyranowski to Mrs. Szkocka's circle, and from time to time there were readings of mystical authors such as St. John of the Cross and St. Teresa of Avila, in whom Karol had begun to take a keen interest. The discovery of their writings was in fact a revelation to him; one might say that he fell in love with a lifelong passion. He had always prayed, but now he did so more than ever. I knew how important prayer was to him, especially the contemplative kind that he learned from those masters of the spiritual life. The impression they made on him was such that I sometimes expected him to become a Discalced Carmelite. I hoped he would not do so, because I feared that monastic life would confine him to a relatively narrow sphere of people and interests and would cut him off from pastoral work, for which I thought him best fitted. That was when I thought of him as a future priest: but at other times I saw him as an actor and stage manager, the creator of a great religious theater in which masterpieces of the spiritual life would be recited and performed.

Meanwhile our "apostolic" work continued to grow beyond our expectations. More and more boys sought to join us, and so we selected from our groups of fifteen those who seemed the ablest, most active and most pious —this word may not be very popular nowadays, but I intend it in the best sense—and appointed them to be heads of fresh groups in their turn. Our own responsibility increased in proportion, and so did the number of hours we spent looking after our charges.

One day Karol came and said, "I'm going up to the Wawel,* would you like to come?" On the way he told

* The royal castle in the old town of Cracow, with a Gothic cathedral and many national treasures.

me that he was going to confess to a priest he had known when a schoolboy at Wadowice.

"He taught us doctrine in my first year at high school. The regular instructor was overworked and asked for an assistant to be sent from Wadowice. I used to serve at Mass, after a time I became chief altar boy, and he's been my confessor ever since then. As I can't always get to him in the morning we make an appointment for later in the day, or I just go at a time when I know he'll be in, and he's always willing to see me."

"Was he transferred from Wadowice a long time ago?"

"Yes, quite a time. He was the first person I came to see when we moved here in 1938. And, as it happens, I was with him in the Wawel when the war broke out."

"How was that?"

"The first of September was the first Friday in the month. I had gone to confession early in the morning, and while I was still there the bombing started."

"Yes, I remember Warszawska Street was bombed."

"So I served Father Figlewicz's Mass to the sound of bombs and antiaircraft guns."

We entered the precincts of the castle, which, being the residence of the Nazi governor-general, was guarded by German police. Father Figlewicz lived in a building opposite the main entrance to the cathedral. We walked up a flight of broad, highly polished wooden stairs and were greeted by a cheerful-looking priest with pleasant manners who gave us tea in a small parlor. He then went off with Karol to another room, and they did not come back for some time. I wondered what could be going on —it seemed too long for confession or for an ordinary chat. Eventually they came back and exchanged a few words of farewell, after which Karol and I set out for home.

"Why were you there so long?" I asked.

Karol did not seem to hear my question, but simply said, "I wanted to tell you that I've decided to become a priest."

I said nothing, but reflected, "Just as I thought."

"That's what I was talking to him about."

I learned afterward that Father Figlewicz had introduced Karol to Archbishop Adam Sapieha,* who had agreed to admit him to the Theological Seminary. The archbishop sent him to the rector, Father Piwowarczyk, who passed him on to Fr. Kazimierz Klosak as director of philosophical studies. Karol did not tell me all this himself because the Nazis had prohibited admissions to the seminary, and both he and I knew that the fewer people one told about such clandestine activities, even one's nearest and dearest, the safer it was for them. The Nazis' motive in banning studies for the priesthood was of course clear enough. They wanted to destroy the Catholic Church in Poland because they knew what a part it played in Polish life and culture, and they hoped thereby to destroy the Polish nation itself.

* Prince Adam Stefan Sapieha (1867–1951), Archbishop of Cracow from 1925 and a staunch opponent of Nazi rule; made a cardinal in 1946.

5

Who Is the Pope?

I looked through the morning papers. All of them featured Vatican news on the front page. The world was still in a state of amazement, but yesterday's events were now in the forefront. The Pope's message to the conclave was commented on at length, and for the most part very favorably. Special interest was aroused by the Pope's remarks about the Council, collegiality and ecumenism. Cardinal Pellegrino, the former Archbishop of Turin, was quoted as saying, "It is a document of the highest importance, especially when it speaks of fidelity to the Council—that alone suffices to indicate its significance."

The press also quoted the final part of the message, addressed to Poland, which for some reason I had overlooked yesterday but which was extremely moving: "May we be permitted, Brothers and Sons, out of inextinguishable love for our native land, to add a special greeting to all our fellow citizens in Poland, *semper fidelis*, and to the priests and faithful of our own church at Cracow—a greeting in which sentiment, nostalgia and hope are inseparably mixed."

The German press gave an impression of relief and satisfaction, recalling with pleasure that the Pope visited West Germany a month ago, celebrating Mass and giving many addresses in German and Polish, at Fulda, Cologne, Mainz, Munich, and so on. The papers admitted, however, that they did not notice him much at the time: he was always in second place, or farther behind, and all the attention of reporters and photographers was concentrated on Cardinal Wyszynski, the Polish Primate. To the Germans, of course, Wyszynski is a living legend, something between a prophet, a national leader and a front-rank politician. Nonetheless it is a remarkable fact that no attention was paid to Cardinal Wojtyla, although, to give Wyszynski his due, he lost no opportunity during the tour of bringing his companion into the limelight and presenting him as his own chief assistant, deputy and successor-designate.

The telephone again, this time the German radio.

"Can you broadcast a talk for us?"

"Yes, certainly."

"They say at Frankfurt that you are the only person competent to give us reliable information about his life."

"That's an exaggeration, but it's true that I have been a friend of his for thirty-eight years, and I knew him especially well during the Occupation."

"Is it true that he was in a concentration camp?"

"No, it's not."

"Wasn't he at Dachau?"

"No."

"A priest told us that he had been in the same camp with him."

"It must be a mistake. There was a separate block for priests at Dachau, and the Pope wasn't even ordained then, so they wouldn't have met."

"Perhaps it's something to do with the fact that when the Pope was last in Germany he said Mass at Dachau."

"No, he didn't—that was Cardinal Wyszynski. Cardinal Wojtyla celebrated Mass at Munich."

"Can you please come to our studio at two this afternoon?"

"Yes, I can."

"And would you bring something on paper?"

"Yes, I have something ready."

"Is it true that the Pope used to write poetry?"

"Yes, he published it under the name of Andrzej Jawien."

I reflected that if Karol Wojtyla had not become Pope, only a small group of the initiated would have known who Andrzej Jawien was. Now suddenly everything private in his life would be a prey to the journalists, who would ferret and poke about relentlessly, seeing things that were never there and weaving conjectures without foundation.

During the morning I listened to various bits of news on the radio. I knew that at ten o'clock the Holy Father would be receiving the College of Cardinals in the Sala del Consistorio: not only the electors, but ten others who, being over eighty, had not taken part in the conclave. Finally I heard a report of this important meeting.

"Venerable brethren, it was an act of confidence and great courage on your part to summon a non-Italian to be bishop of Rome." Then the Pope emphasized that the last two elections had manifested the true universality of the Church. He expressed his thankfulness that Pope Paul VI had given the Sacred College such a large international dimension by appointing so many non-Italian cardinals at successive consistories.

That was about all—an ordinary speech, one might say, nothing very remarkable. All the same, without wishing to be carried away by my feelings, I felt once again that he had spoken unconventionally—not in a diplomatic "Vatican" style but in plain, simple language: one felt that he was addressing people who were close to him, and was talking about things that mattered to them.

Replying to the Pope, Cardinal Carlo Confalonieri welcomed him on behalf of the Roman people and said that all the faithful of Rome understood the significance of the election and, in spite of tradition, fully accepted its result. Rome was the native city of all who believed in Christ, and all Christians might feel at home there.

The radio commentator observed that Popes in the past had always referred to themselves in speeches by the plural "We"; the present Pope had used this form in his first message, but in addressing the College of Cardinals at his first audience he used the first person singular. This was certainly not an accident, and must be connected with the fact that on the previous day the Pope had been speaking about collegiality.

At the end of the audience the Pope, in accordance with tradition, had spoken to the cardinals individually. Finally he gave them his apostolic blessing and, in unison with them, blessed the whole Church.

It was a longish drive to the studio, where I was to record a conversation with an editor in Cologne.

"Have you prepared something in writing, Father?"

"Yes."

"How many pages?"

"Seven."

"Oh, that's too many. But could you answer some questions extemporaneously?"

"Certainly."

"Could you tell us briefly what you think are the Pope's main characteristics?"

"That's a difficult question." Indeed, I found it very

difficult. Trying frantically to think, I went on, "I'll do my best to answer, but you must forgive me if I don't make my points in chronological order or even in order of importance." Playing for time in this way, and hoping that the right expressions would occur to me sooner or later, I added, "If I say 'first of all,' it doesn't necessarily mean that that is the main thing."

"All right. Please go on."

"Although actually the first thing I'm going to say *is* the most important—and that is, he's a man who prays a great deal. If I had to sum him up in a word, his personality and his essential quality as a priest, I'd say that he is a man on his knees before the Blessed Sacrament."

"Could you explain that a bit?"

"Every day he has special hours reserved for prayer. He goes to his chapel early to make a good preparation for Mass. He says Mass quietly and intently, no matter if there are just a few people present or a great many. After Mass he spends a long time in thanksgiving, and every afternoon he stays in his chapel for several hours."

"What does he do there?"

"Various things. They are known to some extent, although there is, I mean there used to be, an understanding that during those hours the Cardinal—I'm sorry, the Pope—must be left alone and not disturbed by anyone. Sometimes he would even lock the chapel door. All the same, people knew that he made the Stations of the Cross, probably every day. On Friday he did so in the chapel of the Passion in the Franciscan church in Cracow. According to the Primate, when he was in Warsaw for conferences of the Polish episcopate or for other reasons, he used to make the Stations every day; moreover Cardinal Wyszynski said that if anyone wanted to find him at any time, the most likely place was in his chapel."

"Did he do anything else there?"

"He used to write. On the left-hand side, near the altar, there was a prie-dieu and also a small table . . ."

"I don't quite understand. You say he used to write in the chapel?"

"Yes."

"But surely it would have been more convenient in his own apartments?"

"No doubt, but I'm telling you what he did. You may indeed think it eccentric—it wasn't the most convenient place, though at least he was free from interruption. But that wasn't the real reason—after all, he could have put a 'Do not disturb' sign on his study door. Anyway, I can only tell you that he did use the chapel for writing, and I would prefer not to offer an explanation. But the most important thing is that he used the chapel for prayer, in a characteristic attitude—bent forward, with one hand in front of his face, or supporting his head in both hands. He would stay like that for a long time. Sometimes he lay outstretched in the form of a cross. I was told so by his driver, who once went into the chapel by mistake."

"You said just now that he had set hours and forms of prayer. That implies that there were also others."

"Yes, there were."

"Can you describe some of them?"

"Well, the rosary for instance. One often met him walking about with a rosary in his hand. I remember it too from our drives together. He and I traveled a lot by car, especially on the occasions when I visited Rome. They were often long drives to places like Mentorella, Naples or even Vienna, and we always said the rosary together. Then there was the breviary—he made a point of reciting that, and he often did so in the car as he had no time otherwise."

"Could we go on to some other characteristic of his?"

"Well, secondly, he is a man who knows how to work

extremely hard. He has a tremendous power of concentrating on what he is saying or doing. He never misses an opportunity of working—if he isn't talking to someone or dealing with some business, he will start straight away reading or writing, or saying his prayers. He has also worked out a method of doing two things at once."

"How do you mean?"

"He used to take part in all kinds of meetings, symposia and so on, in his own diocese or in Lublin or Warsaw, though he could have got one of his four suffragan bishops to stand in for him. And while the speeches and reports and discussions were going on he would be dealing with his correspondence, writing letters, signing documents and so forth."

"And what did the others think of that?"

"I admit that when he first started they took it amiss, thinking to themselves, 'Here are we doing our best to have a sensible discussion, and he spends his time reading.' But after a time they got used to it, especially when they found that, despite appearances, he was perfectly aware of what was going on—more so than any of them. He would suddenly make a highly constructive contribution, and at the end he would sum up the proceedings in a masterly fashion and draw the most practical conclusion. During a meeting of the Synod of Bishops, John Paul I—Cardinal Albino Luciani as he then was—said to him, 'I remember that during the Council we were sitting fairly near each other, and you never stopped writing.' What he didn't know was that Cardinal Wojtyla wasn't making notes of the Council speeches but was writing his new book. That didn't stop him, however, from taking a very active part in the Council debates."

"Does he never take any time off?"

"Oh, yes, he certainly does. In winter he always skis for at least two weeks, not on easy slopes but on the heights of the Tatras, and in summer he takes a month's holiday—generally a fortnight canoeing and another fortnight hiking in the mountains. In fact he takes strenuous exercise, partly because of an illness he had once."

"What sort of illness?"

"A kind of mild leukemia. He was treated by Stanislaw Koznacki, an eminent doctor and a friend of his and mine, who recommended outdoor sport as a preventive measure."

"When was that?"

"I remember he was still suffragan to Archbishop Baziak, so it must have been around 1960. But to go on about his habits of work and leisure and doing two things at once: during the Council, at weekends or when there was a lull in the work, he liked to get out of Rome. He once took a trip to Sicily with Bishop Pietraszka, who told me that in spite of the beauty of the scenery he never stopped reading. Some people in fact wondered why he bothered to travel. He reads a lot, and always heavy stuff—books and articles on philosophy and theology. But those who know him realize that he pays attention to the view as well."

"Can you tell us anything else about his character?"

"Yes, I can."

"Very briefly, then, if you would."

"All right. Thirdly, he is a poor man—he has practically no property, and takes no interest in material things. I don't just mean that he doesn't collect pictures and furniture or *objets d'art* like rings and crucifixes, or that he doesn't have much money. He literally owns nothing except a few books, and those simply for the purpose of his work. In August, just before he left for the conclave on the death of Paul VI, his driver said to me, 'You know, Father, I'm ashamed that His Eminence is so badly dressed. His cassock is all shiny, he wears a battered old hat and a shabby overcoat. Forgive me saying so, but he hasn't even a decent shirt—the ones he's got have been mended over and over again. I wish you could tell the sisters to get him some new things and look after him better. Here we are going abroad, and what will the people think of us for treating our cardinal like this?' That's what the driver said. I might add that he doesn't sleep in the main bedroom like the last archbishop, but in a little back room. Oh, I'm sorry, I mean that's what he used to do—of course he lives in the Vatican now, not in the residence in Franciszkanska Street."

"So he's a kind of ascetic?"

"I wouldn't exactly say that. It's not that he is poor for poverty's sake, in any exaggerated way, but that his poverty, like his work, is the reflection of his life with God, if I may put it that way, and his imitation of Jesus Christ, the Son of God. When he was a simple priest and even before that, when he decided as a young man to become a priest, he resolved to devote himself entirely to the service of God and his fellow men, and to allow nothing to hinder or distract him from that work.

"Fourthly, he is extremely well prepared for the part he has to play—above all, because his whole life has been spent in pastoral activity in the full sense of the term."

"What exactly do you mean?"

"When he became a university professor or an assistant bishop, an archbishop or a cardinal, he never confined himself to organizing pastoral work, acting through suffragan bishops or the lower clergy—he remained in contact with individuals and families and took a personal interest in them. He performed marriages, baptized children, conducted funerals and visited people at all times, especially holidays and name days. At Christmas he would take part in carol singing and invite people to his home for dinner and the wafer-breaking ceremony.*

"Another way in which he is well prepared is that he has a thorough knowledge of Christian philosophy, which he studied for several years; philosophy, of course, is the mainstay of theology, and also a key to the understanding of the modern world. I should explain that he not only knows St. Thomas, but is an expert on phenomenology. His special branch of philosophy is ethics, and that comprises a whole range of problems that are of the greatest importance to modern man. Among them he is especially interested in the problem of love, and married love in particular. But am I going on too long?"

"No, please go on; in any case we shall cut anything we don't need."

This discouraged me a little, but I continued:

"You should also realize that he attended the Council from beginning to end—every single session, and of course it dealt with all the most important problems of the Church and the world. And he did not just attend, but took an intensive part in the work—especially the last session, which was concerned with the Theological Commission. Then there is Constitution No. XIII on the Presence of the Church in the Modern World—of course it is the Council's draft, not his, but he did a great deal of the work on it. Again, he is well prepared because he served on the Episcopal Synod which has met every two years since the Council and which discussed current questions affecting the whole Church. And it's very important that during the Council and synod he got to know all the cardinals and a great many bishops from all over the world, and made friends with several of them."

* A Christmas Eve custom in which the host or hostess breaks a specially blessed wafer and shares it with the guests.

"How exactly do you know that?"

"I should have mentioned that I was in Rome during the Council, working for my doctor's degree and staying at the Polish College, which was always Cardinal Wojtyla's headquarters in Rome. Besides, I attended almost the whole of the Council's third session and was able to observe him day by day. And another important thing: while he was in Rome he got to know everything and everyone that the word 'Vatican' generally connotes. Each year since the Council he's been in Rome for at least two months. He is also very well equipped linguistically: he speaks Italian, English, French, Spanish, German and Russian.

"Fifthly, he is very good at getting on with people. As soon as he meets anyone he gives the impression that for him, at that moment, there is nobody more important than that person. He knows how to listen, and will do so for a very long time without saying much himself. Once a group of lay Catholics buttonholed him in Warsaw and spent two hours pouring out all their grievances—about theology and the liturgy, cardinals, bishops and priests, the Church in the world, the Polish Church and every local parish. When they'd finished he simply said, 'It's a very good thing for the faithful to tell their bishops the truth.' Another time, after he had preached a sermon, someone he knew said to him, 'You know, Your Eminence, that was all a lot of twaddle.' The cardinal asked him to sit down and replied, 'You and I are both philologists—please explain exactly what you think "twaddle" means.' And then they had a long talk about the word. The Pope has a great sense of humor, and in that way he reveals his humanity in conversation. He is also adept at shifting from a humorous tone to the deepest and most important subjects.

"Those are all the points I wanted to make."

"Thank you very much, Father. We shan't be able to include everything, we'll have to cut a good deal."

"Very well."

At that moment I no longer cared. My legs were stiff and my head felt empty, and my one desire was to get out into the fresh air. I said good-bye to the sound engineer and walked slowly home.

6

Secret Studies

The young men accepted by Cardinal Sapieha for underground theological and philosophical studies worked extramurally under the guidance of professors and seminary lecturers. They prepared different branches of the course with the aid of textbooks and mimeographed lectures, and took their exams when they had studied for the prescribed number of years. The cardinal was well aware that if the Germans got to know of this activity, the consequences for himself would be serious. At the outset there were not many underground seminarists—in fact only seven. As a rule they lived in the country, mostly as secretaries or lay assistants to parish priests. Karol was an exception; he went on living the life of a factory worker in Cracow.

His philosophical studies were by no means easy. The first book he was given was Father Wais's *Theodicy*. One day we were walking, as we often did, along Konopnicka Street in the direction of the Solvay works; he was wearing blue overalls and clogs as usual, and I asked him what book he had under his arm. He showed it to me, but I had never heard of the author or the title.

"Are you reading this?"

"Yes, but it's hard going. I sit beside the boiler and try to understand it—I feel it ought to be very important to me."

Next time we met I asked him how he was getting on with the book, and he expressed discouragement. Later, however, he came to admire it more and more, and said it had opened up a new world to him. I guessed where he had got it from and why he was studying it, but we did not talk about the matter openly.

About that time Karol was in a street accident. I was on the way home from work when one of my boys came and said, "Mr. Karol's been run over."

"How is he?" I asked in alarm.

"He was knocked out, but he's alive. He was taken to the hospital in an ambulance."

"Is he badly hurt?"

"I don't know."

"What kind of car was it?"

"A German Army truck. It didn't even stop."

I rushed to the hospital, where I found Karol with his head bandaged.

"How do you feel?"

"Not so bad."

"What happened?"

"I don't know. I was walking to work along Konopnicka Street, on the edge of the road because there isn't a pavement there, and the next thing I knew I was here in bed with my head bandaged."

"Who brought you here?"

"I don't know that either. Apparently when the truck hit me I fell into the ditch and lay there. Some woman saw me, called the ambulance and disappeared. She asked them to send word to a shop in Krowoderska

Street, to say if I was alive or not, but now they can't find her. It's a mystery."

"What do the doctors say?"

"Not much as yet, but it doesn't sound serious. I expect I'll be out in a day or two."

But Karol was not discharged for several days, and then only because the hospital was bursting at the seams. The doctor gave him a certificate of exemption from work and recommended a period of peace and quiet at home. This was not so easy, as the Kotlarczyks had two small daughters, so Mrs. Szkocka offered to take Karol in. He was put in a bedroom next to the room in which the theatricals were held. Again we hoped that a few days' rest would be enough, but his convalescence lasted a good deal longer.

Meanwhile I was more and more exercised by the question of my own future. I was not one to change my mind easily, and I had entered the school of engineering so as to become a motor mechanic like my father and brother. I was due to take the final exam soon, after which I would do a year's factory training and then take a diploma. But for some time past I had been coming to realize that I had a decision to make between devoting my life to machines or being a priest and helping people to find God, as I tried to do with the boys of the "Living Rosary." Little by little the second choice prevailed. Karol, who had recovered by this time, watched in his usual silent way and knew of my inner struggle. I had not yet made a final decision, but I got in touch with the underground grammar school organization and told them that I wanted to take the final exam in arts subjects, which I knew I would need in order to get into the seminary. I was given a plan of work, a list of additional subjects to be got up and the dates by which I must qualify in each. So, although my daily program was already full, I had to fit in additional studies in Polish, Latin and history. I told Karol, who offered to help me in any of them and asked which I found most difficult.

"Latin."

"All right then, I'll give you lessons. There's no room at my place, as you know, but I'll come to you regularly."

"Fine."

So Karol started coming twice a week; we shut ourselves in a room and ground away at Latin, telling nobody what we were doing. My sisters were full of curiosity; they used to bring us tea with milk and bread with lard and onions, and look inquisitively over our shoulders at our books and exercises.

All this time the war was coming closer and closer. Fighting was going on in Russia and Africa; the Germans were bombing Britain, but the British were also bombing Germany; Japan had entered the war some time ago, and the Far East was ablaze. We and the boys were confident that we would somehow survive the cataclysm and would have to find our feet in the peacetime world. Meanwhile there was the immediate problem of survival. We had to obtain food somehow, which meant taking dangerous trips into the countryside and bartering articles of clothing, small valuables etc.; otherwise we would have starved on the official rations. It was hard enough to get food in exchange for these things, but harder still to bring it back with us, as the trains were regularly inspected and the stations patrolled by policemen with dogs —the Occupation authorities did all they could to starve the city. In winter there was the additional problem of getting coal and firewood. In spite of all our efforts, the Occupation remained in our memories as a time of fear, cold and hunger. We were hungry for five years without a break, and each winter we were desperately cold. All the year round we went in fear of police roundups, deportation to forced labor, or death at Auschwitz. I also had the problem of getting to school. The Germans had moved the technical school from Krupnicza Street to an inferior building farther from my home, in Meisels Street in the former ghetto of Kazimierz. To keep up with my studies I had to read technical books and pore over the designs of bridges, engines and boilers, sitting up till the small hours with a T-square and drawing-board and straining my eyes to trace the intricate details of the design.

I passed the final exam and took a job as apprentice at a factory of railway equipment in Cystersow Street, but by this time I already knew I wanted to be a priest. I told Karol; he was delighted by my decision, and said he had guessed it would turn out this way. I asked him to take me to see the archbishop, and we went to the residence in Franciszkanska Street: through the large black heavy gates, across the arcaded cloisters, up the wide stone stairs into a suite of huge apartments hung with portraits of former archbishops. The cardinal came toward us; it was the first time I had seen him at close quarters. His slender figure was known throughout Poland, in the territories annexed to the Reich and the Soviet Union as well as the *Generalgouvernement*.* His austere classical features and prominent nose were dark as if sunburned; his gray hair was close-cropped. Famous for his courageous resistance to the Germans in defense of the Polish and Jewish population, and for aiding all who were poorest and most threatened, he was regarded as the head of the Polish nation in both religious and secular matters.

"Well, Karol Wojtyla tells me that you want to be a

* The rump Polish territory, roughly triangular in shape, governed as a Nazi domain by Hans Frank at Cracow; it also included Warsaw.

priest." He spoke in a clipped, businesslike tone, in a slightly nasal voice.

"Yes, Your Eminence."

"But I gather you have still to pass the school exam."

"I have taken it, but I need the arts subjects as well."

"And how long will that take you?"

"Something under a year."

"All right then, please come back when you have passed."

After a few more words on general matters we took our leave.

It was now the summer of 1944, and the war in Poland was reaching a critical stage. Although Germany's defeat was a foregone conclusion, the Nazis intensified the regime of terror and reprisals throughout Poland and especially in Cracow. The town was covered with posters bearing the names of hostages who would be shot *en masse* if the partisans carried out any armed attack on German nationals. Anti-tank barriers of reinforced concrete, several meters high, were set up in various parts of the city.

The eastern front was getting nearer and nearer, and we knew the Germans intended to make Cracow a fortress to be defended "until final victory." Soldiers patrolled the streets in groups of three: two with rifles or submachine guns, ready to shoot, and one in the center to check the papers of passers-by. Instead of "Papers please!" the command was "Hands up!", and the soldier himself took the papers out of one's pocket: otherwise the challenged man, if a partisan, might draw a pistol and fire, as had often happened. We felt close to death at all times. I remember the shock I experienced when, in retaliation for the shooting of a soldier on patrol in Lubicz Street, a group of hostages were brought to Topolowa Street near the railway station and shot. I was on a streetcar going in that direction, and several passengers including myself were lined up with our hands against the wall of the Rakowicki cemetery and searched for arms. This was only a beginning; acts of violence became more and more frequent. We did our best to live normally and not succumb to the wave of blind hatred or lose our nerve when the end was so near.

On August 1 the Warsaw Uprising broke out. The whole nation was thrilled by the news that the capital had taken up arms. The first reaction was to feel that the rest of the country should do likewise, but fortunately the government in London did not give orders to that effect.* To us in Cracow the Uprising seemed an act of supreme heroism and madness. The "reptile press"—as we called the Polish-language papers circulated by the Germans—referred to it as a piece of brigandage without military significance, but as we knew from secretly listening to the radio or reading the underground press, or talking to people from Warsaw, in the first few days the insurgents scored notable successes. One after another they gained control of important buildings, streets and districts, and there were thrilling reports of the capture of prisoners and arms. The Germans were retreating from Warsaw, and in a few days the capital would be free—especially as the Soviet troops, with Polish units under their command, were already on the other side of the Vistula. We even wondered in secret, at that stage of the battle, why Cracow and other cities did not follow suit.

* The Warsaw Uprising was unleashed by the non-Communist military resistance movement (the "Home Army"), which recognized the authority of the Polish Government in London. It was believed that the Germans were in full retreat and that the Uprising would be assisted by the Red Army and by air supplies from the Western Allies. However, the Soviet Government condemned the Uprising and after two months of street fighting it was crushed by the Germans, who then razed Warsaw to the ground.

7

Collegiality

The newspapers contain summaries of comment by the Italian press in the last few days, purporting to describe the conclave and the intrigues of certain influential circles and individuals.

Immediately after the death of John Paul I the Italian press was convinced that his successor would be an Italian. The conviction was derived from the previous conclave and was based on the argument that the Pope is Bishop of Rome and that, given the political situation, if he were not an Italian it would play into the hands of the Left and especially the Communists. It was also expected that the conclave would be rather a long one. Three days before it opened, the Italian press favored the chances of Cardinal Siri of Genoa.

Today the press contains various speculations, or rather gossip, about the conclave. Some papers say that there were about ten votes for Wojtyla even at the first conclave, and that he certainly had some at the beginning of the second. Nearly all agree that the first day of the second conclave was dominated by a tussle between Siri and Benelli, with Ursi and Papalardo in the wings.

L'Espres gave a circumstantial account of what it believed to have happened at the conclave ("but of course we cannot know for certain"). Unlike the proceedings in August, which went off smoothly, the second conclave was stormy and full of incident.

The first day was spent in endeavors to get a majority for an Italian candidate. A bloc of at least twenty Curial cardinals formed under Siri's leadership. Benelli, Papalardo and Ursi tried to neutralize this bloc so as to gain votes for Pericle Felici. Another group of about twenty, mostly non-Italians, saw no hope for Felici and therefore voted for Poletti, knowing that he was acceptable to Benelli's opponents. All this led to Siri and Benelli's having the largest number of votes. The second ballot was a contest between them, in which Siri got about twenty-five votes and Benelli forty. In the third ballot Siri's votes switched to Benelli, but even then he did not get the necessary two thirds plus one, though he came very close to it. In the fourth ballot there was a fundamental change as the electors cast about for another solution. Benelli's fortunes tended to decline, while several votes went to Pellegrino, but this did not produce a decision either. During the night of October 15 the group of *"innovatori"* who had originally favored Poletti gave up their fruitless effort and instead proposed Wojtyla, Pirogno, Willebrands, König, Pellegrino or Hume. After some uncertainty the votes concentrated on Wojtyla, who attracted those who had supported Benelli. In the afternoon the international bloc declined in importance and Wojtyla was elected.

Panorama confirms that on the first day Benelli nearly won on the fourth ballot, and says that this alarmed the Third World cardinals, who thereupon went into action. It adds that Wojtyla got 103 votes on the last ballot, and that König worked for him among the German-speaking cardinals.

A few papers try to give a general conspectus of the conclave, according to which its main strategist, as in August, was Benelli. On the previous occasion he played his cards with complete success in favor of Albino Luciani. The second time there was no Luciani, and he decided to play for election himself. He knew it would not be easy, as there had been much opposition to his "hard line" policy as Secretary of State, and he therefore decided to make use of Siri, who also wanted to be elected. Siri was an ultraconservative of whom it was maliciously said that he had not yet grasped the fact that the Council had taken place and that it was doubtful whether he would ever do so. Benelli was able to ensure that Siri gained a large number of votes—enough to frighten many of the cardinals, so that Benelli could then present himself as offering the only chance of defeating Siri. This maneuver was almost successful, but then the Third World again took fright and backed Wojtyla.

The press also quotes some much more remarkable gossip, for instance that after Cardinal Wojtyla had received the required majority he refused to accept the papacy. However, there are four different accounts of what then induced him to change his mind. One of these is that the cardinals again voted for him and that he then accepted. The second theory is that he was persuaded by Cardinal Wyszynski. The third is that he asked for the vote to be repeated so that he could be sure that it had not been an accident or the result of some maneuver by particular groups, but that the cardinals really wanted him as Pope; apparently on the third ballot he got over seventy votes, and on the final one 104. The fourth conjecture is that after being elected he asked for a few hours in which to reflect, and only after that agreed to accept office.

A lady telephones from Bonn—the *Times* correspondent—and I receive calls from Catholic and Protestant dailies and weeklies. Some of the questions are similar to those I answered in the studio yesterday, but there are also new ones. Some refer to press statements of the last few days and hours. They express admiration for the cardinals' action in taking their surprise decision; old men as they are, and fixed in their mental habits, they have nevertheless overcome a whole range of psychological barriers—especially by electing a non-Italian, a man from Eastern Europe and, finally, a relatively young man.

"What do you think about it?" asked one of the correspondents.

"Shall I tell you what I telegraphed to the Holy Father?"

"I'd very much like to know."

" 'What did I tell you? Mietek.' "

"What does 'Mietek' mean?"

"It's my name, short for 'Mieczyslaw.' "

"Oh, I see."

"As for the cardinals, I'm sure they deserve admiration, but at the same time the journalists' reaction shows, I think, that they don't understand these matters very well. In my opinion the only 'barrier' that the cardinals overcame was that of age, and even that doesn't seem to me a very real one. Certainly the cardinals who knew Wojtyla wouldn't have felt that they were overcoming any barriers in electing him. One of them is supposed to have summed it up by saying, 'I'd have voted for Wojtyla even if he had been an Italian.' The fact is that the reporters, and some others as well, were surprised by the election because they didn't know Wojtyla—but the cardinals did."

"What do you think about the fact that the new Pope is a Pole?"

"I think it's an important breakthrough—important for the Italians themselves, and their internal politics. The fact that the Pope is not an Italian places him, as it were, outside the internal affairs of Italy. Up to now the reigning Pope has always been considered an automatic supporter of the Christian Democratic party, and similarly that party has considered itself a supporter and defender of the Papacy, which led it to demand special privileges and prerogatives. This was never spoken about, but was taken as a matter of course for years. And now suddenly it's all changed. A non-Italian Pope is above Italian politics, not in the sense that he isn't interested or concerned, but he is independent of them. One pressman put it by saying, 'The Tiber has got wider'—that is to say, the distance between the Vatican and the Quirinal, the seat of the Italian Government."

"What do you think will be the main tasks of the new Pope?"

"I admit I've been thinking about that ever since the election. There are many of them, very many indeed; one, for instance, is the problem of Church government and the bishops' part in it."

"No doubt you are thinking of the word 'collegiality,' which the Pope used in his first message and also in addressing the cardinals."

"Yes. To begin with, we must give credit to Paul VI for instituting the Synod of Bishops. This was supposed to aid the Pope in his legislative function, to deliberate and put forward proposals for the Pope, as the supreme authority, to approve and transmit to his executive, the Curia. But it must be recognized that the synod has not played the part intended for it. Things have not worked out quite that way. The Curia is supposed to be purely executive, but in the dozen or so years since the Council it has constantly tried to assume legislative authority as well, which of course has been its tendency for centuries past. It remains to be seen how the new Pope will give effect to the wishes of Vatican II in this respect, which represent his own wish as well."

"Do you think he will create some new institution, or rely on the Synod of Bishops?"

"I think the latter is more probable. The secretary to the synod, Bishop Wladyslaw Rubin, is a friend whom he has known and thought highly of for many years, and it should be easy for them to settle various matters promptly."

"What do you think of the idea that has been expressed, that he is a better Pope than a bishop?"

"I have never heard it before, but I think there is some truth in it. What is it based on exactly?"

"Well, in the days that have passed since the election he has shown himself to be simple, forthright and spontaneous, whereas in previous years there was something secret and withdrawn about him. On his visit to West Germany, for instance, he attracted hardly any attention."

"I think you are quite right, and I would add that he was probably happier as a priest than a bishop, because he was freer then than afterward. As a suffragan or archbishop or even perhaps as a cardinal he had to take account of people and circumstances to an almost excessive degree, so that it cramped his freedom of thought, speech and action. Now that he has become Pope he is free from these ties and restrictions and, in a way, is as free again as when he was a simple priest."

"Is it true that he did not govern his diocese particularly well?"

This suggestion made me indignant. I replied, "There wasn't a diocese in Poland so well run as that of Cracow. Only those who are close to him in one way or another can realize how well he controlled it. True, he was deceptively unlike other bishops in some ways; but the essential thing was that he was a director, not a ruler. A tremendous amount was done, and if he devolved some of it, it was not so much for lack of time or specialized ability as because he wanted others to do the work."

"And did they?"

"Yes—along with him, in consultation or under his supervision. And sometimes they were quite unexpected people, not always popular with those around them. It was very important that he did *not* do everything himself; it was enough for him to tell someone who had the authority, or the ability and initiative, that this or that needed doing, and it would be carried out. His own authority was so great, and he conveyed his ideas so clearly, that only a short discussion was necessary before some new organization or institution was created, or some step taken which was of real importance to the Church or society at large, in Cracow or the whole of Poland."

"Can you give any specific examples?"

"Certainly. For instance, the periodic meetings of theologians from all over the country; symposia on various topics, to which the highest lay and clerical authorities, also from all over Poland, were invited by name, often under his own signature; his support for Father Blachnicki's 'oasis' activity, despite opposition from some in his immediate circle; and the organization of the Diocesan Synod with its 'synodal groups,' also with lay participation, a thing no other diocese had dreamed of. Then he set up permanent educational institutions such as the Religious Instruction Board or the Family Institute. These are only a few examples of what I mean."

Another telephone call toward evening:
"What do you think of the Pope's future?"

"That's too general a question to answer."

"Well, so far he's only been a cardinal—how do you think he will develop as Pope?"

"I see what you mean. As you know, I have been a friend of his ever since he was a layman. I knew him when he entered the seminary, when he became a priest and afterward a professor, then an auxiliary bishop, an archbishop and a cardinal. From all this experience I can say that he is a man who adapts himself to whatever role Providence assigns to him."

"Does he adapt quickly?"

"No. At least, not every role suits him from the outset."

"Which one did he take the longest to get used to?"

"You want to know a lot, don't you?"

"It's my job."

"All right, but don't forget that I am speaking off the cuff, I am only giving my own opinion and I may be wrong!"

"Of course."

"Well, I think he took longest to get used to being a cardinal."

"Do you mean it was above his ceiling?"

"There, you see how easily one can be misunderstood. I'm glad you asked, because the real reason was quite different: it was connected with the situation in Poland. When Karol Wojtyla became a cardinal alongside Wyszynski, some people both at home and abroad took it for granted that he was a kind of 'counterweight.'"

"They are quite different personalities, are they not?"

"Yes, of course they are. Wyszynski is a prophet and a politician, a national leader and a man on a pedestal; Wojtyla meets people on more equal terms, as a friend or associate. But that was not the important difference, which was, in a word, a matter of politics. Wojtyla realized that and took it considerably to heart."

"How are you so sure?" my interrogator persisted.

"Because I was in Rome when he came to receive the cardinal's hat. He had no car at the time, so he shared the one I was using and we talked about the situation. He was determined that there should not be a split among the Polish bishops, some siding with him and others with Wyszynski. So he made a point of showing absolute loyalty to Wyszynski—perhaps he even overdid it, if loyalty can be overdone."

"And did that continue to the very end?"

"No, he felt that the danger lessened as time went on."

"Are you saying that just to please me?"

"How sharp you are! I didn't mention that Cardinal Wojtyla appointed me liaison officer, if that is not too pompous a term, between himself and the Catholic press in Cracow—the weekly *Tygodnik Powszechny*, the monthly *Znak* and the publishing house of the same name. I had fairly regular meetings with twenty or so people from Cracow and other towns. At one of the recent ones Jacek Wozinakowski, the head of the Znak firm, remarked to me that over the past year the cardinal had become much more open and spontaneous, expressing his own ideas and wishes about various important matters and not simply acting as a mouthpiece of the episcopate. Before that he had played down his own vision and initiative and had deferred to the ideas of the episcopate and the Primate himself."

"Another question. Do you think the present excitement about the Pope will last?"

"Excitement is short-lived in the nature of things, but I am sure the enthusiasm will last, though again that isn't perhaps quite the right word."

"You aren't afraid people will get disappointed?"

"No. I say that because I know him and what he stands for. I don't know what the Pope will do, but I know he will go on working as he did in Cracow and will continue to be the same marvelous man, admired by all who know him. Of course there will be difficult times and hard decisions, if only on personal and disciplinary matters, for he is a man who knows what he wants. So the going will be uphill at times, but I am sure plenty of people will follow him."

8

War and Peace

On August 6, 1944, which was a fine Sunday, I took a party of boys on an excursion to the Twardowski Hills, which are in fact no more than an outcrop of limestone overlooking the Vistula on the western side of Cracow, in the direction of Pychowice and Tyniec. Karol was to have come with us, but did not turn up; a couple of his boys were in the party. We played football for some time and set out for home late in the afternoon—hot, sweating and tired, but noisy and cheerful: the outing had almost made us forget about the Occupation, though one was never quite unaware of it in those days. I wondered anxiously what had happened to Karol—no doubt he had been delayed, but he did not usually miss appointments. As we were going downhill toward Zakrzowek someone shouted, "The Germans!" Looking down in consternation we saw motorcycles with sidecars, black Marias and jeeps coming toward us along a white ribbon of road, not more than 500 yards away, past the last houses in Zielna Street surrounded by their gardens. Soldiers in dark green uniforms, looking almost black against the white background, jumped out into the road.

"It's a roundup!"

We started to scramble back the way we had come, looking over our shoulders every few moments. However, the Germans did not come toward us, but closed off the street and started to enter one house after another—it was evidently a thorough search, probably for some partisans or stores of ammunition about which they had been tipped off. Someone suggested that we make our way home by way of Twardowski Street, on the other side of the hills, but at first we were too frightened to return to town. As we waited among the bushes, men and boys began to turn up from all the neighboring districts— Zakrzowek, Denniki and Ludwinow—saying that there had been roundups in every street and that they had been lucky to escape to where we were. From the direction of town we heard single shots and bursts of sub-machine-gun fire; from time to time it sounded like a regular battle, but a minute or two later there was ominous quiet again.

I felt more and more alarmed on Karol's account. Had he managed to take cover somewhere, or had the police caught him before he left home? I did not say anything to my companions about this possibility.

From what the new arrivals told us, this was clearly a roundup on an unprecedented scale. People were not only being arrested on the streets, but the police were entering houses, dragging out all the men and youths indiscriminately and piling them into black Marias. This was unusual, and extremely alarming.

"Are they checking papers?" we asked.

"No, but when they take people from houses they tell them to bring their identity cards."

"And nothing else?"

"No."

Karol and I had identity cards marked *"Kriegswich-*

tiger Betrieb," meaning that we were engaged on work of importance to the war effort. This usually meant that in the event of raids we stood a somewhat better chance of not being arrested, or of being released sooner than others; but the fugitives from the town said that this time the Germans were making no distinction. My companions and I discussed with them what to do. Their advice was to wait for the present and see whether the Germans intended to surround the Twardowski Hills. If they did, we should try to escape towards Pychowice, Tyniec or beyond—no one could suggest exactly where, however. Meanwhile night was drawing on. We were in shorts and shirt sleeves; hardly anyone had a coat or a sweater. The boys were getting cold, and I decided that something must be done.

"I'm going to leave you here and make my way back to Twardowski Street. A friend of mine, Ludwik Zurek, lives there with his family; I'll try to find out what's going on in town, and perhaps he can give us shelter for the night."

By now it was quite dark. I did not dare go along the road for fear of running into Germans or informers, so I went through the gardens at the backs of the houses. I thought I knew the gardens and that they were separated only by low wooden fences, but I was mistaken. I went slowly so as not to make a noise, fearing every moment that I could see a German standing behind a house or a tree. Terrified at every sound and every movement, I clambered over high fences and nearly lost my sense of direction, though the starry sky and the outlines of houses gave me some idea of where I was. I heard dogs bark and was scared lest they might be Alsatians trained by the Gestapo to capture fugitives. At last I decided that I had reached the Zureks' house—it was pitch-dark and the windows were blacked out. I knocked at the door, and as no one came I knocked at the window, which produced no result either. The thought that the boys were still in the cold night air, frightened for themselves and on my account, made me feel desperate, and I banged so hard at the window that I thought it would break. At last I heard a voice saying: "Who's there?"

"Malinski."

"Malinski?" said the voice, surprised and rather suspicious. "What Malinski?"

"Mietek, Jozek's brother, from Madalinski Street."

"But Jozek's been arrested."

"Please let me in!"

I heard the key turn, the chain was taken off and the door opened. Ludwik Zurek peered at me in the dark passage and finally took me inside his flat, which was not well lit either. His family was there, and I asked what was going on in the city.

"We don't know."

"How did you yourself escape?"

"I had just gone out to the toolshed, and hid there. We're safe for the moment, but no one knows what'll happen next. But what are you doing here, Mietek?"

I explained, and asked if the boys and I could spend the night at his place. "They can't go home because of the curfew, and it isn't safe where they are, because the Germans may realize that a lot of men and boys have taken refuge there. Besides, it's cold."

Ludwik was reluctant and afraid, and I didn't blame him: he had a wife and several children to think of. But I was desperate too, and at last he agreed.

"But I take no responsibility, mind."

"No, of course not. Thank you."

I dashed back the way I had come, trampling over flower beds and fruit bushes. At first I could not find my companions, but when I did they were delighted to see me; they were cold and hungry and had been afraid for my safety. We went back again by the same route. I told them to make no noise and be as careful as possible; they behaved admirably, but I was scared out of my wits at every whisper of sound. When we got to the house, the Zureks were aghast to see so many of us. There was a shed with a concrete floor which we covered with hay; Ludwik brought a few blankets, and his wife produced a piece of bread for each of the boys. Some of them slept soundly, but most of us were too tired and anxious. I kept waking every few minutes—I was cold and uncomfortable, frightened by every unexpected noise, straining my ears at distant shots and the barking of dogs nearby. I fell asleep in the small hours, and awoke to see the worried face of our host bending over me.

"Has anything happened?"

"No, but you must go now."

"What's the time?"

"Five o'clock."

"Isn't it too early?"

"No, you must go at once. Anything may happen in the daytime. I haven't slept a wink because of you, in case there may be some trouble. There are plenty of dangerous people around here."

I woke the boys and told them we must leave. They were numb and chilled, but were soon ready to set out.

"Go in pairs, or groups of three at the most, and don't hurry," I told them. "If you meet a patrol don't run away, or they'll shoot; but talk loudly so as to warn the others."

We all said good-bye as though we were never to meet again. I had hoped we could mingle with people on their way to work, but the streets were completely empty—it was like a dead city. However, by some miracle we all got home safely.

Luckily my stepmother and sisters were safe and sound. My brother had for some time past been in jail under interrogation; we had tried to get him transferred from the political section to that for ordinary criminals, but had not succeeded. My sisters had been so anxious about me that they had hardly slept all night. They were uncertain now whether to go out to work, but eventually decided to do so, while my stepmother went shopping. I myself hesitated whether to go to the factory or not. The police might round up all the workers and send them off to a camp; on the other hand, if I did not go I might be in trouble for absenteeism. Finally I decided to stay at home. I tried to read, but could not. Suddenly there was a knock at the door. I paid no attention, but it was repeated a second and a third time. Who could it be? It was not an imperious knock; if it had been the police, they would have battered down the door by now. Could it be one of the boys in my group, or a police spy?

"Who's there?" I asked.

"A priest."

"A priest? What priest?" I could not recognize the voice.

"Father Kuczkowski, from the archbishop's office."

I opened the door and asked him in. He was a stranger to me, but had a pleasant smile.

"I came to tell you that His Grace would like you to come to the seminary today to begin your studies."

"But I shan't be taking my school exam for some months."

"Then you can do both courses at the same time."

"Who will be coming besides me?"

"We'll see," he replied evasively. "Someone will come this afternoon to make sure you get to us safely."

After lunch my sisters returned with news of the wholesale police roundup. Apparently the men had been

herded into camps outside the city, and it was not yet
known when they would be let go. But my mind was
filled with other thoughts. There was a knock at the
door, and a lady appeared who introduced herself as
Zofia Starowieyska-Morstin.

"I have come to take you to the palace."

My sisters were bewildered. I explained that I was entering the Theological Seminary.

"What? Where? Oh, no, Mietek, you mustn't!"

They burst into tears. I packed my things silently and
left the house. The streets were almost empty. Mrs.
Starowieyska walked on ahead, and when she came to a
corner made a sign to me that it was safe to follow. I was
scared at the Debnicki Bridge, where soldiers stood on
guard by the anti-tank barriers, but they paid no attention to us. Then came Zwierzyniecka Street, too long for
my taste, after which we crossed the Planty Gardens and
entered Franciszkanska Street. Opposite the palace was a
high-walled building containing police stores, with a sentry outside; then another gate, an annex to the residence,
also occupied by the police, and another sentry. We
passed these in fear and trembling, and finally got to the
main door of the palace, where I almost fell into the
arms of a tall young man whom I had not met before.

"Is Karol Wojtyla here?" I asked him.

"Yes, he is."

At that moment Karol came running out of the clois-
ter, and we embraced each other like survivors from a
shipwreck.

"Where were you during the roundup?"

"Imagine—I was at home all the time, but luckily no
one came."

The other young man came up and, smiling broadly,
said, "I'm Staszek Starowieyski—it was my aunt who

brought you here. Come upstairs now and see where you're going to live."

Our quarters were in one of the enormous first-floor rooms, with a separate entrance off a hall next to the chapel. The furniture consisted of some metal beds, a desk for reading and writing and a few chairs. To my surprise I discovered that since the beginning of the war this had been the home of the clerical students whose seminary at 8 Podzamze had been taken over by the SS. Owing to the German ban on admissions, those who were still here were in their fifth and last year of studies. There were only three of them, but it gave us a chance to mingle with some of our seniors.

Karol told me that his own guide to the palace had been Mrs. Szkocka, that they had no trouble on the way and that he had been there for the past few hours. I asked him if he knew why the archbishop had sent for us.

"The Russians are advancing at a great rate, and it looks as if they'll enter Cracow or surround it a few days from now. The archbishop was worried about us, and he thought we'd be safer here. Besides, he wanted us to begin our studies, after a fashion anyway."

"Why 'after a fashion'?"

"Well, we shan't be taught by professors of the first rank, because the university professors are not allowed to teach informal groups."

The main thing was, however, that we would at last be studying in a regular way. Next day we were joined by a few more young men whom the archbishop had sent for from the countryside and who had managed to get through unscathed. We got on well together; the atmosphere was friendly and full of enthusiasm, but we were anxious about events outside. In due course we found out that the mass roundup was a precautionary

measure against a rising in Cracow, following the example of Warsaw. The idea was to immobilize suspects and
also to show everyone that the Germans were still strong
despite what the communiqués called "withdrawal to
prepared positions."

Gradually life in the city returned to normal. The Germans released, one after another, those they decided were
not dangerous, but all suspects were sent to concentration
camps or to unknown destinations in Germany. The factories and offices that had been paralyzed for lack of staff
started up again, and began to check on those who were
still absent. When I had been at the palace for a few
days my sisters came, still in tears at my decision to become a priest, and also to say that the police had been in-
quiring for me.

"What did you tell them?"

"We said you'd left home on Sunday and hadn't come
back."

The police returned a few days later, saying that they
had checked in all the camps and I wasn't there. My
sisters stuck to their story, but the police threatened that
if I didn't come forward one of my sisters would be held
in prison or at Auschwitz as a hostage. The Soviet offen-
sive would have put an end to all this anxiety, but it was
held up on the river San a hundred miles to the east.
The archbishop, too, was in a difficult situation, with several young men sheltering under his roof. If there were
any kind of check or if the Germans entered the palace
for any reason we would be discovered and arrested for
absence from work, if not on suspicion of being partisans; in any case our studies themselves were a breach of
the law. Both Karol and I were in particular danger since
we were registered as engaged in work of importance to
the war effort. We debated what to do, and agreed that if
anyone was arrested on our account we would of course

come forward, but then we would have had to explain where we had been in the meantime. During the next few days the hunt for me appeared to subside, but in Karol's case it became more acute. He said to me, "I know Kulakowski, the head of the Solvay works, through Mrs. Lewaj, you remember? Perhaps he can help me."

"The best thing would be if he could get your name taken off the payroll, but how will you reach him? We haven't yet got our forged identity papers, and in any case if you were recognized, as you well may be in spite of the cassock, you'd be sent to Auschwitz, and the only way out of there is through the chimney."*

Karol put the problem to the archbishop, and suggested that Father Figlewicz might go to see Kulakowski.

One day I was standing at a window with the archbishop, and looking down at the sentry in front of the building where the German police kept their stores, he said, "I prefer not to think what would happen if they ever decided to come in here." For the time being things were quiet, however, and there was no further trouble about Karol, though Father Figlewicz did not hold out great hopes after his visit to Kulakowski; the latter had said he would do anything he possibly could for the archbishop, but unfortunately he was no longer in charge of the factory.

By way of protection it was decided that we would be dressed in cassocks so as to look like priests or seminarists if the Germans should enter the palace grounds—this was at least safer than being in ordinary clothes. So, without any religious ceremony, each of us was attired in a cassock belonging to one of the clergy. Mine belonged to

* I.e., the crematorium

Father Piwowarczyk: it was too big and reeked of to-
bacco, the sleeves were too long and wide, it was tight
at the neck, in fact uncomfortable in every way. So was
Karol's, and his collar, fastened by a metal stud, kept
sticking up at the back of his head. The other protective
measure, apart from clothing, was to provide us with
forged papers. This took a longer time than we had expected, but at last, to our relief, we received them. They
looked as convincing as our old ones—if anything, more
so.

All these problems, however, were really secondary
and demanded attention only every now and then.
What was important were our studies and spiritual exercises. We attended many lectures together, since although some of us were in our first year and some in our
second or third, we were not a large group altogether.
Shortly after our arrival the archbishop introduced Fr.
Stanislaw Smolenski as our father confessor—a quiet, sensitive, kindly man who gave moving addresses and helped
us with our morning meditation and the Way of the
Cross on Fridays.

The rhythm of our daily work was now established.
We rose before six and washed in primitive conditions,
then spent half an hour meditating in chapel; then came
Mass, always celebrated by the archbishop, with two students chosen in rotation as servers. We breakfasted in another part of the building, after which we had a brief
period of recreation in the courtyard, the archbishop
usually joining us. Then came our studies.

The archbishop himself was rector of the seminary:
he took this dangerous responsibility on himself, explaining at our first conference in the chapel that he was personally responsible for everything that went on. Our pre-
fect was Fr. Kazimierz Klosak—a taciturn, quiet man
with a thin, hoarse voice, who looked at us over the top

of his spectacles. He was a bookworm who sat up late at night over treatises on natural philosophy, but he did not himself lecture to us.

We had our main meal at midday, followed by a walk in the garden; then came Adoration of the Blessed Sacrament, followed by private studies. In my case I also had to prepare for my school exam in December.

Karol read a great deal. I used constantly to see him during our afternoon studies, sitting over his books and leaning his head on his hand in a characteristic attitude.

Although there were several of us studying and living in one large room, we observed strict discipline and tried not to get in one another's way. We were conscious of what we were doing in relation to what was happening in the outside world, in the streets of Cracow and especially in Warsaw.

The Warsaw insurgents were in dire straits, and it was increasingly clear that they had no hope of victory. If they had not managed to gain control of the city in the first few days, they would not succeed now. Even the defensive battle was being lost, as the Poles kept retreating and surrendering one district after another. There were fearful tales of murder and atrocities committed by the Germans against the civil population, the shooting of noncombatants, the burning and destruction of houses, and the general devastation of the city.

After the Uprising was crushed, Cracow began to fill with refugees from Warsaw, who had been evacuated from the city to a camp at Pruszkow. The Central Welfare Organization (a Polish body tolerated by the Germans) had its hands more than full, and could not cope with the needs of the poor and the suffering. Organizers of help for those in distress kept coming to the archbishop. We students could not leave the building to take part in the various forms of relief work, but had to concentrate on our studies.

Busy as the archbishop was with problems of protecting the Polish population and the Church in Cracow and the rest of Poland, he did his best to ensure that our studies were as normal and uninterrupted as possible. He not only looked after our philosophical and theological studies, but also took an interest in practical aspects of our training. We were given elocution lessons by Juliusz Osterwa, the great actor and director, whom I had known through Mrs. Szkocka. At our first lesson he greeted Karol with special warmth. He then sat beside me at a table and, after a short introduction, gave me a text to read. I read it aloud; then he did so, and we could all see what a difference there was. He then put Karol through the same test, and went on to explain his ideas on how to preach a sermon.

Another grim wartime winter was at hand. I took my school exam clandestinely in a flat in Kremerowska Street; the examiner was B. Nowodworski, who, as it happened, was the headmaster of the high school I had attended before the war. At night we used to hear the dull roar of aircraft squadrons, and were frequently awakened by sirens. Factories near Cracow were bombed, such as the IG Farben works at Auschwitz. Then, as the Red Army drew nearer, we began to hear distant artillery fire at night. It seemed that we would be freed before Christmas, but it was not to be. We all knew that the Germans planned to turn Cracow into a fortress, but it also became clear that they were making preparations to evacuate if they had to. Sappers mined all the bridges, important sites and monuments, so as to leave nothing behind them but scorched earth and ruins. All offices and factories were evacuated, all valuable books and works of art were removed from libraries and museums. Somehow we did not mind this, provided the Germans were going; but as yet it did not seem certain that they were. Soviet planes began to raid Cracow—not heavy bombers, but small aircraft aiming at precise objectives. They did not meet much resistance except from antiaircraft fire: scarcely any German planes were to be seen. The windows of our room looked onto the street: we were not supposed to look out, but by now one could see at a glance that the Germans were preparing to leave. Trucks laden with all kinds of loot kept passing through the streets without interruption. Then, on the night of January 16, we heard a continuous noise of car engines from across the street—the police were moving out at last, leaving nothing but the army. When day dawned all was quiet and empty, the snow plowed up by tracks in every direction.

The day was clear and frosty. During the morning German soldiers were to be seen, but only in motor vehicles and tanks that rolled slowly through the city. We could not tell whether they were moving in or evacuating. The noise of gunfire became louder and closer. Later the Germans disappeared from the city center, and the streets were practically deserted. We waited, full of suspense. Had the Germans really given up their plan and abandoned Cracow without a shot? Suddenly the rumble of a tank was heard in the distance—German or Russian? The few passers-by dashed into doorways as it roared past, firing a single shot at the palace gate; fortunately no one was hit. A short while afterward the same tank came past again: either it had lost its way or its retreat had been cut off. Then there was quiet for a time, till we heard an outburst of fire from guns of different caliber, followed by a tremendous bang. Windows were shattered, tiles fell off the roof. This was the blowing up of the railway bridge, and sometime afterward the "third bridge" was blown up. During evening service in the chapel we were startled by another fearful explosion, far louder than the first two; it blew out all the windows and must have shaken every remaining tile off the roof. This time it was the Debnicki Bridge. The archbishop stopped the service and told us to go down to the shelter. The upstairs room was uninhabitable anyway; it was freezing cold and there was a bitter wind. There was no light, as the power station was out of action. We boarded up the windows with shutters and went down to the shelter, a huge barrel-vaulted place. We could still hear the sound of guns, but it was not so earsplitting as when we were upstairs. We prayed and sang hymns. The archbishop remained in his own room, accompanied only by his chaplain. After nightfall, when the danger had reached its height, he sent the chaplain down and remained upstairs alone, until a still louder outburst of fire induced him to come down and join us.

9

The Apostolic See

I got up fairly early. It is about twelve miles from the center of Münster to Greven Airport. Gunther took me in his car. It was not misty, but a cold, windy day with a leaden sky. We could not take off for Frankfurt on schedule, as apparently there was an autumn fog there and we had to wait till it cleared. I did not mind; I used the time to catch up with the writing I had not finished the night before because of packing. It was a small departure lounge, as only small aircraft go from there. The atmosphere was cozy: people knew one another or soon did, and chatted away freely. As the hours went by, one person after another gave up hope of the flight and went home. I sat there absorbed in memories, only from time to time noticing the airport police in dark green uniforms with submachine guns slung over their shoulders. By this time I was practically alone. The next plane was not due to take off until 10:25; if it got to Frankfurt on time, I could catch the plane for Rome at 12:20. But it was not on time, as, although the fog had cleared, priority was being given to planes arriving from other continents.

At last we left Greven, flying first in gray clouds and

then in bright sunshine. At Frankfurt, as we awaited our turn to land, I went on writing my reminiscences of the Occupation. Finally the memory became oppressive, and I looked through the porthole at the huge city below with its magnificent layout, tall buildings and bold modern architecture. I noticed how much forest and agricultural land there was around the city, and how well the villages and townships fitted into the landscape.

After circling for an hour we finally landed; there was no fog but no sun either, and I had a long wait before I could fly on to Rome. The airport was like a small city with its complex of lounges, corridors, escalators, luggage conveyor belts, shops, bars and restaurants. I looked around for a place to write, and found a small table in a restaurant served by what seemed to be Turks and Greeks. It was dark, and the broad expanse of window was like a screen on which I could see aircraft landing and taking off, filling up with gas and discharging passengers. I looked at the fairy-tale sight with unseeing eyes—my mind was too full of the horror of the Occupation days.

At last I got on board a Boeing 747, and we took off punctually.

When we arrived in Rome it was quite dark, and raining. The plane circled for some time before making a soft landing. I did not wait for my suitcases but went straight to the bus, which left for town almost at once with hardly any passengers. I was not sure if I would get a room "at home"—that is to say in the Polish College, where I had lived for nearly two years. Later I had gone on to Munich and Münster to complete my studies, but as I had a four-year grant I continued to use the college as a base and had a permanent room there. However, I knew that innumerable priests and at least fifty bishops would be coming to Rome for the Pope's inauguration on Sunday; institutions like ours would certainly have to put some of them up, and I had only announced my arrival two days ago. At Termini Station I got out of the bus and went into the enormous central hall, simple yet monumental with its tremendous vaulting, and a host of memories crowded in on me. I felt spellbound as I remembered all the times I had arrived at the station or left it with Karol by day or by night, the first *cappuccino* on arrival in Rome or the last before departure. I went to the underground, traveled three stations to Circo Massimo, came up the steps to the Viale Aventino and turned by the FAO building into the Via Aventina, where I knew by heart every house, every tree, even the cars standing in front of the college. Not only *I* knew them, but *we* knew them—Karol and I had so often walked that way together. I came to the gate marked Collegium Polonorum and rang the bell. It was answered by Dr. Jozef Michalik, the new rector, a delightful priest and an old friend of mine who had also been at the Angelicum. Seeing his face recalled me to reality, and I asked if there was a room for me.

"Yes, of course."

We walked along a narrow path, at the end of which was an illuminated statue of Our Lady; beyond this was the small college garden. In the dim light I could also see the metal table and chair at which Karol had been sitting and writing when I arrived a month ago, just before the conclave that elected John Paul I. Jozef told me who had arrived and who was still expected. We passed the ground-floor apartment that Karol had last used, and I went upstairs to my room. I met various friends on the way, and had scarcely had time to deposit my traveling bag before they started to buttonhole me and give me all the news. They had all been on the piazza waiting for the famous puff of smoke on each occasion, and had heard Cardinal Felici pronounce the words: *"Annuntio vobis gaudium magnum. Habemus papam."* They could not stop telling me how exciting it had been.

"You can imagine what we all felt."

"You have no idea how delighted everyone is in Rome."

"At first we couldn't believe it."

"We thought it couldn't be true, that we must have heard wrong."

"When he came out on the balcony, the scene in the square was terrific. Everyone shouting, calling out, applauding, crying, waving handkerchiefs."

"And when the people around us heard we were Poles they embraced us and fell on our necks with joy."

But I had heard enough now of what had happened on that great day. It was late; I did not want to keep my friends up, and I wanted to be fresh in the morning. I had done some writing on the journey, and decided to do no more that night. Indeed I could hardly have added another word—I could not bring myself to recall the war years in those surroundings.

In my room I turned on the radio and heard an account of the Pope's reception of the diplomatic corps at eleven that morning in the Sala del Consistorio. A speech of congratulation was read by the Guatemalan ambassador, Luis Valladares y Aycinena, on behalf of all the diplomats accredited to the Holy See. The Pope in his reply spoke first of the excellent relations which Paul VI had had with the diplomatic corps. "This was the effect of that great Pope's sense of responsibility, full of respect and benevolence, for the general good of nations, and his understanding of the high ideals of peace and development which inspire them." After speaking warmly of John Paul I the Pope extended a welcome to everyone present, both personally and as a representative of his country. "If there is any place where all nations should coexist peacefully and find respect, sympathy, a sincere desire for their dignity, happiness and progress, it is here at the Apostolic See in the heart of the Church."

The Pope added that in their meeting not only were governments represented, but also peoples and nations. Some nations were young and some old, but the Church had always recognized the wealth and greatness of cultures, histories and languages. Called to be the successor of St. Peter, he would endeavor to show to each nation the respect that was its due. As to his own nationality he said, "The particular nature of the country of our origin is henceforth of little importance: as a Christian, and still more as Pope, we shall continue to give proof of universal love, showing the same favor to all and especially to those who are undergoing heavy trials."

He emphasized that diplomatic relations did not signify approval of this or that regime or of all that was done in the conduct of public affairs. "They do not necessarily imply on our part approval of one regime or another—that is not our business—nor, of course, approval of all they do in conducting their affairs. . . . The Holy See appeals to all governments represented by diplomats to show more and more understanding of certain needs. The Holy See does not ask this for itself. It does so, in union with the local bishops, in order that Christians and other believers in your countries should be allowed, without special privileges but in all justice, to deepen their faith, practice religion and, as loyal citizens, play a full part in the public life of their countries." Then another significant sentence: "The Holy See does this in the interest of all peoples without exception, knowing that freedom, respect for the life and dignity of individuals—who are never mere instruments—fair treatment, professional conscientiousness and the joint pursuit of common good, a spirit of reconciliation and openness to spiritual values are all basic conditions of harmonious social life, progress and civilization. . . . There is still too much physical and moral suffering due to indifference, selfishness, blindness and insensitivity. The Church wishes to contribute to the lessening of these sufferings by peaceful means, moral education, and honest behavior by Christians and all men of good will." Finally the Pope said that in this spirit he hoped to maintain sincere and fruitful relations with all the countries there represented.

After his address the Holy Father surprised and pleased the diplomats by talking separately to each of them. This, the radio reporter observed, was a new style of papal audience, similar to his address to the College of Cardinals. The Pope spoke fluently in English, French, German and Spanish, but still more notable was the atmosphere of warmth, sincerity and humor, and the personal approach to each of the diplomats present.

Having heard the full description of the audience, I breathed a sigh of relief and satisfaction—another important step on the long and difficult road had been successfully accomplished. I went to bed and slept soundly.

10

Reconstruction

The first Soviet soldiers reached our underground shelter late at night. We welcomed them with tea and bread, which was all we had. Only now, when we saw them with our own eyes, did we realize that the nightmare of the Occupation was over.

In the morning we set to work feverishly clearing away broken glass and tidying up the disorder caused by the night's events. Karol and I decided to visit our homes, if only for a moment, to find out whether our loved ones were still alive. We had to be back soon, however, to help fit in new windowpanes; there was not a single one left in the palace, but new glass was expected shortly.

For the first time in six months we went to see our relations in Debnicki. The streets were crammed and it was hard to get through the crowd. Masses of military vehicles, great Studebakers, Dodges and Fords, machine-gun carriages, peasant carts drawn by two ponies or one, and streams of soldiers on foot wearing fur caps and felt boots and carrying submachine guns. At the end of Zwierzyniecka Street we turned into the embankment by

what had been the Debnicki Bridge and were able to realize the force of the explosion that had destroyed a
whole section of it. We climbed down and walked across
the frozen surface of the Vistula, whence we had a full
view of the contorted steel girders pointing up at the sky.
Soldiers' bodies were scattered on the ice, and there were
a few broken-down tanks.

Luckily everybody at home was well.

We made our way back through the streets jammed
with soldiers and civilians, tanks and handcarts. As we
got to the palace a group of military vehicles drew up
and some officers alighted—evidently of high rank, to
judge from the red insignia on their coats. We followed
them inside, and they went up to the archbishop's apartments. It turned out that they were Marshal Konev, commander of the Ukrainian front, and two generals; they
had come to pay tribute to the archbishop's anti-Nazi
stand throughout the Occupation.

Two days later we witnessed a similar scene. Three
jeeps drew up; soldiers piled out of the first and third,
and Marshal Zymierski* emerged from the second, attired in prewar Polish uniform with a general's insignia and the distinctive four-cornered cap, with riding
breeches and a saber. Accompanied by his adjutants, he
had come to the palace to meet the archbishop and pay
his respects.

As we worked busily to reglaze the windows and retile
the roof, day after day hundreds of the most varied people filed through the palace, as delegates and representatives came to submit a multitude of problems or to
give vent to their joys and sorrows. Everyone wanted

---

* Michal Rola-Zymierski, commander of the "People's Army"
recognizing the authority of the government set up in Poland under Soviet auspices in 1944; minister of national defense, 1945–49.

help in some form. We went to the headquarters of the Theological Seminary, previously occupied by the SS; there were still some French prisoners there, but they had started to leave for home. The building was in a frightful state. Not only were its windows blown out and the roof stripped, like ours, by the Debnicki explosion, but the central heating had failed some time ago; water had frozen in all the pipes, and the inmates had had to keep warm by lighting open fires in the rooms. The state of the lavatories was appalling, with piles of frozen excrement that had to be chopped up and carted away. Karol and I and a few other students volunteered to do this. The stench was dreadful, and we found the only way to keep from vomiting was to breathe through the mouth. It was quite a long job, as there were three lavatories on each floor. After that we had the easier task of carrying tiles up to the roof, where they were fitted by a small team of experts.

We continued to live in the palace, where we were joined by other students who had applied to the archbishop previously but had had to wait. There were also some "late vocations," including two remarkable men: Dr. Staszek Kownacki, a physician who played Chopin beautifully during recreation hours, and a lawyer, Dr. Stanislaw Stomma. Both of them fitted in admirably with our group, though we were so much younger, and they became special friends of Karol's.

A new rector was appointed, Father Kozlowski, who tried hard to get the seminary back onto a normal peacetime footing. He had only partial success, as various special tasks kept cropping up. For instance, we were asked to help reorganize the university library, which was in a state of total confusion. The Germans had removed the more valuable books and consigned the others to various sheds and junk heaps, some in the open air. It was a formidable task to sort through the piles of books, pamphlets and periodicals, arranging and cataloguing them as best we could. Our help was especially required in organizing the theological faculty, housed on the ground floor of the Collegium Novum, on the left-hand side; at present there was nothing to be seen but bare walls and a heap of rubble on the floor. The new rector of the university, the dean of the theological faculty, the professors and the rector of the seminary were all anxious to get the university going as soon as possible, and we managed after a fashion to organize the various departments and their libraries. One of the first to get going was the theological faculty, where lectures and seminars were soon being conducted by professors of the very highest caliber: for instance Fr. Konstanty Michalski, for many years rector of the university, for philosophy, Fr. Marian Michalski for basic theology, and Bishop Godlewski for church history. However, the organization was still provisional and very far from ideal.

Karol and I attended many lectures together, although he was in his third year and I in my first. We were crowded into small rooms, and I often sat next to him. As in former days, he used to head every page of notes, on the left, with initials such as J+M (Jesus and Mary) or OAMDG (*omnia ad majorem Dei gloriam*—all to the greater glory of God).

As the university began to get into its stride again, a vigorous student life developed. Student self-government was carried on through the organization known as Bratniak, on which the faculties were represented in proportion to their numbers. Among those appointed from the theological faculty were Karol, Staszek Starowieyski and myself. Andrzej Deskur, another "late vocation," soon joined us from the law faculty. Karol was elected

vice-chairman of Bratniak, while Staszek and I belonged
to the auditing committee. It was our first contact with
university students, and we saw for ourselves how many
of them were poor, even destitute, and in what wretched
conditions they lived. Many had no financial support, as
their parents had been murdered under the Occupation
or were in territory now part of the Soviet Union. Some
had neither suits, shirts nor boots to wear: they dressed
in rags, were half-starved and lived in cellars or hovels—
but they kept on studying. Many were very ill and in
need of recuperation, especially those who had come
from POW or labor camps in Germany, not to speak of
escapees from extermination camps. Luckily we were not
powerless to help them. UNRRA (the United Nations
Relief and Rehabilitation Administration) sent goods in
ever-increasing quantity: powdered milk, lard, conserves,
huge parcels of used clothing. Our task was to distribute
these according to need, to send off the most gravely ill
to mountain sanatoria, and in general to relieve distress
as much as we could. It was often late at night before we
returned to the seminary from Bratniak meetings, and
the rector would mutter crossly that "this must be the
last time."

An event in our home in Debnicki was the arrival of
my aunt and cousin from Lwow: she had decided to
leave her home town, which was on the Soviet side of
the new frontier, and settle in Cracow, while my cousin
was to study at the technical college. Two of her sisters
turned up from Lwow, and also an aunt on my father's
side. They would have liked to stay in Cracow too, but
could find no room, as the town was crammed with refugees from Warsaw and Poznan. Those who had fled
from Lwow were obliged to go farther west, and my own
relations, like many others, settled in Lower Silesia.

We finally left the archbishop's palace, though with regret, and went to live at the Theological Seminary. Life was getting more and more normal. An event that delighted all Poles was that in 1946 the archbishop received a cardinal's hat.

On one occasion he said to me after returning from a visit to Rome, "I have nobody left there now. All my old colleagues are dead. I ought to send some young men there, but I don't know where they could study: the Polish College and Institute are already full."

We organized a celebration in his honor at the seminary, including prose and poetry recitations in the style of the "rhapsodic theater." I was to recite the passage in Sienkiewicz's *Quo Vadis* where St. Peter is persuaded by the community to leave Rome for fear of execution, and meets Christ as he is leaving the city. I practiced it for hours under Karol's direction. Fr. Bronislaw Mazur designed a handsome backdrop; we cut out various symbols and signs in silver paper, which he stuck onto sheets of cardboard. It was curious to think that a wing of the seminary, immediately adjacent, was still in ruins.

Jan Tyranowski used to visit us from time to time, smiling and cheerful as ever. He apologized for not coming more often, but said he and his friends were busy studying. I asked what subject, and he replied, "Theology. As we are all laymen and can't go to the seminary, we are organizing our own theological courses."

"Who is going to teach you?"

"The same professors as are teaching you—so there's nothing make-believe about it. There will be end-of-year exams, degrees and everything." He was full of his usual enthusiasm.

"Have you got many applicants?"

"Yes, more than we have places. We've had to weed them out."

Not long afterward Karol said to me during the recreation hour, "Rozycki has suggested that I write a doctoral thesis."

"The professor of dogmatic theology?" Our year had not yet studied with him.

"Yes."

"A doctoral thesis?" I said in some surprise. "Somehow I never thought of you as becoming an academic."

"Well, it wouldn't mean that straight away."

"How did the idea come about?"

"There are only a few of us in my year, so we have closer contact with the professors. Rozycki examined me once or twice, he was pleased with my work and asked me what I was reading for myself, what interested me most."

"Well, you read all kinds of things, don't you?"

"Yes, but I mentioned St. John of the Cross, St. Teresa of Avila and St. Teresa of Lisieux. He remarked that they were writers who are not often the subject of academic writing, and suggested that I take as my theme 'The theological virtue of faith in St. John of the Cross.'"

"It sounds more like a subject in moral theology, in Father Wicher's field."

"Perhaps on the borderline between dogma and morals."

This was perhaps the first signal that our paths were about to diverge. I had never thought of myself as an academic; I wanted to be a priest so as to help people in a direct way, not through books. Soon afterward came a second shock: the archbishop was sending Karol and Staszek to Rome for further studies. Karol's ordination was to be advanced so that he could go there as a priest, while Staszek would be ordained after his return. I was upset and rather saddened by these surprises.

Karol prepared for ordination in a six-day retreat conducted by our father confessor. The ceremony took place in the archbishop's chapel; no one else was present. It was a gray, gloomy day, as the first of November—All Saints'—often is in Poland. On the following day, All Souls', he said his first Masses at the Wawel, with myself as server: one in St. Leonard's chapel and two at the shrine of St. Stanislaw. Only a few others were present; Father Figlewicz guided him through the ceremonies. It was another dark, wintry day, and I felt as if our ways were parting. On the following Sunday there was a solemn Mass at the church of St. Stanislaw Kostka in Debnicki, attended by some of those who had belonged to the "Living Rosary," and whose comrades were now scattered all over the world. Father Figlewicz preached, and afterward Mrs. Szkocka gave a lunch at 14 Szwedska Street. Karol, in accordance with Polish custom, had asked his godmother, Mrs. Wiadrowska, to hold a small reception at her home in Florianska Street, but she had too little room and did not think the entrance imposing enough. So Mrs. Szkocka had spoken up:

"It's no problem for me, I've plenty of room. It's just a matter of moving the big table."

"In which room will you have the reception?"

"The room Karol convalesced in—the 'theater' room isn't available at the moment."

Among those who came were Tyranowski, Father Kuczkowski from Wadowice and a fellow student called Staszek Truszkowski, who had also formerly belonged to Tyranowski's "Living Rosary." It was all very nicely done, with speeches and congratulations and good wishes for Karol's new life, but there was a touch of melancholy about it because Karol was going to leave us for two years. Of course we consoled one another by saying it was only two years—though someone kept insisting that this was a long time; there would be letters and post-cards, and he would surely come back for the summer holidays and perhaps even for Christmas, as there was a longish break then and where could one celebrate Christmas properly except in Poland? We partly believed all this, and partly pretended to.

Anyway, Karol went off; we missed him greatly, and I was very unhappy. Cards and letters started to arrive, and we shared his news. He and Staszek had not found rooms in any Polish institution but were at the Belgian College, which was good for his French. He wrote to me that he had started at the Angelicum, where the lectures were in Latin, and was continuing the thesis he had begun in Poland about St. John of the Cross; between lectures he was learning Spanish so as to understand his beloved author better. But, although he realized that the time would go quickly, he was not confining himself to study.

One day when I called on Mrs. Szkocka she showed me with pride Karol's latest letter, which said, "One's first experience of Rome simply cannot be described in a few sentences—there are so many aspects, so many different levels. One associates them with some detail or another and feels more enriched day by day; but I am a long way from having systematized my impressions."

About that time Jan Tyranowski fell ill. I heard disquieting reports and went to see him. I found him with a bandaged hand, but cheerful as usual, and pleased to see me.

"I was afraid you were confined to bed, but I see it doesn't look too serious," I said. "What is the trouble exactly?"

"An infection. The doctor told me to stay in bed. I haven't been going out at all, but staying in bed isn't so easy, as I have so many visitors."

I too felt that a mere infection could hardly warrant staying in bed, and after a short talk I went away, feeling relieved. But a little later I heard that he was in the hospital. I asked what was the matter, and was told that it was still the trouble with his hand. Much alarmed, I went to see him again. He was still smiling, but his forearm was swathed in bandages. The tips of his fingers were sticking out: they were swollen and bluish-yellow. Some visitors were sitting by his bed.

"My arm has swollen up like a watermelon," he told me, "and the suppuration won't go down. The doctors say that the only hope is a new drug called penicillin, but it isn't made in Poland yet; it has to be gotten from abroad."

"Then we'll get it by hook or by crook. Does the arm hurt?"

"A bit."

One of the visitors put in, "It must hurt badly, the doctor said."

"Are they giving you painkillers?"

"Yes."

"And are you taking them?" I asked suspiciously.

"No," he replied in a hesitant tone.

"Why, are they bad for you?"

"I am lying here doing nothing, but I still want to work for the salvation of the world, as you people are doing at the seminary—I don't want to remain idle. So I am offering up my pain for the benefit of all those in need—and for Karol as well," he added.

I could find no words with which to reply.

Shortly afterward I went to see him again. This time Mrs. Szkocka was there—brisk, cheerful and energetic as usual. She announced that she had a letter from Karol in Rome.

"There are two letters in this envelope, one for me and one for you." Tyranowski took the letter she handed him and pressed it to his breast, while Mrs. Szkocka went on:

"I must read you a bit of my own letter, which is about you as well—would you like to hear it?"

"Of course."

"Then listen: 'Dear Granny,' [that's me, she added for our benefit] 'Thank you very much for the precious'— yes, 'precious'—'news about Mr. Tyranowski.'" She paused for a moment and went on, "'I enclose a letter for our beloved Job'—that's what he calls you. Ah, yes, this bit isn't about you, but here's some more. 'Please pray that I may, to the best of my ability, become an imitator of Christ and of those who reflect him so perfectly.' That means you, of course," she concluded.

I asked Tyranowski if the penicillin had helped.

"No—it changed the color of the pus, that's all."

"Are you having injections for the pain?"

"As long as I can stand it, I don't want them."

I left, realizing that he was in a bad way. A few days later I heard that his arm had been amputated almost to the shoulder.

I hurried to the hospital, where I found him still cheerful, with a kind of inner calm. That was the first impression he gave, but when I looked closer I saw that the long illness and the operation had pulled him down terribly. The empty sleeve of his shirt hung limply. His calm and serenity, however, were amazing.

The operation was probably carried out too late, but

perhaps in any case it would have done no good. A few days later he lost his hearing, and three days after that he was dead. His funeral was attended by crowds of those whom he had instructed in faith, hope, charity and contemplative prayer, teaching them the secrets of inner life, above all his own example.

Karol, like all of us, was much upset by Tyranowski's death. He did not come home for the vacation, however, as it turned out that the cardinal had given him and Staszek a sum of money and told them to "travel about Europe." In July 1947 we received a postcard saying: "I am writing from Paris for a change, having got here by way of Marseilles and Lourdes. The archbishop wants me to spend the vacation visiting France, Belgium and perhaps Holland, to study pastoral methods. How far I shall succeed will depend on the grace of God and, subject to that, on my own powers of observation. Then there are all the sights to be seen here—northern France and Flanders with their Gothic architecture." He also wrote about the French bishops' efforts to re-Christianize Paris and the appointment of the best pastors to important urban parishes. Later he told us briefly of his contacts with Polish mine workers in Belgium, and especially Father Cardijn and his Young Christian Workers' movement.

Two years later Karol came back as though from another world. He seemed somehow refreshed and different, yet still his old self. The archbishop appointed him curate at Niegowic, which rather shocked his friends. "Fancy sending you, with all your gifts and now with a doctor's degree, to a remote place like that!" Karol only laughed at such comments.

I went to see him there. Niegowic was indeed a small

parish at the end of the world, or at any rate of the diocese. The old church was surrounded by big linden trees; the priest's house had no electricity; there was a well, a kitchen garden and orchard, a cowshed and chickens. More important, however, the parish priest was one of the finest in the diocese. Here again the cardinal's hand was to be seen: valuing Karol as he did, he wanted to give him the best possible start in his pastoral career.

Karol asked me many questions, but first we talked for a long time about Tyranowski. As I spoke of his terrible illness I could still see his face, serene amid all his suffering.

"Do you like it here?" I asked.

"Yes, it's fine."

We went for a walk round the church. The leaves rustled and the birds sang. Every now and then someone came along and greeted us from a distance, not venturing to interrupt our conversation. Children came boldly up and kissed Karol's hand; in reply he stroked their heads, close-cropped or plaited and ribboned, and sometimes kissed their foreheads, which they raised expectantly.

"What do you do?" I asked with the curiosity of one who knows that before long this way of life will also be his.

"The same as any curate. Early Mass, confessions, breakfast, doctrine classes, after which I go back to the presbytery. The afternoons are more flexible, but I have to be available in case of a sick call."

"That doesn't sound so bad—you have a bit of time to read or write?"

"Yes, except that people keep coming in, especially children and young people, to borrow a book or, really, just to chat. Then after Christmas there's the carol singing. The first time I went on it I remembered the days in Wadowice when I used to go round from house to house with our parish priest there. It's fun seeing the people in their homes, and teaching the children doctrine there as well as in church."

"But it must be tiring going about like that all day long."

"Yes, it is, when you're plodding through the snow in a surplice and biretta and a cassock and overcoat. The snow sticks to the hem of your cassock and melts when you're indoors, and then in the open air it freezes so that the cassock is stiff and heavy and interferes with walking. By evening you feel you can hardly go a step farther, but you have to because you know there are people who have been waiting for this visit all year."

"What do you do when you enter each home?" I asked, still curious.

"You go in and say, 'Praised be Jesus Christ,' you greet the whole family who are standing round, you pray with them and sprinkle the cottage with holy water, and the stables too so that the cattle will prosper during the coming year; then you go back into the house and you can't escape sitting and talking to everyone for a bit, though the sacristan keeps reminding you that it's late and you have other houses to visit. After all, the people have been waiting all year and they're entitled to it. Then in springtime there's Lent, of course."

"Do you have many extra devotions then?"

"The main thing is confessions—they're very important, but also very tiring. Imagine sitting all day in the confessional, from morning to evening, with a short break for lunch."

"Yes, but it's only one day in the year."

"Oh no, it isn't. To hear confessions for the whole parish in one day you have to call in over twenty priests from neighboring parishes, and then you have to go and do the same for them."

"Yes, I see the number of days must mount up."

"Besides, it's not just a question of long sessions in the confessional and freezing in unheated churches—the important thing is the contact you have to make with the person kneeling behind the grille. Most of them aren't used to receiving the sacraments often—they usually begin by saying, 'My last confession was a year ago,' or it may be ten years, or even more. So you can't just polish them off rapidly, first turning to one side and then the other; you have to have a really serious, heartfelt talk with them. Confession, in a way, is the acme of our activity as priests, and it is there that we encounter human beings in the depths of their personality. But I wonder if we shall be able to preserve these pastoral values during the next stage of development of our Polish culture."

"How do you mean?"

"I am thinking of the danger to any pastor, that if he does not have a deep inner life he will imperceptibly turn into an official, a kind of bureaucrat."

"Do you say that because of what you have seen in the West?"

"Partly, but you only have to look around in this country to see the same thing, especially in cities. In the villages a priest of the 'official' type may hold his own for a time, but in town he will very soon disappear completely. France is a sad example, both the towns and the countryside—in fact, I don't know which is worse."

I asked Karol about his travels, and he enlarged on the subjects, mentioned in his postcards, of the "Mission de France" and the Young Workers' movement (known in French as JOC). He had met Father Cardijn in Rome, when the latter had lectured at the Gregorianum on his idea of the duties of a modern pastor toward various social groups; but it was the Mission de France that impressed him most of all.

"Was it in Paris that you first heard about it?"

"No, I came across a book by the founder or inspirer of the movement, Father H. Godin, called *La France, pays de mission.* He is a priest working in a suburb of Paris, and he was the first to make people realize how far Paris had ceased to be Christian. He divided the population into three categories. First those who are still practicing, and these, as he showed, are terribly few. Secondly those who do not practice but who remain in the Church's orbit in some way or another, and these are numerous. Thirdly those who have completely lost touch with Christianity, of whom there are many and who are increasing at a fearful rate. Take this example, for instance. A group of lads come upon a statue of Christ on the cross, and study it with interest. They see the letters INRI over the top, and one of them says, 'Inri, was that the chap's name?'"

"How did Father Godin begin his career as a priest?"

"I should have told you that in the port area of Marseilles, at about the same time, there was another priest called Father L'Oeuf who discovered much the same state of affairs as Father Godin, and together they worked out new methods—or rather they are very old ones, but applied in a fresh way. A group of priests live in a kind of community, meeting every day to pray together, to compare notes and discuss their problems. Instead of the usual division of rank between parish priest and curate, they work according to their different specialties—whether they have to do with children, young people or adults, or according to geographical areas."

"Something like the original idea of canons regular?"

"Yes, exactly. Secondly, their motto is *'témoignage,'* or bearing witness to Christ by their daily lives, especially unselfishness and poverty—they aim to have the same standard of living as those to whom they minister, or even a degree lower. Thirdly, the liturgy: they want it to play its original role of initiating people, of drawing them into active life."

"And is it true that they also work in factories?"

"That is a secondary aspect of the movement; the main points are those I've mentioned. Of course there are various groups within it, and some of them regard factory work as essential; but as I say, it is only one aspect among several."

"And what do *you* think about the worker-priest idea? It's spoken of here as a revelation."

"I think it's going too far to make it a *sine qua non*. Of course there are some places where the only way to begin is by working alongside people—but in general, circumstances are against it, as a priest simply hasn't time to do a manual job."

I could see that the Mission de France was still an object of keen interest to Karol.

"How is your doctorate getting on?"

"My thesis has been approved, to all intents and purposes, at the Angelicum, where I took my exams; but it has to be formally accepted by Fr. Wladyslaw Wicher of the theological faculty of the university in Cracow."

"Not Father Rozycki?"

"No."

My own seminary course was completed in July 1949. Staszek Starowieyski and I were ordained together in the cathedral and I said my first Mass in the Debnicki church, Karol preaching the sermon. He spoke of the sacrament of priesthood and of the part that can be played by individuals in the development of a vocation—not only priests but laymen, such as Tyranowski and the "Living Rosary."

The first parish to which I was appointed was Rabka,

about fifty miles south of Cracow. Karol, after a year at Niegowic, was transferred to a curacy in the parish of St. Florian, one of the best in Cracow, with fine traditions—fresh evidence of the cardinal's interest in Karol's future.

I dropped in to see him during my visits to the city. The presbytery was in the center of town—a trifle gloomy, but ideally quiet.

"Do you like it here?"

"Yes, I do."

"Who is the parish priest?"

"Fr. Tadeusz Kurowski, a fine chap."

"And the curates?"

"Also first-rate: Czeslaw Obtulowicz, Jozef Rozwadowski and Marian Jaworski."

I already knew Father Rozwadowski, known as "the soul of optimism," from the days when he used to substitute for the archbishop's chaplain, Fr. Julian Groblicki; at the university he was assistant to Fr. Konstanty Michalski. His special subject was psychology, under Szuman. In due course I met Father Obtulowicz, a man sober beyond his years, whom Karol especially admired, and Father Jaworski, a quiet, meditative priest who was Karol's devoted friend.

11

Freedom of Speech

I got up at six, as was my habit when living in the college. Two months ago it had been light at that hour, but in October it was still dark.

The sacristy was full of bishops and priests helping them to robe; another sacristy was full of student priests. In August, I recalled, there had been four or five of us at most, and Karol had been the celebrant at early Mass. This time the Mass at 6:45 was concelebrated, the chief celebrant being Archbishop Stroba, the new ordinary of Poznan—and Karol was no longer with us.

At breakfast we were able to talk to those who had just arrived from Poland. There was a noisy, festive atmosphere as they vied in giving us the latest news.

I went up to the apartment that had been Karol's, and was now occupied by one of the visitors. Then I came away, lest I should be accused of sentimentality. I went into the garden, where there was a faint smell of cypresses; it would be stronger once the sun got up. In the corner of the garden where I had seen him last time, the white-painted metal table and chair were still there and looked as if they had not been moved. I could still see him writing, his cassock buttoned up to the neck. I went back to my room so as not to miss the radio report of his meeting with the press, a very important occasion.

About fifteen hundred press, radio and TV correspondents were assembled in the Hall of Benedictions when the Pope appeared at 11 A.M. He walked up and down for at least fifteen minutes in the space between the barriers, greeting and talking to individual journalists. When Jerzy Turowicz, the editor of *Tygodnik Powszechny,* knelt and kissed his hand, he bent over him and said, "Well, they're putting me through the mill today, and no mistake!"

His formal address to the journalists was in French, and from the very beginning he established friendly contact with them.

"I welcome you heartily, and I thank you all for all you have done and are doing to present to a wide public, through the press, radio and television, the events in the Catholic Church which have brought you to Rome more than once in the past two months." He thanked them for their friendly attitude toward Paul VI and John Paul I and added, "I thank you, too, for your presentation of the last conclave, of my election and the first days, the first steps taken by me under the heavy yoke of the pontificate."

He then spoke of the dangers and difficulties encountered by journalists in telling their readers of events in the Church. "It is so hard to discern events and convey them to others. In the first place, they are nearly always complicated. It suffices to overlook a single aspect, to ignore it or belittle it intentionally, or alternatively to exaggerate it, and the whole picture of reality or prediction of the future is falsified. . . . At the same time you must arouse the public's interest and attract its attention, as your employers frequently demand sensational news above all else. Some reporters are tempted by anecdotes, which are down-to-earth and can be very useful, provided they are significant and in true proportion to the nature of the religious event. Others plunge boldly into a far-reaching analysis of the problems and motives of Church personalities at the risk of passing over the most important aspect, which, as you know, is not political but spiritual."

I thought to myself, That could only have been said by someone who is himself a careful reader of "religious" articles in the press; and I remembered at once how Karol wrote for the *Tygodnik Powszechny* and how avidly he read it. When I came to Rome for the August conclave, one of his first questions was whether I had brought the latest issue with me. And I remembered all the discussions and arguments he had presided over, or which we had in our weekly meetings at his place in Cracow.

The Pope continued, "You attach great importance to freedom of speech and information, and you are right. Consider yourselves happy that you enjoy it. Use your freedom well, so as to pinpoint truth . . . I venture to appeal to you to show an understanding and fair-minded attitude; when you report on the Church's life and activity, try even harder to understand the profound spiritual motives of its thought and action. The Church for its part will give heed to the objective testimony of the press concerning the demands and expectations of this world."

In conclusion he said, "I am pleased and happy at my first contact with you. I assure you of my understanding, and I venture to count on yours." Then, in English: "I address my greetings and blessings not only to you, but to all your colleagues throughout the world."

A dozen or so journalists were then presented to the Holy Father. Jerzy Turowicz was one of them, and the

Pope said to the director of the Vatican press bureau who was standing by, "We two are old friends."

The Pope then spent nearly an hour walking up and down among the journalists, chatting and answering questions—not always of the most intelligent—into the microphones that were held toward him. From time to time he himself grasped a microphone and spoke into it—to the amazement of his suite, to whom such a thing was quite new.

Among the questions and answers were:

"Does Your Holiness feel like a prisoner in the Vatican? What is the atmosphere like?"

"Well, I've had five days of it. If it goes on like this, I can stand it."

"Will Your Holiness have other press conferences like this one?"

"If they'll let me, but we'll also have to see how you people treat me."

"Will Your Holiness go skiing?"

"I'm afraid I probably won't be allowed to."

"Will Your Holiness go to Lebanon?"

"That would be a good thing, but we must find a solution there first."

"Will Your Holiness go to Poland?"

"If I'm allowed."

The Pope replied to each questioner in his own language—Italian, English, French, German, Russian and of course Polish. When, after an hour, he concluded his "walkabout" conference he suddenly said, "Oh, I forgot to give you my blessing."

It may safely be said that there had never before been such a meeting between the Pope and the press corps. The journalists were delighted, and one of them said, "We were seduced by the Pope."

Lunch, like breakfast, was a noisy and hurried meal; the refectory was crowded with strange faces. The rector gave out tickets for next day's ceremony.

After lunch I went out onto the roof terrace to walk about alone, as Karol had often walked there with me or others.

Alojz Cader came up, evidently for the same reason. He said, "Do you remember the first time we went to Terminillo?"

"Look at those hills over there—that's Castel Gandolfo, and farther on is Castelli Romani, where we used to walk."

Indeed, I remembered our walks well. We would leave the college in the afternoon and go to Castelli, where we walked around the lake. Karol would generally walk by himself, reading or meditating, while we others—two or three of us—spent the time in conversation. On the way home we would eat lasagna or spaghetti in some little trattoria.

"Do you remember how often we used to eat in Roman restaurants?" I said to Alojz.

"Especially our meals with Bishop Lubowiecki."

"I forget why he used to give so many suppers."

"It was to keep up Prince Sapieha's tradition—you remember how he admired him. When Sapieha was in Rome he used to entertain Polish priests to dinner, and I once pointed out to Lubowiecki that he could afford to do the same. I used to choose the best dishes for everyone, and although he was stingy by nature he used to slap me on the back and say, 'You're quite right, Alojz, that's the way.' And Karol used to like it because it gave him a chance to talk to people."

We went down to my room so as to be with Karol a little, if only in memory.

In the afternoon I went to the basilica. Thousands of chairs were still set out on the piazza. Workmen were erecting a throne near the entrance to the church, and there was an open-air altar by the steps leading down to the square. I went in, and was engulfed by the enormous building. I stopped for a moment to contemplate Michelangelo's Pietà, and then went along the left-hand nave and up toward the sacristy, near the entrance to the papal tombs. I joined a small queue and we went down some steps, past the Lithuanian chapel with Our Lady of Ostra Brama* and the Polish chapel with Our Lady of Czestochowa,† where the Pope prayed on the first day of his pontificate. I stopped for a moment in front of the tomb of John XXIII and the tombstone of Paul VI—the two namesakes of the present Pope—and also the tomb of John Paul I. On the way out I passed a dark, empty niche, where no doubt John Paul II would one day rest.

* A shrine at Wilno (now Vilnius) in Lithuania, invoked by the poet Mickiewicz in his best-known work *Pan Tadeusz*. Poland and Lithuania were united before the eighteenth-century partitions, and Wilno belonged to Poland between the two world wars.

† Another famous shrine and place of pilgrimage, about sixty miles northwest of Cracow. The walled monastery with the miraculous picture of Our Lady withstood a Swedish siege in 1655.

12

Karol's Expeditions

On one occasion when I dropped in at St. Florian's, Karol said to me, "We don't often meet or have a chance to talk and pray together. What if we take a trip into the mountains some time?"

I was delighted, and on the appointed day we set out for the Beskids.* Our first destination was Prehyba. It was a beautiful autumn day, and the woods were a riot of color. At first it was a stiff climb, but later the going became easier. We talked or fell silent as we felt inclined, and at one point we knelt and prayed in the long grass. When we got to the mountain hut it was practically empty; but the sun was still well up in the sky, so we continued on our way. Before long, however, it was later afternoon and we had to find a lodging for the night. We came to a signpost, but were not sure whether the name on it denoted a mountain peak or a village. The distance appeared to be a short one, but after about an hour or so it was clear we were going steadily uphill, and we sadly concluded that the path was leading to an-

* A range southeast of Cracow, on the border with Czechoslovakia

other peak. There was nothing for it but to turn back. By the time we reached the signpost again it was dark; we wanted to get downhill as fast as possible, but it was easier said than done. We did not know the terrain, the forest was dark and we had no flashlights—only afterward did we realize how ill-equipped we were. We were afraid of straying from the path and never finding it again, and we were certainly not equipped for a cold autumn night in the woods. As we wandered desperately from tree to tree, trying to identify the markings that denoted the tourist trails, we suddenly heard voices, and in a few minutes the forest was full of people. We were immensely relieved and also surprised, as we had met no one on our route all day. What could they be doing so late? It turned out that they were women on the way back to the village from picking mushrooms; they had lost one of their number and were searching for her. Luckily she was found, and we too were rescued. We were hungry, cold and thoroughly exhausted, and decided to ask the village priest to put us up for the night. We found the presbytery, where a light was still burning.

"Stay here," I said to Karol. "I'll go by myself."

"All right."

I found the housekeeper clearing up in the kitchen, and asked if the priest was in. She looked at me suspiciously and said, "Yes, what do you want?"

"I'd like to talk to him."

"I don't know if he'll come down. It's late."

"Would you mind asking him?"

She went off, and returned saying that the priest would be down in a moment. When he came he said inquiringly, "Yes?"

"Good evening, Father. I'm a priest."

He looked surprised and angry. I went on, "I've been walking hereabout with a friend of mine, and we wondered if you could put us up for the night."

"Have you got your identity card?" he asked suspiciously.

Fortunately I had. He examined it and said, "It's a disgrace for a priest of this diocese to be wandering about at night dressed as a layman. I shan't report you for it, but I'm not having the likes of you in my presbytery overnight." Turning to the housekeeper, he said, "They can sleep in the barn."

We slept like logs. In the morning we said Mass—our clerical dress was in our knapsacks—and set out again without breakfast.

On other occasions Karol and I went out with a party of male and female university students from various faculties who had attached themselves to him. I asked how the group originally came together.

"Rather by chance. It started when the Sisters of Nazareth in Warszawska Street asked if I would lecture to their girls, and sometime during the winter they suggested that I take a party out skiing—although I wasn't very expert at the time. That's how it all began."

Karol's young companions called him *"Wujek"* (uncle). There was no vestige of formality, and the whole atmosphere was one of comradeship. It seems strange today when one attempts to describe it—words, no doubt, are inadequate to any reality, and especially so when the reality is something new and unusual. Every word that I add in the hope of giving a clearer picture of those days seems to distort or impoverish them. For all the frankness and simplicity of the young people's behavior, they genuinely respected their "uncle"—even, for instance, when they laughed at his attempts to ride a bicycle: one of them usually had to ride in front of him, because if he relapsed into meditation, or "turned off," he was liable to run into a tree, and if they were not careful they would lose him for good. Apart from that, they would all pray and say the rosary and sing hymns together, and he would say Mass every day. On their first outings he did so in churches along the route; later, once or twice a year, they went on longer expeditions, for a fortnight or so, and then he would say a "field Mass" by the roadside, in or outside a tent or in a peasant's cottage.

Karol's expeditions were of various kinds. He would go hiking in the western or eastern Beskids, or skiing, or canoeing on the Brdza or Czarna Hancza rivers, sometimes with close friends, sometimes with a group of mathematicians or physicists or the like. But always there was time for prayer and meditation as well as keen discussion and argument concerning the true nature of man.

After a time I ceased to accompany Karol on his group expeditions, since, as I explained to him, I felt that two priests was one too many; moreover I had my own young people at Rabka to look after. But of course I remained in touch with Karol in other ways. I used to drop in at St. Florian's at various times. When I asked for him I was often told, "Oh, he'll probably be in the confessional." Sure enough, he generally was there: not necessarily hearing confessions, but reciting the breviary or reading, or just meditating. The confessional was a means of escape from the people who beset him at all times—there was always somebody wanting to see him or talk, but he also needed time for prayer and recollection.

Meanwhile a fresh problem was looming. "You know," he said to me, "I have an important decision to make."

"What about?"

"Father Rozycki suggested that I take the qualifying exam for a university lectureship."

"And what did you say?"

"I realize, of course, that it's something beyond a doctorate—it means embarking on an academic career, and I don't see myself as an academician. I can't imagine myself not carrying on some kind of pastoral work, if only with students."

In the end he discussed the matter thoroughly with Archbishop Baziak (Sapieha's successor; the latter died in 1951). Describing the conversation, he told me, "The archbishop put his foot down firmly, as he knows how to do, when I suggested that I might have it both ways. He said, 'I won't agree to any half-and-half solution. You will not be allowed to do pastoral work except with my personal permission on each occasion.'"

The subject of Karol's "teaching" thesis was the possibility of basing a Christian ethical system on the philosophy of Max Scheler. "Look what I've got to cope with," he said, pointing rather dejectedly to a pile of books. "I can hardly make it all out, my German is poor, and there are a lot of technical terms I don't know how to translate. Do you know what I'm doing?" He showed me an exercise book. "I've started to make a translation of the whole book—there's nothing else for it."

On the archbishop's instructions Karol moved out of St. Florian's altogether—both the church and the presbytery—and went to live with Father Rozycki in Kanonicza Street, while saying Mass at St. Mary's. He had a large, dark room hung with huge reproductions of stained-glass windows by Bronislaw Mazur, a friend of Father Rozycki's. As his reading progressed he became more and more engrossed in it. "It opens up a new world," he told me, "a world of values, and a fresh view of mankind."

Although he was not allowed to do regular pastoral

work among students, no one had forbidden him recreation, and trips into the country were his favorite pastime. So he took his group of young people all over the place, to the Silesian or "island" Beskids, the Gorce Mountains or Babia Gora. The group was not always the same, as old members disappeared and new ones arrived. Those who remained were content with its size and composition at any given time. And so Karol and his young friends would pray and sing, laugh and joke, roast potatoes at an open fire, discuss the past and future and refashion themselves, the world and Poland.

After two years, in 1953, Karol passed his teaching examination and began to lecture at the Theological Seminary in Cracow and also at the Catholic University of Lublin. He would not go to live in Lublin (about 150 miles northeast of Cracow), but preferred to travel there regularly. All this meant extra work, but the conclusion of his studies with the teaching exam gave him a sense of independence and stability.

In those days I was teaching young people of high school age at Rabka. I asked Karol to come and give a Lenten retreat there, and he agreed; he was interested in the rather special atmosphere of the place. After early Mass we ate breakfast in the tavern run by the famous Teodor Kliminski, who, as soon as he saw us approach, would call to his wife, "Maryska, get the liver out of the icebox." Afterward I went off to teach while Karol stayed in my rooms, reading and writing. At noon we met again for lunch at Teodor's. In the afternoon I generally went back for a short spell of teaching, after which we went to the spa chapel where Karol addressed the young people. He spoke of matters that were really too advanced for them, but I could tell that he was holding their attention. Afterward he would stand by the door and talk to them in a light, joking way about everyday matters, as was his custom.

That was the pattern on the first day, and the others were very similar. On the first day he announced that he would be free directly after lunch if anyone wanted to go to confession or have a chat. This was not the usual custom, as confessions were generally heard at the end of the retreat, on Saturday. When I arrived in the afternoon I found him already talking to the young people. As they turned up he would walk with each one up and down the avenue of tall pine trees in front of the chapel, while the others sat on benches or strolled about. The pines rustled, the blackbirds sang; every now and then a red squirrel scampered along a branch, scattering bits of bark and pinecones. It was like being in a big church, but even more beautiful.

Karol told me at that time that he wrote poetry.

"Why don't you publish it?" I asked.

"I do."

"But I've never seen any."

"I write under a pseudonym—Andrzej Jawien."

"Oh, yes, I remember seeing something by you in *Tygodnik Powszechny* in 1950 or thereabouts."

"Yes, I did publish two poems in that year."

"What are you writing now?"

He showed me, and I remarked, "This is in the same style as the ones I read—more like a meditation than a poem, perhaps rather in Norwid's manner, but not quite. Are you going to publish it?"

"I expect so."

But I was not really much interested—I was thinking of something else: of his direct contact with my young pupils and those for whom I was responsible, and the Mass and sermon that were to conclude the retreat. He knew that I attached great importance to sermons and had devised a special short form of my own. He once asked me if it was true, as rumored, that I had once preached the shortest of all my sermons at Easter, consisting simply of the words: "Christ has risen, but you will not believe. Amen." I laughed and replied, "No, it was a little longer. What I said was, 'Christ has risen, and you too will rise from the dead. Yet you do not believe.' And there was no 'Amen.'"

In the evening we had supper with the families of one or another of my pupils. Next year, when I asked the young people whom they would soonest have again out of all the priests who had given Lenten retreats, they replied "Father Wojtyla"—and so he came for the second time. My schedule and his were much the same as before: in the evening we dined with pupils' parents, both those who had entertained him the preceding year and others—the Malewskis, for instance, or the Romanowskis. As before, he spent most of the mornings reading and writing. He said he could actually get more done here than in Cracow, as it was quieter and he had the mornings all to himself.

He told me about his work at Lublin, the people he met and his fellow teachers. He spoke of the new school of philosophy that had begun there, mentioning names I had not heard before such as Krapiec, Kurdzialek and Kaminski. It was clear that he felt thoroughly at home at the university.

"What are you working on?" I asked.

"It's hard to say exactly. I write various articles, but what seems to me most important at the moment is to reconcile Thomist philosophy with that of Max Scheler, who of course was Husserl's disciple. I am fascinated by Scheler's theory of values and of human nature. Phenomenology seems to me a fine philosophical instrument, but no more than that. It lacks a general world view, a metaphysic if you like, and it would be worthwhile to create one."

The following year my pupils again said they would like Father Wojtyla to give the retreat, and I invited him to come.

"All right, with pleasure. But aren't they tired of me by now?"

"Not in the least. They really pay attention to what you say. Of course it's a bit above their heads, but they've got used to your style and your basic ideas, and they want to hear more about them."

Altogether he came to Rabka six years running. The early spring is not the pleasantest season there: the roadsides and mossy banks were covered with melting snow, it was cold and the sky was generally gray and overcast. To Karol's delight, however, his contact with my pupils did not end with the Lenten retreats. "Those who come to Cracow as students," he told me, "have started to look me up. They come along and say, "We remember the retreats you used to give at Rabka.""

13

The Pope's Inauguration

SUNDAY OCTOBER 22, 1978

A cloudy, rather gloomy day. If only it doesn't pour! Staszek and I leave the college early and get to the piazza about eight—it is already crowded. Our tickets are closely scrutinized. Suddenly someone calls to me: it is Fr. Stanislaw Kluz, an old friend who worked on the *Tygodnik Powszechny* and is now studying pastoral theology at Vienna. He arrived yesterday especially for the ceremony and is in a tense, excited state. We find fairly good seats in the piazza, opposite the altar and the Pope's throne.

We watch the heads of states and diplomats arriving one by one to take the seats reserved for them on the right-hand side near the altar. There are Prince Rainier and Princess Grace of Monaco, Henryk Jablonski the president of Poland, President Carter's aide Zbigniew Brzezinski; the tall, straight figure of King Juan Carlos of Spain with his queen, and President Pertini of Italy. "Look, there's Kirchschläger," Staszek said to me.

The foreign dignitaries continue to arrive: Africans, Japanese and many others, some in colorful national dress, others in black, the men in tailcoats and the women in long, elegant dresses. The left-hand side of the altar, where the bishops sit, is a great expanse of violet. Next to them are more exotic costumes, black or colored: these are the representatives of the non-Catholic churches—the Ecumenical Patriarchate of Constantinople, the Coptic and Moscow Patriarchates. To my surprise I also catch sight of Archbishop Coggan of Canterbury and Brother Roger of Taizé. These are all I can recognize, but Staszek comes to my aid, as he knows many of the "separated brethren." He points out the Catholicos of Armenia, the Lutherans, Methodists, Presbyterians and some Jewish notables. On the square itself, near the steps, is a large group of Poles in national dress, the white-and-red flag of Poland fluttering above their heads.

It is nearly ten o'clock, and the piazza is filled to overflowing. I look behind me, and can see the crowd extending beyond the Piazza Pio XII right into the via della Conciliazione. There must be about three hundred thousand in all—apparently the same number as for Pius XII's funeral. TV cameras can be seen in various places: yesterday evening's papers said the number of radio and TV networks that have applied for facilities beats all records. Staszek talks in a whisper of the new era that this pontificate signifies. We agree that the Pope is an outstanding representative of Poland's thousand-year-old civilization and a symbol of the Polish people. Staszek points out that he is important not only for his general pastoral activity but because of his meetings with diplomats, statesmen and others who play a major part in shaping the present-day world and who may be influenced by his personality. Staszek compares our age with that of St. Francis, which bore the imprint of the great saint's personality.

"I always believed Karol would rise to the top, but I did not foresee in what way."

Staszek tells me that he has already formed student groups in Vienna. I ask him what he spoke to them about. He replies that he himself has not yet a clear conception of the future, nor has he altogether fathomed the secret of the great man's personality.

"But, as far as you have done so, what would you say is the new Pope's most important quality?"

"I would call it the faculty of listening to others, of paying attention to what is going on in society and in the world. He likes listening to people, and he tries to anticipate their questions."

"What else?"

"Forgive me if I don't go on just now—it's nearly ten, and I wouldn't have time to finish. Before I left Vienna I read that poem by Slowacki."

"The prophecy?"

"Yes."

"Look at the empty throne up there. Isn't it amazing that Slowacki, more than a century ago, should have written the lines:

'He has made ready the throne for a Slav Pope,
He will sweep out the churches and make them
    clean within,
God shall be revealed, clear as day, in the creative
    world . . .'"

I suddenly thought of Mrs. Szkocka, who died in 1971 at the age of ninety-two—and who, many years ago, showed me that in her copy of Slowacki she had written opposite those lines: "This Pope will be Karol."

The hour strikes, and the choir begins to sing the *Veni Creator*. The liturgical procession emerges from the basilica. The cardinals, wearing white miters and preceded by the cross, advance in pairs to the altar, kiss it and take their places on either side. At long last the Pope appears at the end of the procession, wearing a gold miter and holding the crosier that belonged to Paul VI. A burst of applause breaks out as he blesses the crowd and seats himself on the throne.

Then comes the ceremony of investing the Pope with the pallium as a sign that he is Bishop of Rome. Cardinal Felici comes up and places over his shoulders the long woolen band marked with black crosses. Next, the *obbedienza* or homage of the cardinals—an ancient ceremony, in which they kneel and kiss the Fisherman's Ring, and receive from him the kiss of peace. The cardinals form a line, with Cardinal Confalonieri at the head; he kneels, kisses the ring, the Pope bends over him and the cardinal moves on. Next comes Cardinal Wyszynski. At first everything is as before, but when he kisses the Pope's ring the Holy Father presses his face to the cardinal's head and then kisses his hand—a quite unexpected gesture, which moves the onlookers profoundly.

The homage continues. The Pope behaves with great simplicity: he helps some of the older cardinals to rise to their feet, and prevents others from kneeling at all; with each he exchanges a few words or even has a brief, rapid conversation.

When all the cardinals have paid homage, the Mass begins. It is concelebrated by all the cardinals from their places; only two are at the altar itself, one being Cardinal Wyszynski.

The choir sings the Gloria; then comes the collect, which the Pope intones in a strong voice. Staszek remarks to me in a whisper how strong and beautiful his voice is.

The Pope prays to God that he may worthily perform his duties as Vicar of Christ. Next come the readings. The loudspeakers announce that the first and second of these will be in English and Polish, while the Gospel will be sung in Latin and Greek. The English text is read by a redheaded priest, the Polish by Father Marian of the Polish College, who comes from the Pelplin diocese. He reads admirably, in a slow, clear voice. Then comes the Gospel with St. Peter's reply to Christ's question: "Who do you say that I am?—Thou art the Christ, the Son of the living God."

There is a pause, and I wonder whether the Pope intends to preach a homily. For some reason I expected him to advance to the lectern whence the Gospel was read, but nothing seems to be happening there. After a few moments of suspense, however, he speaks from the throne on which he is seated, with a miter on his head and holding a text in both hands. He speaks slowly and very clearly; according to the TV news at 8 P.M., he made only three mistakes in stressing the Italian words. He says that Peter's confession was an act of faith on his part and also on the part of the whole Church: we ourselves are participants in his recognition of the Christ. Speaking of St. Peter's coming to Rome, the Pope says that no doubt he would have preferred to go on living by Lake Gennesaret, but that he obeyed the Lord's call and came to the city. Staszek whispers to me, "The Pope too would have preferred to stay in Poland, in his own Cracow, doing the same work as hitherto and enjoying his holidays on skis, or hiking among our own mountains and lakes."

Suddenly the Pope's address, which has so far been in a quiet key, turns into an impassioned appeal to the whole world. The whole style and tone are different; the voice is one of urgent entreaty.

"My brothers and sisters, do not be afraid to accept Christ and his authority. Help the Pope and all those who desire to serve Christ, to serve man and all humanity. Do not be afraid, open the doors wide to Christ and his saving power. Open the frontiers of states, economic and political systems, wide realms of culture, civilization and development. Do not be afraid. Christ, and he alone, knows what is in men's hearts."

Then, with another change of tone, the Pope speaks movingly in Polish: "I turn to you, my beloved countrymen and countrywomen, pilgrims from Poland: bishops headed by your great Primate, priests, sisters and brothers of Polish orders, and representatives of Polish communities all over the world. And what shall I say to you who have come from my own Cracow, from the see of St. Stanislas,* of whom I was the unworthy successor for fourteen years? What shall I say? All that I could say would be insignificant compared with what my heart feels, and your hearts feel, at this moment. So let us do without words—let there be only a great silence before God, that silence that is true prayer."

The Pope then spoke again in Italian, saying that he had just addressed to his compatriots an appeal and invitation to prayer, and that this was meant for all other nations as well. Finally he greeted the whole world in French, English, German, Spanish, Portuguese—each language calling forth applause from a different part of the square, according to where the national groups were standing. Greetings in languages that few understood— Slovak, Russian, Ukrainian, Lithuanian—also aroused joyous applause from all present. Never, since Popes and the Vatican have existed, can all these tongues have been heard at such a scene as this. I sat as though in a trance, thinking of all those who were hearing the Pope in their own language. I looked at my neighbors with tears streaming down their faces. As the Pope addressed his deeply moving words to the Poles, Staszek whispered

---

* Bishop Stanislas (Stanislaw) of Cracow, the city's patron, murdered during Mass by King Boleslaw the Bold in 1079.

that he must have nerves of steel to be able to complete the ceremony without breaking down.

At last the address, interrupted every moment by wild cheering, is over. The Mass continues, accompanied by the fine singing of the Vatican choir. Two hundred priests distribute Holy Communion to all parts of the square, under the warm sun and sky of deepening blue. Mass concludes with the sonorous "Christus vincit" and Te Deum. The Pope moves to the front of the altar to bless the people; then, contrary to protocol, instead of withdrawing he comes down into the square. He first speaks to a group of invalids in chairs, and then approaches the Polish section, where, to the alarm of the papal guard, it looks as if the crowd would break through the cordon. Small boys come up, some Polish and some not, some with bunches of flowers, and he strokes them on the head and kisses them. Unable to tear himself away, he blesses the crowd again and again, waving in reply to greetings; finally he lifts up the crosier of Paul VI and makes an enormous cross with it. Then he continues to wave—breaking all the rules of protocol and precedent, with what seems to me marvelous assurance. After all, he has only been Pope for six days, and one might have expected him to show some uncertainty or at all events to conform to the directions of the masters of ceremonies, who understand the complicated mechanism of a pontifical Mass. But he shows no hesitation in overriding rules that are secondary in themselves, though no less important to those who are responsible for the whole ceremony—he is not afraid to be himself, and thus to be one with all who have come to attend his inauguration.

Even after he withdraws from the piazza, the Pope's encounter with the crowd is not complete. In a few minutes the clock strikes two, and the Pope appears at the window of his private library, in front of which the tradi-

tional carpet has been hung out, in order to say the
Angelus, although this was not part of the original program—the Mass itself lasted nearly four hours. He begins
by saying, "Dear brothers and sisters, I wish to renew the
fine custom of my predecessors and say the Angelus with
you . . . I wish to express my deep regard for young people, who are the hope of this world, the Church's hope
and mine." He continues in Polish: "I have a few more
words to say to my countrymen and to all pilgrims from
Poland. Today you are reciting the Angelus with the
Pope. Soon you will be going back to Poland. When you
say the Angelus again—and I ask you to say it often—say
it together with the Pope, who is your brother and a son
of our country."

The Poles in the square applaud and shout deliriously,
"Long live the Pope! Long live the Holy Father!"

The Pope concludes in Italian, "We really must finish
now, it's time for dinner"—and he repeats his words in
Polish. After pronouncing the Apostolic benediction in
Latin he appears at the window three times more, blessing and greeting the crowd with outstretched arms.

But this was not the end of the day. In the afternoon
the Pope received the delegations of the non-Catholic
Christian churches who attended the inaugural Mass.
He first spoke to them individually in his private library
and then addressed them all together; his speech included the words: "Your presence bears witness to the
mutual desire to strengthen the bonds that unite us and
to eliminate all that has divided us in the past. We must
recognize that that division is a real scandal and a great
hindrance to the proclamation of the Good News. I wish
to declare to you that we shall pursue the road indicated
by the Second Vatican Council. Much has already been
done, but we must not stop until we achieve the aim of

bringing about that unity of the whole Church for which Christ prayed.

At 4:30 that day Cardinal Krol celebrated Mass in the Gesù, the preacher being Cardinal Wyszynski. The church was crammed with Poles and some Italians. There was not room for everybody inside, and some could not last out the long service. During Communion quite a number went outside and sat on the church steps in the darkening air, or stood or walked about talking in front of the church. I saw priests and lay families whom I knew from Cracow, Warsaw and Lublin. Among the crowd was Franciszek, the aged butler from the arch-bishop's palace at Cracow, whom I remembered from Prince Sapieha's time. He was dressed as he always used to be for big receptions, in a dark suit with a cheerful tie, and his eyes twinkled as merrily as ever.

"It was a great sign," I said to him, "when the portrait of Paul VI fell on your head just before he died."

"Yes, it made its mark on my skull all right."

Mucha, for many years chauffeur to Bishop and Cardinal Wojtyla, was there. I asked if he would go on driving the new Pope.

"Not likely. There must be some better drivers here who know their way about Rome."

A maid from the palace said, "Yesterday morning I opened the gate at five. It was still dark, and I was startled to see a candle on the pavement, and a man beside it kneeling and praying."

All these people had been invited by the Pope by telephone. I met a group of lecturers and assistants from the Catholic University of Lublin, friends of mine since the days when we attended lectures by the present Pope; some of them I had also met later in Cracow. To these people the Pope's election meant something different from what it did for the ordinary faithful: it meant the loss of a professor who had held the chair for years, educating not only the mass of students who had passed through his hands, but also his own assistants. The loss was too great to express in words, nor did they need to explain it to me. Someone whom I had known as a girl, and who was now a wife and mother, kissed me on the cheek without a word; her face was swollen with weeping. Other friends told me what it had been like in Cracow on the evening of October 16 and the ensuing days. The excitement, they said, was indescribable: crowds in the streets, seminarists playing guitars, Masses at night, adoration of the Blessed Sacrament, prostration in the form of a cross—all this with thanksgiving and prayer for God's grace upon their beloved pastor. The palace doors and those of the archbishop's curia were thrown open wide—after all it was *his* curia, *his* palace and his own people: they had a right to see the place where he and his closest assistants had lived and worked. They threw open the chapel where he used to say Masses daily and to pray for hours on end. The crowds came to look and pray and to lay wreaths of flowers. There were flowers everywhere, inside and outside the building—almost as though someone had died, as indeed the archbishop had died to the diocese and to Poland, yet at the same time he was, so to speak, newly born to the whole world.

14.

Bishop Wojtyla

Bishop Stanislaw Rospond, a suffragan in the Cracow archdiocese, died in the summer of 1958. The names of various successors were mooted, and it was rumored more and more strongly that Karol might be appointed. I thought this very unlikely—surely the archbishop had not directed him into an academic career in order suddenly to make a bishop of him, and anyway he was not thought of as *episcopabilis*. Nonetheless, on July 4 the news of his appointment came through.

"How did you first hear of it?" I asked him.

"I was on a walking tour with my troop of young people when I got a telegram summoning me to Warsaw, and then to Cracow. I told the archbishop, however, that I must go back and say Mass for them on Sunday. They asked me if I was no longer to be their 'uncle,' but I reassured them. However," he added to me, "I'm afraid you'll have to get somebody else to give Lenten retreats at Rabka."

Karol received episcopal orders at the Wawel on September 28 from Archbishop Baziak, Archbishop Kominek of Wroclaw and Bishop Jap of Opole. I wondered what would become of his academic work, since he could hardly combine being an auxiliary bishop with teaching in another diocese, even at the Catholic University. However, when I asked Karol he said, "I shall go on being a professor at Lublin, if only because there's no one to replace me, and anyway I want to continue what I've been doing there."

"And what does the archbishop say?"

"He agrees."

"Well, that's the main thing."

I had not expected such crowds to be making their way to the cathedral for the consecration ceremony, and I had difficulty getting through the traffic on my Lambretta. Arriving somewhat late, I pushed my way through a group of people awaiting the archbishop at the main entrance and almost ran into the bishops standing at the end of the nave. Karol was among them—his head bowed, his drawn face wearing almost a look of suffering. I turned into a side aisle, and in a moment heard the choir intone *"Ecce sacerdos magnus."* "The archbishop has arrived," I thought, and went quickly to the sacristy, past a serried group of smiling nuns wearing cornets of various shapes. I left my overcoat, and begged a sacristan whom I had known when a seminarist (nothing ever changed in the cathedral!) to lend me a cotta—but alas, all the spare ones had been borrowed by others before me. I therefore decided to go into the chancel in my cassock, but now it was too late, as my way was barred by a great crowd which had poured into the cathedral as the archbishop entered. Suddenly I saw a sacristan going around behind the high altar by way of a secret passage that I had used in my student days. I made my way toward him by dint of smiles and loud apologies and, I am ashamed to say, elbowing aside ladies and gentlemen, country folk and mountaineers, young people and students of both sexes. They all had a good right to be there, since after all Karol came from Wadowice and had been a curate at St. Florian's and Niegowic. At last I got to the narrow passage and came out beside the altar, where the archbishop was robing while the sacristan finished lighting seven candles as a sign that the Ordinary was in the cathedral. In the canons' stall I saw Monsignor Niemczewski, who, unlike me, was an expert on all kinds of liturgy and ceremonial. I smiled across at him, and when he smiled back I went and sat on the step beside him and asked him to tell me what was going on. He said, "The chancellor is reading out the papal bull of appointment. Before that, one of the bishops requested the consecrator, that is to say the archbishop" (how precise he is, I thought to myself) "to raise Father Karol to the dignity of a bishop. The consecrator replies, 'Have you an apostolic mandate?' and, in answer, the chancellor reads out the bull. After that comes the examination."

"Examination?" I inquired in some surprise.

"Yes," he said. "Here, you can read the text." He handed me a small volume; it looked rather antique, and its date proved to be 1657. He explained that it belonged to the Chapter. Meanwhile the archbishop was speaking:

"We ask you, dear brother, with sincere love whether you are resolved to dedicate all your wisdom, as far as lies in your power, to the study and teaching of holy scripture."

Karol replied, "With all my heart I intend to be obedient in all things."

"Is it your desire by word and example to impart what you have learned from holy scripture to the people for whom you are being consecrated?"

"It is."

Then came questions and answers about fidelity to the
Fathers of the Church, obedience to the Pope, morality,
piety and hospitality. I followed the printed text as the
archbishop continued, "May God grant you these and all
other graces and protect and strengthen you in all that is
good." To which my companion and others who knew
the ceremony added "Amen." As the dialogue proceeded
my companion asked for a copy of the ritual, but we did
not need it as the archbishop spoke clearly and I could
hear everything. He asked Karol whether he believed in
the Trinity, the Church, the Resurrection and the revelation of the Old and New Testaments, and finally said,
"May God increase this faith in you, beloved brother in
Christ, for your true and eternal happiness." Once more
the congregation said, "Amen."

After the examination, Mass was concelebrated by the
archbishop and the new bishop. I had never known of
this elaborate ceremony, though I ought to have, and I
was now able to witness it. After saying the initial verses
and responses with the archbishop, Karol and some of
the servers went to the altar of St. Stanislas, while the
Mass continued in their absence as far as the lessons and
the Alleluia. The archbishop then sat and waited for
Karol to return: he, it appeared, had meanwhile vested
for Mass—he had been wearing a cope—and had himself
read the portion of the Mass as far as the Alleluia. He
came back to the high altar and prostrated himself, while
the archbishop and servers knelt and the litany of the
saints began.

How many memories this conjured up for me, for
Karol and for all priests! I remembered his ordination,
when, wearing an alb, with a chasuble folded over one
arm and a candle in his other hand, he lay prostrate in
the cardinal's chapel in Franciszkanska Street. *"Kyrie*

eleison, Christe eleison; Christe audi nos, Pater de coelis Deus, miserere nobis . . ." Years in the seminary, weekly retreats, the decision to devote one's whole life to God as a priest—it all seemed only yesterday, yet it was ten years ago. How much had happened in that time in his life and mine, in Poland and in the world! But the litany today was no different from the one that had accompanied his ordination to the priesthood. Years ago, the question had been, "Does God really want me for a priest?", but today's was a no less momentous decision: "Shall I do as the Apostolic See requires? Does God want me to become a bishop?" It must have been all the harder for Karol to make up his mind, as he had now been a priest for some time and knew how difficult the priestly life could be.

The litany was nearly over. The archbishop rose and, holding a crosier in his left hand, made the sign of the cross and said, "That thou mayest bless this thy bishop-elect . . ." We replied, "We beseech thee to hear us, O Lord."

"That thou mayest bless and sanctify him . . ."

"We beseech thee to hear us, O Lord."

"That thou mayest bless, sanctify and consecrate him . . ."

"We beseech thee to hear us, O Lord."

The litany ended. Karol rose from his prostrate position and knelt on the altar steps before the archbishop. Through the moving crowd of servers we could see the archbishop open a book of the Gospels and lay it on Karol's head and shoulders. While an acolyte held the book, two bishops came up and, with the archbishop, held out their arms over Karol and said, "Receive the Holy Spirit." It was as though time had turned back in its course and we were in the days described in the New Testament, when the apostles laid their hands on those who were to be their fellow workers. The archbishop, with uncovered head and outstretched arms, now recited a form of preface, certain words in which constituted the formula of consecration. Not remembering which they were, I whispered to my neighbor, who replied that when we got to them he would lay his hand on my arm. He did so at the passage: *"Comple in sacerdote tuo ministerii tui summam et ornamentis totius glorificationis instructum coelestis unguenti rore sanctifica"* (Confer on thy priest the fullness of thy ministry, adorn him with all glory and sanctify him with the dew of celestial unction). After this the archbishop intoned the Veni Creator. Everyone in the cathedral rose and joined in the chant. I looked around curiously. The mixed throng of secular and regular clergy and laity included people from every period of Karol's life—his townsfolk from Wadowice, fellow students of philology, friends from Debnicki and Tyranowski's circle, seminary priests, young people from St. Florian's, students of his from Lublin and journalist colleagues from *Znak* and *Tygodnik Powszechny*. The only discordant note was struck by photographers, both lay and clerical, who surged forward with their flashbulbs at the moment when one of the acolytes bound a strip of linen around the new bishop's head. This was to prevent the sacred oil from dripping onto his face and neck as the archbishop anointed him, saying, "May heavenly blessing anoint and sanctify you in the office of a high priest, in the name of the Father, the Son and the Holy Spirit, Amen."

The archbishop then rose and chanted in the tone of the preface: "Grant him, O Lord, the grace to convert others by word and action . . ." and so on to the petition: "Increase on him thy blessing and grace, so that he may always implore thy mercy and be pious by thy grace." Next the new bishop's hands were anointed, the archbishop saying, "Be thy hands anointed with holy oil and the chrism of salvation; as the prophet Samuel anointed the king and prophet David, so mayest thou be anointed and sanctified."

A crosier was placed in Karol's hand; the archbishop placed a ring on his finger and handed him the book of the Gospels, after which all the clergy and servers gave him the kiss of peace. The consecration was over.

The new bishop returned to his own altar, still with the bandage around his head. Apparently someone exclaimed in alarm, "Good gracious, what have they done to him?!" In a minute or two he returned, without the bandage, to continue Mass. The crowd was such that I could only just see the acolytes in front of him carrying bread, two small vessels of wine and a candle, as in the good old times of Christian antiquity.

The rest of the Mass followed its normal course in profound quiet; the congregation was clearly deeply moved. After the *"Ite, missa est"* the archbishop consecrated a miter and placed it on Karol's head. It was of new-fangled design, less tall than usual, and Monsignor Niemczewski growled, "It's ugly!" So did one of the canons and another prelate whom I recognized. I did not think it respectful to agree with them aloud, but said to myself, "Yes, it is." The archbishop intoned the Te Deum, and the whole congregation joined in the chant, while the new bishop moved about the cathedral blessing those present. There were so many of his friends and acquaintances, people he knew or who knew him, that we had to wait some time after the end of the hymn, long though it is, before he came back to the altar. He looked somewhat tired as he solemnly blessed the whole congregation and thanked the archbishop in moving words.

The ceremony was over, and the cathedral slowly emptied. I saw a little group at the sacristy door, evidently waiting to offer congratulations, but for some reason I did not feel like joining them. I turned around and stepped out of the cathedral into ordinary life. Riding homeward on my Lambretta, I felt happy that Karol had become a bishop and happy that I was returning to my own parish of Rabka.

Karol came to Rabka to confirm a group of my young people. I had been preparing them for the sacrament for some months, instructing them to take stock of their lives and contemplate the future in the light of our Lord's example.

Outside the parish church, where the ceremony was to be held, we arranged an elaborate reception. There was a triumphal arch of fir branches and flowers inscribed "Welcome to our Bishop."

The choir, under the organist's direction, had practiced appropriate songs, and the fire brigade provided a brass band. There was a group of highland men and women in regional costume, including an old couple with bread and salt on a tray (the traditional symbols of hospitality). Children in highland costume carried bouquets of flowers. In short, everything was as it should be. True, Bishop Wojtyla was said to have indicated that he did not want any special treatment, but our reply was that things had always been done that way and that the bishop must be welcomed properly. I awaited his arrival with curiosity, as it was the first time I had seen him carry out any episcopal function. We were all on tenterhooks—the dean, the organist, the choir, the band and the rest of the faithful—you didn't see a bishop every day, and it was five years since he'd first come here. As the children waited to hand their bouquets and say little poems, their mothers anxiously straightened the wreaths

on their heads or the ribbons with which their braids
were tied.

At last Karol arrived, in violet attire and a short surplice. He seemed a bit nervous at first, which did not
surprise me, as the reception started with a bang. The
band played, the choir sang, the children recited poems
and presented flowers, the old couple offered their bread
and salt, the dean came forward with a holy-water sprin-
kler and a crucifix for the bishop to kiss. But the main
thing was that everyone was delighted Karol had come
and we were all together.

I was afraid that he might be in a hurry and might
pass over some details of the ceremony for which we had
all prepared so carefully; but no, he managed to attend to
everything. He even showed special deliberation, as
though to make sure that he was not carried away by the
general excitement, and that no one should miss playing
the part assigned to them. He listened attentively to the
children, who stammered from nervousness. He accepted
the tray of bread and salt and replied to the old couple's
words of welcome. He kissed the cross with fervor, and
sprinkled holy water vigorously over those present. All
the time he was full of smiles. He made a joke of some
sort about the triumphal arch, as I saw his suite look up
at it suddenly, but I could not hear what he had said because of the singing and the brass band.

Before confirming the young people, the bishop was
supposed to question them. For some reason I had completely forgotten this part of the ceremony, and as it was
about to begin I felt a sudden panic. If he put questions
in catechism style as some bishops did, the result would
be disastrous, as my boys and girls had learned no for-
mulas by heart except a few of the most basic definitions.
Formal questions requiring set answers might paralyze
them with fear, especially as they had never seen the

bishop before. I went toward a group to whom he was talking; from a distance things seemed to be going well enough. I did not go close enough to break the circle, but I could hear the tone of their voices and could see his eyes and theirs. I breathed a sigh of relief; it was not an examination, but a conversation—part serious, part humorous, as I knew to be his way, but I had not yet known that he could talk thus informally at a liturgical ceremony.

The dinner that followed was long and accompanied by flowery speeches. Afterward he and I went for a walk in the vicinity of the church.

"You shouldn't mind," he said, "that dinner took so long. It was a way of meeting everybody, and I couldn't hurry it without giving the impression that I hadn't time for them.

"You wonder if I begrudge the time that I have to spend on canonical visitations, 'counting pigs and chickens' as you call it, seeing what a state the farm buildings are in and agreeing that it is high time for the church roof to be repaired. But it isn't really a matter of checking, it's for the sake of the man who has all these worries day by day and looks to me to encourage and approve his activities.

"You ask, too, about my conversations with parish priests and curates. It isn't really such a bad thing that they have to live in presbyteries together. There must be tension, of course—it's the meeting of two worlds, two generations anyway. You don't have these problems in Rabka, but it wouldn't be surprising if you did. It's all right so long as you don't get the parish priest saying, 'I'm the one who decides here,' and the curate thinking, 'What's the use of talking to the old fool?' In any case I can see the point of my meetings with them. It's really a form of pastoral activity among the clergy—they need it, even though they're pastors themselves."

I was impressed by what Karol had to say about his new duties—I had not realized that he would learn to be a bishop so quickly.

Not long afterward, Karol fell ill. Staszek Kownacki, who was one of the doctors treating him, told me, "When I spoke to Archbishop Baziak he said, 'You must look after Bishop Wojtyla just as carefully as if it were myself.'" Staszek was touched by this, but, characteristically, had replied that as a conscientious physician he tried to do the best for all his patients.

To prevent a recurrence of the illness, Karol was advised that for the rest of his life he should take plenty of vigorous exercise in the summer and winter vacations, which should not be less than a fortnight each. From then on he obediently spent two weeks canoeing or hiking in the mountains in summer and skiing in winter— which, in fact, was what he did already, but now he had a medical justification for it.

My time at Rabka came to an end after eleven years, and I was transferred to St. Stephen's parish in Cracow, as a curate with special responsibility for young people of high school age. Karol was responsible for pastoral work among the student population in general, to which Archbishop Baziak attached great importance, and so our lines converged again.

The priests concerned with pastoral work among school pupils and students met from time to time to discuss current problems. In each parish we held regular weekly meetings with groups of young people, consisting of a talk followed by discussion, and in addition we maintained extensive personal contacts with the students.

A year after I came to St. Stephen's, Karol presided over a meeting to discuss plans of pastoral activity for the coming academic year. When I began to speak he interrupted me and said, "This doesn't concern you anymore, does it, as you will be studying for your doctorate this year."

I was astounded, as I had heard nothing of this. After the meeting I asked Karol what it was all about.

"Ask the archbishop, he can tell you better. I thought you knew about it. He asked to see you today—come down afterward and we'll have a talk."

I protested that I had no wish to take up academic studies again; it was ten years since I had left the university, I had forgotten a great deal and lost the habit of academic work. However, I went to see the archbishop and he explained his plan.

"You can choose any college or subject you like, but I want you to take a doctorate because it's the custom in this diocese that anyone who, for instance, delivers reports at the national conference of the clergy, or writes regularly for *Tygodnik Powszechny*, should have a doctor's degree." He told me to let him know my decision within a fortnight.

Still feeling rebellious, I went down and told Karol what the archbishop had said. He urged me to agree, pointing out that a lot could change in the field of theology in ten years. "You ought to bring yourself up to date, and it's a big chance for you if you want to go on seriously with what you are doing now."

I wanted to go to Rome for my further studies, but was refused an exit visa. The alternative was the Catholic University of Lublin—a quiet place, the most easterly of Polish towns, where the people had singsong voices and a gentle melancholy disposition. Karol asked me what I would most like to study, and I replied, "Something on the borderline between philosophy and theology, some fairly basic subject."

"Lublin isn't much good for theology at the moment—if you're going there I should do philosophy. As you know, I've been visiting the place for some years, and I can assure you the standard is pretty high. So now you are starting to follow in my footsteps, only a bit behind," he added laughing.

The train to Lublin left Cracow late in the evening. Unfortunately there were no sleeping cars, only couchettes. My students saw me off, and during the long, uncomfortable journey I wondered what Karol's university world would look like. I was awakened at four and found myself in Lublin Station at five, an hour when one does not know whether to start the day or try to get some more sleep. It was a long way to the university, and there was a crowd of passengers waiting for taxis, so I took the streetcar.

I went first to the hostel, which was full of priests and members of religious orders from all over Poland. It had been built many years ago and was already too small. I was given a room that I shared with a fellow student. The refectory and common room were in the basement. On the ground floor were some poky guest rooms, in one or another of which Karol had stayed on his trips to Lublin. Off the passage was a cold, dark communal bathroom and washroom.

The university proper was a rectangular building with a large inner courtyard. The broad passages had windows looking out onto the yard, while on the other side were doors leading to the lecture rooms. On the ground floor were the offices of the different faculties, each with a secretariat, a small library and reading room.

I was curious to see the professors of whom Karol had spoken highly to me at Rabka and Cracow, and to get to know the university where he had taught, but I wanted to stand on my own feet and not to be helped by him. We had agreed on this in a conversation we had in a car during my last days in Cracow, when Karol said, "I've heard that some priests imagine I've helped you because we are old friends, but I can honestly say I've never done anything special for you." I replied that that was the way I wanted it to be, as long as he and I should live.

Gradually and shyly I became acquainted with my new world. I kept making discoveries that filled me with surprise and delight. The first striking fact, which of course I knew beforehand but now saw for myself, was that the students were of all kinds: lay people, secular and regular clergy, monks and nuns of various orders. It was a pleasant surprise to see the broad, light corridors full of them, the priests wearing cassocks as they still did in those days. I was also greatly impressed by the quality of the professors. Karol and I had agreed that I should study theoretical philosophy—a broad foundation after which I could branch out in any direction. The professor of metaphysics was a Dominican, Fr. Albert Krapiec—a close friend of Karol's, a fine man and a first-class teacher. He was an expert on Aristotle, as I found out at his seminars, when we read texts and discussed particular words and sentences. He was remarkably young in appearance, and no doubt remained so all his life. A fine lecturer, he often spoke extemporaneously, showing all the more clearly his wide range of experience and the profundity of his thought.

I was interested in exploring problems of faith from the existential viewpoint, and decided to write my doctoral thesis under his supervision. After some thought and discussion I chose the title "Transcendence in the philosophy of Gabriel Marcel." The work progressed rapidly, and by the end of 1963 I had already produced a first draft for seminar discussion.

Another impressive figure was Father Kaminski, who taught mathematical logic and the methodology of science. He was a bustling man with a rather shrill voice, always with a joke on his lips, and especially fond of teasing students of both sexes. He knew his subject well and was a formidable examiner, failing candidates right and left.

An eminent lay professor was Stefan Swierzawski, a historian of medieval philosophy. As he was a scholar and teacher, his methods differed widely from those of the other two. He was fond of delivering special lectures on matters he was currently studying, and brought to the lecture room piles of reference cards which he read out carefully.

Another outstanding lay professor was Mieczyslaw Gogacz, a man of great energy and probably of pastoral inclinations. He wrote impressive academic discourses and thoughtful articles, even for quite popular journals.

The regular lectures given by these teachers were full of conviction and authority and were always well attended. Apart from these there were seminars and special lectures, which interested me greatly from the point of view of method and subject matter.

Then there was Karol himself. If I mention him last it is partly because although he taught philosophy, the subjects on which he lectured were not a compulsory part of the course I was following. Nonetheless, I often attended them and was able to see him in action as a teacher. As in ordinary conversation, he generally began on a light, humorous note and then passed without effort to the deepest analyses, observations and deductions, summarizing existing material and transforming it into a coherent whole. I saw the effect of the work he had been doing on Max Scheler's philosophy: a new way of thinking and of observing humanity. I use this general term rather than speaking of "human experience" or the like, as I fear this might be misunderstood. Karol was not concerned merely with emotions and experiences but with the whole of human personality, including will and intellect as well as feeling. The more I listened to him, however, the more clearly I realized that he was presenting his own philosophy of mankind and not just that of St. Thomas, Scheler, Husserl, Heidegger or Ingarden. Elements of his thinking might be traced to one or another of those great minds, but it was a personal philosophy and not simply an eclectic one. He was always keenly interested in human personality, and this gave direction to his academic studies. Above all he was interested in the supreme experience which is love—both love in general, if one may put it so, and particular forms of it such as married love. Listening to him, I realized more and more clearly that the field of experience on which all his abstract thinking was based consisted in his day-to-day contacts with all manner of people, and especially the young folk whom he took on outings and whose pleasures and mutual relations he witnessed at first hand. He was able to see how feelings of attraction gradually developed into love; he was there when couples made the decision to marry and start a new kind of existence, and when their lives were again transformed by the advent of children. With his penetrating mind he strove to observe and analyze human behavior and so arrive at an integrated conception of humanity.

It might be thought that this habit of observing and analyzing the young people with whom he came in contact would have made his relations with them artificial and self-conscious. But when I think back to those days and his relations with young people in general, I am convinced that there was no such effect. Nothing was artificial, nothing merely for show or for sale; everything was as natural, simple and genuine as could possibly be imagined.

What was true of his young friends in Cracow was also true of his students in Lublin. He and they were a group of friends, engaged with all their hearts and minds in studying problems in which they were deeply interested. They were a family united not only by lectures and seminars but by daily life together: the affairs of one were the affairs of all, and members of the group would help and support one another in everything—whether it was money, or finding a place to live, or at time of sadness or joy in family life, such as the death of a relative or the birth of a baby.

When Archbishop Baziak of Cracow died in June 1962, it was realized how much he had been loved and respected by all around him. A reserved and difficult man, he was the model of an old-fashioned prelate who saw himself as father, teacher and shepherd of his flock and believed in ruling them with a firm hand. However, his severity of manner and method could not conceal his kindness and warmth of heart. Although my own experience of him was slight, I knew a lot about his character from Karol, who worked with him day by day and of whom he thought highly, as others in the Curia told me. Eugeniusz Baziak came to us as an "exile" from Lwow, of which he had been formerly archbishop.* While attending a bishops' conference in Warsaw he died at the Hotel Roma of a heart attack, so suddenly that he was unable to call his secretary.

* Lwow (Lvov), like Wilno, was in the Polish territory ceded to the Soviet Union after World War II. Archbishop Baziak was expelled by the Soviet authorities in 1945.

After the funeral, which was attended by huge crowds of the faithful from Cracow and former inhabitants of the Lwow diocese from all over Poland, the question was who would be appointed to the country's second most important see. Some people thought of Karol, but this was more a matter of sentiment than of reason: his youth seemed to rule him out, as it was usual then to appoint as archbishops men of long pastoral experience; moreover Cracow was a cardinalatial see. True, Prince Sapieha had ruled it from an early age, but this was not a precedent, as he had been nominated by Pius X himself after being a domestic prelate to His Holiness. Another obstacle was that Karol was an auxiliary bishop of the diocese, whereas it was customary to appoint an archbishop from outside.

Matters remained in suspense for several months, and the names of various candidates were bandied about until finally the news came that Karol had been appointed, beating all records as far as age was concerned. In 1958 he had become the youngest auxiliary bishop in Poland: his appointment took place on July 4 and he was consecrated in the cathedral basilica of the Wawel on September 28, being then aged thirty-eight. Less than four years later, on July 16, 1962, he became vicar capitular and thus the youngest man in charge of a Polish diocese, albeit in a temporary capacity. Then, when Paul VI appointed him Metropolitan Archbishop of Cracow on December 30, 1963, he became the youngest archbishop in Poland.

15

A Polish Pope

On Monday October 23, Rome Radio announced that the Pope had that morning received in private audience Henryk Jablonski, chairman of the council of state of the Polish People's Republic and thus titular head of the Polish state. Afterward he received the government delegations from different countries which had attended the inaugural Mass on the previous day.

After the general audience, the Pope had a further conversation with the Polish president and his suite. The manner in which this news was announced indicated that it was felt to be a mark of special consideration for the Polish delegation, and its head in particular.

The Pope thanked the government representatives for attending the inaugural Mass, and declared succinctly, "There can be no lasting peace without a disinterested search for cooperation and unity among nations. The Church, through the evangelical love which it proclaims, can make an effective contribution to restoring the unity of mankind and intensifying the spirit of universal humanity."

Karol and his mother

Karol's father

As a schoolboy

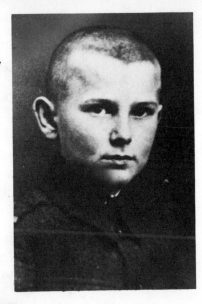

As a first communicant (Uzan/
Gamma Photo, Liaison Agency)

Karol in 1946 (Uzan/Gamma Photo, Liaison Agency)

The building of the Cracow ghetto (Uzan/Gamma Photo, Liaison Agency)

Karol meditating in solitude

With Stefan Cardinal Wyszynski, en route to the conclave
that elected Wojtyla as Pope. (Wide World Photos)

Polish newspaper headlines, October 1978 (Wide World
Photos)

At noon the radio announced that the Pope had invited the Polish bishops and some priests, mostly also from Poland, to lunch with him at St. Martha's College in Vatican City. This is a hostel run by nuns for various Vatican officials, and the large restaurant on the ground floor is used by many who live and work in the area. I knew the hostel well, as Bishop Andrzej Deskur had lived there for some years. The news that the Pope was actually lunching with his guests must have caused a sensation in Vatican circles, and in the wider world as well. Hitherto the custom has always been for the Pope to take his meals alone; only quite recently have there been exceptions, and only in the case of persons close to the reigning pontiff. Now suddenly everything is different. But in the last few days novelty has started to become the norm. The rigid, hieratic character of the papacy, developed and cherished through the centuries, has suddenly changed to a simple regime bearing the imprint of a new personality. It has become common knowledge that when the present Pope decides that something is artificial he makes no bones about changing or abolishing it. Everything to do with the latest successor of St. Peter is natural, genuine and spontaneous.

At 4 P.M. the Pope gave an audience for Poles in the Sala Nervi (named after its architect). There was to have been a general audience followed by one especially for people from Cracow, but almost at the last moment it was announced that as there was no suitable separate hall the Pope would address the Cracovians specially in the course of a single audience. I arrived at the piazza well before four, and on the left-hand side of Bernini's colonnade found a large group of Poles waiting to be admitted. We entered the building by degrees, guided and supervised by Swiss guards and attendants. The huge modern hall, well lit and with excellent acoustics, seats over seven thousand, but can be filled or emptied in a short time thanks to a well-devised system of corridors and side entrances. Among the throng I met many old friends who had come by charter plane from the United States. Everyone was in a state of joyful excitement, relating their experiences of the day before. It was now nearly four, and the raised platform was crowded with bishops and monsignori, while press and TV reporters with their cameras were in enclosures on either side. Someone announced that the Pope would be a few minutes late, as he had had a full day receiving the government delegations in the morning and entertaining the Polish bishops and monsignori at lunch. A Polish hymn was struck up, after which we said the rosary. Suddenly the lights began to flash in the press enclosure to the left of the dais, and the Pope entered amid wild applause. Smilingly he waved in greeting and took his seat on the throne, a high armchair upholstered in light gray velvet. The crowd sang the congratulatory chorus *Sto lat* (A hundred years!), after which Cardinal Wyszynski came forward and began to speak. The Pope, instead of remaining seated, stood up, as did everyone else present, until the cardinal had finished his address. He said:

"We know, Holy Father, what a costly decision this was for you. We know how dearly you love your country and your city of Cracow, the Tatra Mountains, the forests and valleys, and the solitary walks that gave you joy and renewed your strength. All these things you have laid on the sacrificial pyre of your loving heart."

Amid recurrent applause the cardinal thanked the Holy Father for his work in the Cracow diocese and at the episcopal conference, and for his activity at the Catholic University. He promised that the whole of Poland would offer prayers for the Pope, and begged for a bless-

ing on himself, on all present and on our fellow countrymen everywhere in the world. After finishing his address he approached the Pope to do homage. He knelt,
kissed the Fisherman's Ring—and then came another surprise like that of the day before. The Pope knelt before
the Primate, kissed the latter's ring and then embraced
him. Thus for a few seconds the two greatest men in recent Polish history remained locked in each other's arms.
The exaltation of the spectators—weeping, cheering and
applauding—knew no bounds. Later the Primate said, "I
wanted to free myself, for it was quite wrong that the
Pope should kneel to me. But he realized it and clasped
me so hard that I couldn't move—I couldn't even
breathe."

The Holy Father read his reply to the Primate from a
written text. He apologized for doing so, but explained
that he had important things to say and did not want to
overlook or forget anything, though he realized that his
words would be far from adequate in any case. After this
preamble he did not start to read at once, but spoke of
the reception for government delegates that morning.
After telling us that he had had a separate conversation
with the president of Poland and the rest of the Polish
delegation, he added, "I could feel how deeply this
event, brought about by the will of Christ, aroused in
those to whom I spoke the awareness of our nation's history, its past and future and the indissoluble bonds between the Church and the Polish people."

After these words the Pope resumed his seat and asked
us to sit down likewise. He read out two messages, one to
be read—if the Primate and the episcopate agreed—in all
churches in Poland, and the other addressed to the archdiocese of Cracow. We listened intently as he began the
first message:

"My beloved countrymen: I write these words to you

on the day on which it has fallen to the lot of a son of our dear motherland to assume episcopal office as the successor to St. Peter. . . . The Church in Poland has become an object of great interest by reason of the conjuncture of circumstances which is of such importance to the aspirations of contemporary humanity, of so many nations and states. It has become a church of special witness, toward which the eyes of all the world are turned. Without realizing this fact, it is hard to understand that the Pope who speaks to you today is also a Pole."

Then followed perhaps the most moving passage in the whole speech: "Most reverend and beloved Cardinal Primate: allow me to speak my mind in simple terms. There would not be a Polish Pope in the see of St. Peter today if it were not for your faith, which did not shrink from prison and suffering, and your heroic hope."*

As all Poles are well aware, this was no more than the truth, but it was a momentous thing for the Pope to say. I looked at the Primate's slight figure and his deeply wrinkled face, and could see how deeply he was moved. Still addressing him, the Pope continued:

"When I say this to you, I speak at the same time to all my brothers in the episcopate, to each and every priest, to all brothers and sisters in religion and to all my beloved countrymen in Poland and throughout the world . . . I speak to all Poles without exception, with respect for the convictions and philosophies of all of them without exception. Love of our country unites and must unite us beyond all differences."

With rising emotion the Pope addressed words of farewell to his native land:

"It is not easy to accept the fact that one cannot return

* Cardinal Wyszynski was placed under arrest in September 1953 for resisting government measures aimed at subjugating the Church. He was released in October 1956.

home . . ." At this point his robust, sonorous voice, with its clear stressing of every phrase, perceptibly broke into a kind of recitative. A long burst of sympathetic applause enabled him to recover his composure.

". . . But since it is the will of Christ it must be accepted, and I do so. I ask of you that my departure may unite us more than ever. . . . Do not forget me in your prayers. . . . I beg you, too, to resist anything that impairs human dignity and diminishes the moral health of society."

Finally he imparted his blessing: "I do this not only by virtue of my episcopal and papal calling, but from the deepest necessity of my own heart."

Next came the message "To my beloved archdiocese of Cracow." After a few introductory words the Pope said, "Believe me, when I came to Rome for the conclave, my greatest desire was to return to you." The main theme of the message was one of thanks.

"Allow me to thank you for all those years of my life, as a student, priest and bishop. I think of my beloved parents, who died long ago, and the parish at Wadowice dedicated to the Presentation of Our Lady, and my primary and secondary school, and the Jagellonian university,* the faculty of theology, and the Theological Seminary. And what shall I say of my great predecessor in the see of St. Stanislas, Cardinal Prince Adam Stefan Sapieha, and that great exile Archbishop Eugeniusz Baziak, and all the bishops and priests and devoted shepherds of souls, the learned professors and the exemplary monks and nuns? What of all the layfolk I have met in the course of my life, my school friends and fellow students at the university and seminary, the workers at the Solvay plant, the intellectuals, artists and writers, people of all

---

* The University of Cracow, founded in 1364 by King Kazimierz the Great and extended in 1400 by Wladyslaw I Jagiello.

professions, married couples, young people engaged in apostolic and missionary work, and all the young men and women who, with the Gospel in hand, sought the meaning of life, and some of whom finally chose to become priests or enter religion? All these I bear in my heart and, in a sense, take with me: the whole of my beloved church in Cracow . . . May God bless you all! Once again I commend you to Christ through the maternal hands and heart of his blessed Mother."

There was a burst of applause as the message ended. But this was not all: the Pope wished to take his leave of those present. He left the dais and moved down the aisle, formed by cordons, to the far end of the hall, escorted by attendants in snuff-colored dress coats, while the assembled Poles struck up a medley of patriotic and religious songs, including one concerning the sorrows of a mountaineer leaving his native land. The Pope stretched out both hands to those who wished to touch or embrace him; again and again he caught sight of a known face and exchanged a few rapid words, or answered questions put by complete strangers. He then returned up the other aisle, from the main entrance back to the dais: the whole procession took about an hour. Near the dais itself there was a transverse aisle. Some mountaineers from Koscielisko, standing close to me, began to sing a song they had composed for the occasion, but the general uproar was such that they could not be heard. The Pope passed close to where I was and saw me: he stretched out his hands and, shouting in order to be heard, said, "Well, you've had your way—but you came to the wrong conclave. Come and see me as soon as you can!"

The Pope moved on again, answering more questions, talking and shaking hands. He was smiling and cheerful, yet one had a sense of inner peace amid all the acclaim. Finally he stepped back on to the dais and said, "It's a pity, but we must part now—the Primate is short of time, he's pressing me to go." The whole assembly burst out laughing as the Pope concluded, "I shan't say any more, or the Congregation of the Faith may be after me." Then he disappeared amid a last flashing of lights.

16

The Council

I finished my studies at Lublin in May 1963, having completed the course in two years instead of three, and began to work hard at my doctoral thesis. The state authorities gave me permission to travel abroad. I told Karol, and he asked me what I wanted to do next.

"I'd like to go to Paris and meet Gabriel Marcel—he's quite old, and I'd like to make contact before he dies. Then I'd stay there for a short time to finish my thesis, which is well in hand already, and after presenting it at Lublin I'd come back to Cracow."

Karol replied, "You have an invitation to Rome, so let's meet and talk there. I haven't time now, but I have to be in Rome for the second session of the Council." Accordingly I went to Rome and met him there in September.

I stayed at the Polish College, which is pleasantly situated on the Aventine and is a convenient place to study. The fragrant cypresses, the recreation ground with a pond and a basketball court, the little garden with narrow paths and shady corners to sit in; a comfortable room, good Italian-Polish meals cooked by nuns, and pleasant companions. And, most important of all, the rector, Fr. Wladyslaw Rubin, a man of great charm and genuine kindness. He had come from Lwow to Rome by way of Siberia and the Middle East* and, after completing his theological studies, remained to minister to Poles abroad. He was an ideal rector, who treated us all like friends of a younger generation and helped us greatly by his experience, knowledge and contacts. We enjoyed his company, and I believe he enjoyed ours.

Although the college was a delightful place, I disliked it on this occasion because of the impact of the Council. A number of bishops stayed there for the duration of each session and inevitably made calls on the time of their diocesan priests, with whom they discussed various matters. As a result the college was in a state of constant bustle, with conferences, correspondence and errands of all kinds—shopping to be done, people to be shown around—and I determined to get out of the hurly-burly as soon as I could, so as to complete my work in peace.

After supper one evening I walked on the terrace with Karol. The black vault of the sky was studded with stars, and we could just discern the dark ruins of the Baths of Caracalla. Farther off was St. John Lateran, and in the other direction the dome of St. Peter's, Trastévere and the E.U.R. district (the former exhibition ground)—in short, a complete panorama of the city. The distant noise of motor traffic did not disturb the placid scene.

Karol said, "You know, I think we have enough philosophers in the church in Poland, and what we need

---

* I.e. he was among the many Poles deported to Siberia after the Russians occupied eastern Poland in 1939; a proportion of these, with their dependants, were released to form the Polish army under General Anders, which was evacuated to the Middle East in 1942 and subsequently fought in Italy.

now are good theologians. And there's a new subject that is just beginning to develop as a result of the Council and is sure to become very important, and that is ecclesiology. I would like you to study it."

This was quite unexpected. I replied, "But I've just done the philosophy course, and I'm halfway through my thesis."

"The philosophy you have done is bound to be of use sooner or later in ecclesiology."

I did not care for this new idea, but Karol continued, "I've made up my mind about this, and I think you should study at the Angelicum. It did me a lot of good and I think it will you, especially as you are a bit of a left-winger in theology. They'll give you the real St. Thomas there, not just Thomism. I'm sure you'll find it a good thing."

There was not much I could say. He continued, "Don't look so unhappy about it. It's a good university, and not such a great machine as the Gregorian—there are not too many students, and there is more chance for the professors to work with them. Unfortunately my old teacher Garrigou-Lagrange has gone, but the Dominicans are good at getting first-class people from all over the world—they have plenty to choose from. Apart from that, there are great things going on in Rome at present."

"You mean the Council?"

"Yes. It's something which is going to shape the whole future of the Church. It would be a pity for you to leave Rome without seeing anything of it. Later on, if you really want to, after taking your doctorate at the Angelicum you can take one in philosophy as well."

I enrolled at the Angelicum, and was curious to see what "Karol's university" would be like. I could get there on bus No. 90 or on foot via the Circo Massimo, the Colosseum, across the Piazza Venezia and up the Quirinal, turning right instead of left as for the Gregorian. It was a rectangular building with an inner courtyard, as at Lublin, but smaller and painted a warm orange color. I registered for the doctoral course and started attending lectures. These were supposed to be in Latin, like the exams, but the professors, a fine team from all over the world, also used Italian and sometimes French, German or English.

Meanwhile the second session of the Council had begun. The Polish bishops stayed either at the college, like Karol himself, or at the Istituto Polacco on the via Pietro Cavallini, as did Cardinal Wyszynski. Those in the college were mostly lodged in large rooms on the first floor, or on the second floor near the chapel. Karol had no fixed abode there at first, but toward the end he moved into a fine ground-floor apartment with a view of the garden pool and the statue of St. Christopher bearing our Lord in his arms: the saint stands in water up to the ankles, with goldfish swimming around.

At the outset I did my best to have nothing to do with the Council, knowing that if I did not get well into my studies at the beginning of the academic year I would never catch up. Every day at eight I dutifully attended the prescribed lectures for the doctoral course, and if anyone suggested any other activity in the morning I excused myself on the ground of studies. The lectures were not easy in themselves, and there was the additional difficulty that they were in Latin. I had to acquire the language perfectly for the final exams, including the oral defense of my thesis.

But circumstances were stronger than I. The afternoons remained free, and people could always get hold of me at lunchtime. There were urgent jobs to be done— drafting, translating, copying and so forth—and I was involved willy-nilly in work connected with the Council.

I gradually found my feet at the Angelicum, and even learned to understand the Latin spoken by English, French and Spanish lecturers—in effect, three different languages. I took a liking to the American Professor Powers (yet another kind of Latin!) and chose him as my director of studies. Cautiously and by degrees I raised my eyes from purely academic concerns, though I still avoided Council matters as much as possible. I did not go near St. Peter's in the mornings, as the piazza and the via della Conciliazione were thronged with bishops, cardinals and theologians of all races, besides reporters and photographers. I resisted the temptation to visit the Sala Stampa, though I would have liked to see my friend the editor of *Tygodnik Powszechny,* who was reporting on the Council and on Church events in general.

I had many opportunities of talking to Karol. Hard-working as he was, he enjoyed a break and would often invite me to join him on an outing, which I always did if my university work permitted. We would get into Alojz Cader's little car and travel to the seaside or the Vatican beach or some farther destination. Karol was a good swimmer, especially sidestroke. He would chat with us on the way out, but after our swim he would leave us for a time or sit without talking; sometimes he lay in silence for quite a time with a towel over his head. On the way home we would eat at some little pizzeria or trattoria where they served *porchetta* (suckling pig roasted out of doors).

In winter we went to the sports resort of Terminillo. We left Rome on a cold but sunny winter's day: the oranges were ripening, and one could manage without an overcoat, but after sixty miles or so we were in real winter weather. It was frosty, the snow lay deep, and a bitter wind sprang up which drove the tiny flakes into our faces. Karol, not in the least daunted, put on skiing clothes and disappeared for half the day. He did not take exercise merely because he was under doctor's orders to do so: it was clear that he thoroughly enjoyed it.

At other times we would go on visits outside Rome. For instance, one day Karol said to me, "Let's go and see the Resurrectionists* at Mentorella—they must be getting bored to death." We drove out, left the car where the road ended and walked two or three miles up a steep path—Karol clearly enjoyed this too. Mentorella, a Marian shrine of great antiquity, is on a spur of land which projects, like a ship's bow, into a deep valley. At the top is a solitary little church and monastery set among green forests, with a marvelous view of mountains round about. The sanctuary was given by the Vatican to the Resurrectionists when the Benedictines withdrew. Thanks to their care and dedication it has continued as a hermitage, a place of quiet visited only by occasional pilgrims.

Karol greeted the fathers and brothers warmly, and spent an hour or two praying in the little church. After eating a meal prepared by our hosts we returned home.

On other occasions Karol visited people to get to know them or to make acquaintance with some new social development. One day he said, "Let's go and see the Little Sisters at Tre Fontane." We went there, and came upon the founder of the community with a rake in her hand, helping some novices to tidy the square. During our drives he would read or talk or recite the breviary, or we would say the rosary together.

We talked about all kinds of things, but most often of the Council and the Popes connected with it. We talked of John XXIII, that wonderful man whom experts and

---

* A congregation of priests founded in Paris in 1836 to minister to Poles in exile.

non-experts at first thought of as a stopgap or "transitional" Pope, while children called him "grandpa" and enjoyed his jokes and stories.

Karol recalled the occasion when John XXIII was asked how many people worked in the Vatican, and replied, "Probably about half." Or again, having taken care to find out the proper way to address Jacqueline Kennedy, he startled his entourage by calling her simply "Jacqueline." Apart from stories of this kind, true or false, the most important surprise that the Pope had sprung on the world was when, on January 2, 1959, he declared to the assembled cardinals with an innocent air, in his nasal and rather indistinct voice, that he had a matter of great rejoicing to announce to his episcopal brethren, namely his intention to hold a Council.

"I don't know," Karol added, "how far he realized what an avalanche this would mean, but probably he wouldn't have shrunk from it in any case."

As I listened to what Karol had to say I realized that in Poland I could never have formed an idea of the tremendous machinery of the Council and the volume of work it represented. Here in Rome, although I had tried not to become involved, I began to see what a great event it was and how much had already been accomplished. First there was the arduous preliminary work leading up to the first session, which opened on October 11, 1962. When that session closed on December 8, there was at first a sense of disappointment, as people thought the Council was over, but they soon found that it was only a beginning. Pope John, it was thought, wished to conclude the Council after the second session, but he died before it was convened. By that time the Council had acquired such momentum that he probably could not have stopped it in any case. When he died, in June 1963, I imagine that there were few who wished to succeed him: it would not be easy to follow such a predecessor and to steer the Council for the remainder of its course. The conclave elected Montini—Paul VI—as had been expected, if only because he was the closest collaborator of the late Pope, and it fell to him to preside over the Council's most momentous sessions. He was quite a different type from John XXIII—a highly sensitive intellectual, who had spent all his life in the papal diplomatic service or the Roman Curia. He knew, however, what he was taking on and how the Council was likely to develop.

I saw more and more clearly that it was time for me to enter into the great world of the Council, and when I returned from my vacation I had made up my mind to volunteer to take part in some way. I said to Karol, "As I am to study ecclesiology, I think I ought to take a close look at the Council, which is the greatest thing that has happened to the Church in our time." Karol agreed.

17

A Conversation in the Vatican.

On Tuesday October 24, 1978, I telephoned to the Pope's secretary, my friend Staszek Dziwisz, at a Vatican number known to few people. I told him of the Pope's invitation, and asked if I might come to the Vatican that day.

"The Pope hasn't time this morning, he's seeing Pertini, the president of Italy."

"What about the afternoon?"

"He's busy."

"Tomorrow, then?"

"Not a chance."

"The day after tomorrow?"

"No, there's a public audience in the morning, and in the afternoon he's going to Castel Gandolfo."

"Then perhaps it had better be next time I come to Rome. I haven't any especially important business to talk about."

"Come to lunch today. He'll be alone."

"Fine."

"Only don't say you're lunching with him, say it's with me."

"All right. What time?"

"Half past one. Come from the direction of St. Anne's; there's a little elevator at the entrance."

"Right."

I took a bus, and entered the Vatican Palace from the Via di Porta Angelica. The first person on duty let me through, as a member of the clergy, but the second asked my business and referred me to the porter, who struggled with my name and then telephoned for a minute or two. Finally he wrote out a pass. At the inner gate I was checked by a Swiss guard, and at the elevator door by another. I went up to the second floor, into a hall with fine frescoes. Another Swiss guard escorted me to yet another, who led me through a magnificent vaulted apartment and entrusted me to the care of some footmen. One of these, as he escorted me further, made vain attempts to pronounce "Dziwisz" properly: it came out as "Chiviss." He complained that Polish was written one way and pronounced another—I had always thought this was true of Italian, but I did not tell him so. He took me to another small elevator; I went up to the third floor and was welcomed by Staszek, who was, as always, cheerful, cordial and knowledgeable. He asked me to wait for a while, as I was a little early.

The waiting room was small and windowless, with a central light; some small armchairs and cupboards stood against the walls. I noticed a passage leading to a small chapel, which I entered. It was of a handsome modern design. Behind the altar was an image of the crucified Christ on a semicircular slab of black marble. There was a bronze throne and several prie-dieus upholstered in gray velvet. On the walls to either side of the altar were sculptured reliefs of the martyrdom of St. Peter and St. Paul. The heavy doors of the chapel were also of bronze. I went back to the hall, off which several doors opened into small rooms filled rather untidily with presents received by the Pope. While exploring I ran into a sister of the Sacred Heart of Jesus whom I had known in Cracow —I already knew that the Pope had brought three nuns from his residence there. I asked her where the others were, and she led me to the kitchen, which was small but conveniently arranged. I was struck by the small scale of everything compared with Cracow—a single room in the archbishop's residence would have contained all the rooms I had just seen and the kitchen as well. The chapel there was also huge compared with the one I had just been in.

"The Poles are frightened," I said jokingly, "that some wicked people may poison the Pope."

"Well, we cook everything ourselves."

"Or that they might shoot him."

"They would have to shoot us first."

I went on and came to the Pope's private library. This, at least, was a room of some size. There was a Louis Philippe desk and, on the wall above it, a huge picture of the risen Christ. Beyond was a fair-sized table with chairs on either side. Four large bookcases, four crystal chandeliers and a few modern pictures completed the furniture.

I heard the Pope's voice some way off, talking to Staszek. In a moment he came in and greeted me in his old style; then he went off again, saying, "I must prepare myself—it won't be easy with Mietek!"

He came back and we sat down to lunch—myself facing the Pope, with Staszek and an Italian secretary at either end. The butler brought us soup while the Pope talked about the Italian president's visit, which had just concluded; in two days, he told me, he would be meeting President Giscard d'Estaing. Then he said, "Well, Mietek, what's your news?"

"Could I ask a few questions?"

"What about?"

"I would like to write some short reminiscences of Your Holiness."

"Very well, go ahead."

"And I want to write them very quickly, in a month or so. Others will be writing more thoroughly in the next few years, but I would like to write my book at once."

"Then bring it along when it's ready, so that I can see what you've written."

"Splendid—I'm leaving Rome now and I'll be back in three weeks with the text. But there are a few gaps I'd like to ask you about, Your Holiness. (Please forgive me if I'm not using your title rightly, but it's always hard at the beginning.)"

"What do you want to know?"

"First, about the development of your philosophical ideas."

"Goodness me, that's a big subject! Well, to begin at the beginning, as you know there was St. John of the Cross and St. Teresa of Avila, and the other St. Teresa."

"And what about Scheler?"

"Wait a minute, go easy or we'll get lost. I would say that in my life I've had two great philosophical revelations—Thomism and Scheler. So it all really began with Wais's book."

"I remember, and I've already written about how Your Holiness read Wais, sitting beside a boiler at the Solvay factory."

"Yes, and it was no easy matter. It was Father Klosak who first gave me Wais and told me to study him for an exam. For a long time I couldn't cope with the book, and I actually wept over it. It was not until two months later, in December and January, that I began to make something of it, but in the end it opened up a whole new world to me. It showed me a new approach to reality, and made me aware of questions that I had only dimly perceived. St. Thomas gave me answers to many problems, and Scheler taught me a lot about personality and methods of investigation. I translated nearly the whole of his principal work—an enormous tome, but I couldn't see any other way of getting to grips with it."

"I remember the time when Your Holiness was working on it."

"I should say, too, that I have never studied philosophy in a regular way or attended a course of lectures. Of course, at Cracow University we had Konstanty Michalski, who was a great philosopher, but I only heard him once, delivering a paper of some kind. But you surely went through a whole course of philosophy under him, didn't you?"

"Yes, I did metaphysics and the history of philosophy, and he supervised my master's degree on St. Thomas."

We reminisced about Lublin, Debnicki, St. Florian and rambles with students in the Beskids. Among the many old friends we mentioned often were Father Figlewicz and Tyranowski. We also talked about books.

"Does Your Holiness expect to travel anywhere in the near future?"

"Yes, I want to visit the patron saints of Italy, and go to Assisi and Siena. I want to put down roots in this country."

The short meal came to an end. After we had gotten up from the table I asked if he would talk to me some time about his ideas concerning a bishop's diocesan work.

"What can I tell you? You were there and you saw it all."

"But I would like to hear about it from Your Holiness —and also about the council of the Polish episcopate."

"Well, that would take a very long time."

"I don't mean now, of course, but some other day."

"Come and see me anyhow. You'll be in Rome, so come when you've nothing else to do."

I went back to the College, loath to speak to anyone. Next day I was returning to Poland. I sorted through a batch of newspapers and returned some to the rector. I felt that I ought to copy out some headlines and keep at least some photographs of the last few marvelous days. I looked helplessly at all the material. My meeting today was part of history, and so was yesterday's unforgettable, miraculous audience for Poles—the cheers and applause, the whole assembly singing "A hundred years!", and the two great men of our country, the Pope and Cardinal Wyszynski, embracing on the dais.

I knew that I could never manage to remember it all. Life would resume its course and would blur my recollection of those days with their unique atmosphere and enchantment, and above all my meeting with that great man.

People would be asking me what it was all like, what he was like, how the Italians, the French or the Germans had taken it all; and I would have to think up some comment to describe the indescribable and relate something that could never be related. I knew that I would be angry with those who made me do so, and that whatever I told them would impoverish me forever. For every time I was asked the same questions I would play the same record, repeating the same words in the same tone. I would know what most interested and affected people, what they wanted and expected me to say—and I would repeat it over and over again, distorting it more and more each time. And in the end I would come to believe that what I was saying was the whole truth, whereas the reality was so much richer, so much greater, so much more beautiful.

18

At the Council

The third session of the Council opened on September 14, 1964, and I was able to attend it in the role of an usher or *assignator locorum*. This was the only possibility: I could not be called a *perito* (expert), as I was still a student, and the Polish Catholic press was represented by Fr. Szczepan Wesoly. As it turned out, I was freer than I would have been in any other capacity: I could go wherever I liked without being challenged, as people assumed I had legitimate business there, which was not always the case. At first an attendant might stop me with "*Prego?*" or "*Padre?*", and I would show him a small pass, but after a time they all knew me. Thus I could enter rooms to which the Council experts were not usually admitted, and where the bishops did not always have business either.

Everyone living at the college attended early Mass at 6:45. At breakfast Karol always ate the kind of Roman rolls with a hole in the middle: once when I passed him some bread, he said jokingly, "Don't you know that I come to Rome especially to eat the local rolls, and you offer me bread!" We left the college by bus at eight and got to the basilica shortly before Mass was said there at nine. I used to wait in a seat in the top row of the block of about sixty seats for which I was responsible.

The hall, measuring 100 by over 20 meters, separated the main nave from the rest of the basilica. There was a wide passage down the middle, and on either side were ten rows of seats, upholstered in dark green with desks and kneelers—2,200 places in all. Some of the priests sat in the arcaded balconies still higher up. The seats were allocated on a permanent basis, according to rank and age, all nationalities being mixed up together: first cardinals, then patriarchs, archbishops, bishops, abbots and prelates *nullius,* the heads of religious congregations, proxies representing some of the priests, and the *periti* (experts).

Karol's place was in one of the middle rows of my sector. On the way to the Council he would sometimes enter the chapel of the Blessed Sacrament or kneel to pray at a side altar where Mass was being said, or he would meet and talk to someone. Once he got to his seat he nearly always began writing.

As the minutes went by, the hubbub of voices grew louder and one could hardly see a square inch of the white marble floor, covered as it was by a multicolored crowd of Council priests talking, smiling, greeting one another or, most frequently, arguing.

The list of those entitled to attend, drawn up by the Central Committee of the Council, contained 2,850 names, including 85 cardinals, 8 patriarchs, 533 archbishops, 2,131 bishops, 12 abbots, 14 prelates *nullius* and 67 heads of orders and congregations. Pope John had appointed 195 experts in theology, canon law and other specialized studies, who cooperated with the commissions and were allowed to take part in the Council debates to the extent of answering questions put to them.

To begin with I did not know any of the priests, other than Karol, in my sector, but identified them by the numbers of their seats. The Archbishop of Paris sat in the bottom row, next to a Malaysian. I had three blacks: one with gray hair in the bottom row, and another four rows higher, a tall, slim man who looked about twenty. Next to Karol was a huge man with a short beard, wearing a long robe with a red lining and a black head-covering with a black veil down to his shoulders; this, however, he only wore outside the hall. A dignified elderly man with a gray beard, in similar attire, sat in the next to the top row: he wore around his neck a heavy chain with a fine enamel image of Our Lady. At the opposite end of the third row was a priest in almost identical costume, also with a beard, but wearing a kind of cowl with a silver cross in front. He would make notes on little cards, in Arabic script. There was also a Portuguese, and Enrico Dante, the Pope's master of ceremonies.

The occupants of my sector already sufficed to show that Vatican II demonstrated the universality of the Church in a way no previous Council had done. Only a third of the world's bishops were Europeans; North and South America accounted for another third, and the other continents made up the remainder. For the first time in Church history Africa was represented by a native hierarchy. I noticed that Karol talked a good deal to the black bishops, especially those in our block. Again, it was the first Council attended by non-white cardinals—a Chinese, an Indian, a black African, a Japanese and a Filipino—and by many representatives of the separated churches: the World Lutheran Federation, the Presbyterians and Quakers, the German Evangelical Church, the World Assembly of Disciples of Christ, the World Congregational Council, the World Methodist Council, the Old Catholic Church, the Copts, Syrians and Abyssinians, and the World Council of Churches representing over 170 communities. All these bodies were represented by observers at the Council.

Before nine o'clock the strong TV lights were turned on—they were not tiring, but were directed from a great height and created an atmosphere of tranquility.

Each day, Mass was celebrated by a different member of the Council. It was a dialogue Mass, the other priests answering in unison, and portions were sung by the choir.

After Mass, an old volume of the gospels was brought into the hall by a priest and two acolytes, while the schola cantorum sang a psalm. The volume was placed on a lectern on the altar at which Mass had just been celebrated, after which the secretary-general announced who would be presiding over the day's deliberations on behalf of the Holy Father: this office was performed in rotation by one of a presidium composed of nine cardinals. The presidium sat at a table in front of the shrine of St. Peter; next to them, at a separate table, was the secretary-general with five other secretaries, while the stenographers' desk was some way behind them. All present then repeated the invocation to the Holy Spirit, a sixth-century prayer attributed to St. Isidore of Seville: *Adsumus Domine*—we are present and we beseech you to descend upon us. The secretary, Pericle Felici, then pronounced the *Exeant Omnes*, calling on all who were not entitled to attend the Council to leave the basilica. I handed out cards—*schede*—to the individual priests, who signed them in pencil; I then collected them and inserted them in the counting machines. Then I distributed the texts of the schemata to be discussed that day. Monsignor Felici announced whether amendments would be voted on or whether it would simply be a day of speeches. I listened to the speeches whenever I could; one could always tell from the pronunciation whether the speaker was English, French, Spanish or Italian. Each was allowed ten minutes, after which the moderator of the day would interrupt with: "*Reverendissime pater, tempus tuum iam exhaustum est.*" This did not matter greatly, as the speaker had previously given his text to the secretariat either in full or in a shortened form. At each congregation there were usually some twenty to twenty-five speakers. They generally spoke from notes, not from a rostrum but from the body of the hall: microphones were placed at intervals along the front row, and the speaker would go to the nearest one. The acoustic arrangements worked admirably. Speeches at the plenary sessions had to be in Latin. The priests expressed themselves with great freedom, and the most conflicting views were heard, with extreme traditionalists and radical innovators contending incessantly. The audience showed their opinion of the speeches clearly: some were received in silence, others with loud applause. Some speakers were awaited eagerly and listened to in rapt attention, as they were expected to say something of importance.

At eleven there was a short interval during which the priests left their seats for conversation or coffee. Karol generally stayed where he was and went on writing, his head bent over the desk, but when I saw that the interval was being prolonged I would go up to him and say, "Come on, let's get something to drink." Then he would either come at once or wait to finish something.

"What are you working on?" I asked him one day.

"Several things: my speech to the Council, a Polish broadcast from Vatican Radio, a book I am writing, lectures for Lublin—a bit of each, one after the other."

"What are you going to speak about this time?"

"Religious freedom. I think the subject ought to be mentioned again; it's important to the present discussion."

"Did you speak at the previous sessions?"

"Yes."

"What about?"

"The sacraments."

"Do you decide yourself what to speak about, or is it coordinated with the whole Polish episcopate?"

"We discuss it at our meetings under the Primate's chairmanship, but of course the basic initiative is mine."

"When will you speak?"

"Sometime in September."

We went outside the basilica and talked, mostly about the speeches we had heard. We did not always manage to reach a bar, as Karol would engage someone in conversation or vice versa.

"How did you get to know all these people?"

"Mostly at the Council itself—after all, it's the third session. Of course there are some people I knew at the Angelicum or the Belgian College, but mostly I have met them during the debates. There are a few bishops of Polish origin, too. The simplest way of making contact, whether with old acquaintances or new, is through the speeches themselves. There is always someone who would like something explained or expanded, or would just like to talk about what one has said. Besides, at the first session especially we Polish bishops were something of a curiosity, like the black ones, and people wanted to hear from us how the Church fared in the Eastern bloc. In that way we made new contacts. And some people are particularly interested in Cracow and in me as its spiritual head."

Sometimes we were able to get back to our places without being held up. The way led through a chapel and a small corridor, through the smoke of cigarettes, cigars and pipes, loud conversations in every language; people drinking an espresso or a cappuccino, milk, tea, Coca-Cola, orangeade, eating cakes—everybody standing up, as the space was cramped. Karol usually had a cappuccino, or occasionally a Coca-Cola if he was hot and thirsty.

Besides the Polish bishops, some of those attending the Council were Poles living permanently abroad. I came across some of these at the very beginning of my work. Almost on the first day one of the priests asked me to find out who was the first speaker. I was not quite sure whom to ask, but turned to an archbishop sitting at the secretaries' table. He told me what I wanted to know, but was evidently intrigued by my bad Italian and asked which country I came from. When I said Poland, to my astonishment he replied in our own language, "Then why didn't you ask me in Polish?" It turned out that he was Archbishop Krol of Philadelphia, and was one of the secretary-general's deputies. Later I often saw him and Karol chatting together during sessions.

After the morning break the hall presented a different appearance. The tiers of seats emptied, but on the floor of the hall were groups of priests and experts conversing —*auditores* and *auditrices*—little groups of two, three or four people standing or walking about. There was an incessant hubbub of conversation, argument and the exchange of views, and this was doubtless just as important as the speeches. Karol, like the others, often did not go back to his seat but remained below to meet or talk with someone.

Looking at the scene, I felt that the Council was really a kind of retreat or seminar for the episcopate of the whole world—it was not only a matter of exchanging views, but of the equalization of levels. Some bishops were extremely well prepared and had come with their own theologians, or were in regular contact with the most eminent theologians in the world. It was these who took the initiative and set the tone for the Council. Other bishops had not concerned themselves with theoretical matters for years, if only because they were too busy: they were still at seminary level, or at best on a par with university students. This did not prevent their being, in many cases, far better pastors than the others; they knew the ordinary people in their home parishes and had evolved ways of reaching them. One great advantage of the Council was that it enabled contact to be made between theoreticians and the pastoral clergy. The organization was such that even those who did not speak on a particular topic had to make up their minds about it. There was constant voting on schemas presented by the commissions, either on a whole document or on detailed points, and each bishop had to say "Yes" or "No" or "Yes with reservations." Each one had to compare his views with those of others and find arguments with which to defend them.

Karol was not a typical member of the Council. On the one hand he was one of the bishops who were also professors, but he was a philosopher by training, not a theologian, although he showed increasing ability to cope with theological problems. Having a well-thought-out mental system, he was capable of assimilating any subject without delay. At the same time he was a practical man in constant touch with his flock, and consequently was well acquainted with modern man.

The general discussion would end sometime after noon, when the secretary-general uttered the words: "*Proxima sessio crastina die, hora nona. Deponatur sacrum Evangelium.*" Everybody rose as one of the priests, designated beforehand, lifted the Gospel volume from the richly gilded lectern and carried it away. Those present sang *"Gratias agimus Tibi"* and the Angelus, and the day's session was over. The priests moved slowly along the aisles to the main exit, in a broad violet stream varied with trickles of white and red. I left my own place and joined the throng making for the sunlit piazza.

Karol knew from experience that it took time for the building to empty, and he nearly always waited in some quiet place such as the Blessed Sacrament chapel, where he knelt and prayed, often reciting the breviary. Sometimes, however, he would be buttonholed by a bishop or theologian or would stop someone he wished to talk to.

The cardinals left the basilica by a side door, while all the other priests went straight out into the piazza. By about 12:30 over two thousand of them had poured out of the main door, and the steps appeared from a distance to be covered by a carpet of flowers. The dominant color was violet, but there were also the black or white robes of Eastern bishops and curious forms of headgear—a kind of turban or a round black or red hat such as I had never seen except in pictures. The variety of ecclesiastical robes, especially from the Near and Middle East, was amazing, and provided a field day for the photographers, while journalists and theologians lay in wait for priests who had played an important part in the debates. More interviews, brief or extensive, and more conversations about the course of the discussions, the prospects, difficulties and possibilities. The life of the Council in fact continued outside the debating hall, as bishops, theologians and journalists met one another, and the subjects that had been discussed in dignified Latin were now thrashed out in every language of the world.

But alongside this normal, rational debate there was a mysterious underground campaign of gossip and slander, conducted by unknown forces using every means, legitimate and otherwise—*per fas et nefas*. It took the form of whispering, of anonymous leaflets and little cards distributed in front of the basilica itself, and even of ostensibly serious articles which were in fact full of malice and brutality—a ruthless battle with the sole aim of compromising, ridiculing and destroying the adversary, whoever he might be. For instance, I came across an attack on Cardinal Bea, who was concerned with relations between the Church and the Jews and had sought to link this question with the schema *De Ecclesia*. In a pamphlet of a few pages he was accused of being the leader of a Jewish-Masonic conspiracy at the Council; for good measure he and his staff were said to be Jews themselves, and so forth.

We returned to the college in our own bus, which was waiting for us on the piazza. On most days there were guests for lunch, invited by Karol or another of those staying at the college; the guests were usually bishops or theologians, and on most afternoons there would be a short lecture or discussion with them. We students were invited to these meetings, but their main *raison d'être* was to provide contact between the visitors and our own bishops as members of the Council. Of all those who addressed us in this way, the one who impressed me most was Fr. Yves Congar, whom I had met several times at the Council itself. I was struck by his expressive and humorous face, like that of a clown or an actor, his typical French clarity and lightness of touch, and his extreme sensitivity to his audience.

Karol used to take a short siesta and work in his room for the rest of the afternoon, unless he was going to some conference or committee or subcommittee meeting. He usually ate supper at the college unless he was invited out by some bishop or religious house. At times he would take me with him on these occasions. As always he was cheerful, humorous and openhearted, taking full part in the conversation. After eating at the college he would generally walk about on the terrace, saying the rosary or talking to me or another companion. We used to discuss events of the day or general questions affecting the Council, the Church, Poland or Cracow. It was dark on the terrace and around our building, but in the neighboring gardens we could discern pine trees, cypresses and exotic shrubs. Even late at night we could hear the muffled roar of the busy city. Our little fountain with the statue of St. Christopher splashed peacefully, and on the horizon we could see the lights of far-off suburbs. If the dome of St. Peter's was illuminated for some holiday, and especially when a southeast wind was blowing up, we could often see it from our terrace, so clearly that it seemed as if one could have stretched out a hand and touched it.

I waited with impatience to hear Karol's speech. I watched him go down to a microphone fixed to a desk in the bottom row of seats, and wait with the text in his hand until he was given the word to start. He spoke quietly, distinctly and with expression. He said that the Council's declaration on religious freedom should explain more clearly the link between freedom and truth. It should also bring out the positive aspect of freedom and not confine itself to the negative idea of tolerance. His speech fitted well into the framework of the debate, as the notion of religious freedom had been the subject of lively discussion. Many priests were suspicious of it, fearing lest the impression be given that all religions were equally good and should enjoy equal rights, for which reason they thought it safer to speak of "tolerance." Anyone who listened attentively to Karol's words could perceive the importance of his attempt to base the discussion on a fuller understanding of the relation between truth and freedom. He did not prolong his speech but finished within the time limit. There was no applause, and I myself found the speech a little dry; it seemed better suited to a theological discussion than a public debate.

When we went to have a cup of coffee I said to him, "It's a pity you didn't develop the idea of truth and freedom a bit further."

"There wasn't time," he replied. "I could never have said all I meant to."

But he too probably felt he had not managed to put his point across. I changed the subject and asked if he intended to speak again.

"Yes, on Schema XIII [the Church's role in the modern world]."

"That is your special subject, isn't it?"

"Yes, I think it's a very important schema, both in itself and for the Council as a whole."

"The Polish episcopate have brought a draft of their own, haven't they? But I'm told it is mainly the work of Cracow theologians under your direction."

"That's true, Cracow did most of the work; but that isn't the main point. I think it's a good draft."

On October 19 Karol was to give a talk on Vatican Radio. The usual practice was for such talks to be recorded a few days earlier at Via dei Penitenzieri. This was partly for the speaker's sake, lest he should get nervous or repeat himself or talk too fast or too slowly for the time allowed. But it turned out on this occasion that the recording studio was under repair, so Karol spoke live. I had some experience of broadcasting, as I had given talks for young people every Saturday for nearly a year. As we drove toward the studio through half-empty streets, I asked what he was going to talk about.

"The dignity of the human person, and humanity in general. It seems to me a kind of foundation for Schema XIII, which is to be debated for the first time tomorrow and which in my opinion is, or should be, the main theme of the whole Council; but the subject may get lost in the heat of discussion. It won't be a matter of revealing any important new truths, rather of reminding people—but I think this is to a large extent what we are here for."

"One thing I should warn you about. When you get to the end, even if the clock says 8:30, don't move or say anything that isn't to be broadcast, because they sometimes extend the time."

"Have you had any awkward experiences like that?"

"Yes. On one occasion I spoke too quickly and finished a minute early. I sat there till 8:30 and then said, to myself as I thought: 'Too bad, I spoke too fast.' A week later I heard about it from listeners in Poland."

We entered the palace by way of the piazza, lit only by the four fountains which, illuminated from below, looked like crystal chandeliers; Bernini's colonnade was in darkness. We passed the Swiss guard at St. Martha's gate and walked upward through the quiet, empty gardens along winding, lamplit paths; the atmosphere was unreal, almost fairylike. We got to the little building of Vatican Radio at the top, and climbed to the large studio on the first floor that I knew so well, with the glass box in the middle. Karol sat at a small table as the clock slowly ticked off the seconds to 8:15. The machine played *"Christus vincit, Christus regnat, Christus imperat,"* after which Karol read out the ritual formula: *"Laudetur Jesus Christus*—praised be Jesus Christ. This is the Polish service of Radio Vatican." Turning to his text, he began:

"When we speak of the human person we do not think of man's superiority to other created beings, but above all of what, or rather who, he is in himself."

I could tell that he was very tense, but also calm and collected, so that his voice showed no trace of nervousness. He went on:

"Intellect and freedom are the essential, inalienable attributes of the human person and the whole natural foundation of his dignity. To recognize the dignity of man is to place him above everything that proceeds from him in the visible world. All man's works and deeds, crystallized in civilizations and cultures, are only means to the attainment of his proper end. Man does not live for technology, civilization or even culture, but he uses them as aids to his own purpose, which is closely linked with truth." He was speaking rather in the style of a lecturer, and a shade too loudly for studio conditions.

"Neither the concept of *homo faber* nor even that of *homo sapiens,* understood purely functionally, is sufficient here. Human dignity is much more an objective or a calling than something which men have already achieved either individually or collectively."

At first I had perceived nothing of special interest in his talk—as he said himself, it was a "reminder" of known facts—but suddenly this reference to an objective or a calling shone out like a jewel among pebbles.

"The Church and the Council are trying to answer this call, which they regard as the most important of our time. In each of us believers the dignity of the human person is asserted and, as it were, brought to the surface. This is, so to speak, an upward-looking affirmation through religion. At the same time there is a downward-looking affirmation, and this is equally important to people who do not recognize religious truth.

"There remains for all of us a basic question and a basic task: how, given all the circumstances, can human dignity best be preserved? For preserved it must be. If it is not, we shall come into conflict with man's essential purpose and all our quest for means will be useless—they will only turn into means of self-destruction."

Having finished his main theme, Karol added:

"Tomorrow, on St. John Cantius's* day, I shall be celebrating Mass before the Council fathers and I shall pray especially for the particular gift of the Holy Spirit which is called piety, but which is really the gift of duly honoring every creature for God's sake. May it enable us to assert in the modern world the dignity of the human person, which is the basis of all that is good in society and in individual lives."

After concluding with the formula "Laudetur Jesus Christus," Karol left the studio. On the way back to the college I said, "I thought you would be mentioning Schema XIII."

"I spoke about that on St. Wenceslas's† day," he replied.

"Yes, of course. I missed it. I'll listen to a recording; no doubt one of our colleagues has one."

"You can borrow the typescript if you like."

The following passage interested me especially: "In accordance with the Holy Father's ideas, the Council priests at the very first session set themselves two basic questions. The first concerns the Church from within: what do you say in the Church about yourself? Who and

* Polish preacher and theologian (1390–1473), patron of Cracow University.
† Duke of Bohemia and patron of Czechoslovakia, martyred in 929 or 935.

what are you, what is your idea of your own true being? The second question is external and leads to the problem of the Church in the world—not an abstract world above space and time, but the world of here and now—and also the essence of the world itself, not as a work of nature but as the work of man."

When I returned the text that evening he pointed to another typescript and said, "Do you know this? It's a letter to the bishops of the Cracow diocese, to be read there on November 8. Have a look at it if you like."

I read the words: "I appeal in particular to those who are praying earnestly for the Council and enduring much suffering and sacrifice, for in this way the whole Church participates in the work that is being guided by the Holy Spirit." This was what Karol had most at heart, that all the faithful should be united with the Council's work. Then he spoke of a ceremony that had escaped many people's notice:

"I can add with joy that during the present session of the Council I received from the Holy Father, Pope Paul VI, the pallium bestowed on the Metropolitan Archbishop of Cracow. This is not only a token of office but also a special link with St. Peter the apostle, Bishop of Rome and rock of the Church. When the pallium is conferred it is spoken of as a 'pallium from the body of St. Peter,' for it is first laid on his grave before being placed on the archbishop's shoulders. I should add that besides myself, about forty archbishops from all parts of the world asked on September 26 to be vested with the pallium and received it on October 10; they came from Australia, Indonesia, India, Africa, North, Central and South America, Britain, Ireland, France, Spain, Portugal, Italy, Yugoslavia and Hungary. This universality has an eloquence of its own, and I rejoiced that our venerable church of Cracow was thus united with the community of God's people in all nations throughout the world (Mark 16,15)."

Reading this message, I thought how typical it was of Karol in several ways. It was like him to share his own experience out of a sense of responsibility for the community under his charge. It was like him to draw his hearers into the heart of the matter by pointing out the significance of some object or event, such as the bestowal of the pallium, which might have escaped their notice altogether. Finally it was typical that all the appurtenances of his position did not impair his humility: he accepted them as belonging to him on behalf of the community he represented—he, the obedient servant of his flock.

At this point it struck me what an industrious writer he was. Every letter or talk of this kind represented a lot of hard work, and he could expect much more as the session continued. People all over the world would listen to what he had to say—strangers whom he was striving to contact through his writing, so as to make them think and act and model their lives on that of Christ.

Next day, October 20, Karol was to celebrate Mass for the Council. We left the college at the usual hour. When we arrived, Karol went straight to the sacristy. Unfortunately I could not go with him, as my duties kept me in the body of the hall. It was a joyful and moving sight to watch him at the altar, and I thought how happy he must be. It was not the usual Mass of the Holy Spirit but was in honor of St. John Cantius, patron of the Cracow diocese and university. That day the Council began its debate on Schema XIII, the role of the Church in the modern world—a new problem, in a sense, and one to which Karol attached such great importance.

On October 28 Karol was to make his second speech of

the session. I knew how much it meant to him, and noticed that he was more preoccupied than usual. He spent much time in prayer in the Blessed Sacrament chapel. When the day came he spoke from the same place as before; as usual there was a background of subdued noise in the hall, as though the priests were only lending half an ear to the speaker.

Karol said that the Council must unquestionably prepare a document on the Church in the modern world—if they did not, it would be a loss to the world and to the Church as well. The world desired the presence of the Church in some ways, but wished to exclude the Church from everything it regarded as its own province. It was for the Church to bear witness to itself by means of Schema XIII.

Nothing new so far, I thought impatiently. If he goes on like this, the chairman will interrupt him on the ground that it's all been said before, and he will look foolish. I longed for Karol to get to the heart of the subject.

He went on to say that the term "world" had many meanings. Human life was so diverse that one should really speak of several worlds, with different social, economic and political systems. The Church ought to have something to say to all of these, but their diversity was not brought out in the text of the schema, which ought to be reconsidered.

At this point the background noise died down and I realized that the Council had begun to pay attention. Karol went on to criticize the schema on other grounds, saying that it was too didactic and patronizing: the Church possessed the whole truth and expected the world to do as it said. The draft ought to be modified in the sense that the Church was not only teaching the world from a standpoint of authority but wished to cooperate with it in seeking right and true solutions to the difficult problems of human life. The point to bring out was not that the Church already knew the truth, but how the world could be brought to recognize the truth and accept it.

Karol continued in a clear, firm voice, arguing in a tone of conviction that a heuristic method should be found—that is, the world should be encouraged to find out the truth for itself. This meant eliminating all that smacked of the ecclesiastical mentality, such as lamenting over the unhappy state of the world or ascribing credit to the Church for everything that was good in it. I was surprised at the firmness and boldness with which Karol argued, albeit in moderate language, that the existing draft ought to be scrapped. He did not confine himself to criticism, however, but showed on what lines it should be replaced.

He pointed out that the heuristic method enabled students to follow a lecturer's arguments provided they were clear and simple and acceptable to common sense. Arguments on moral questions ought to be based on the law of nature. A moralizing and preaching tone, of which there was much in the present draft, should be avoided. The main emphasis should be on rational inquiry; theological arguments might also be used, however, since after all it was the Church speaking.

As Karol ended his speech I saw the priests looking at him as, with bent head as usual, he returned to his seat. The hum of conversation grew louder. Unquestionably his words had made a strong impression. I thought to myself, "Well, if anyone did not know you before, they do now."

19

The Modern Age

One day after supper Karol came to the college and gave
a general talk on the Council and its work. The rector,
Father Rubin, announced that morning that he had
agreed to do so at the students' request. I knew nothing
of such a request, but reflected philosophically that man
is not always aware of all his own desires. It turned out
that the suggestion had come from Janusz, a zealous
young student who had broached it to the archbishop of
his own accord. In any case it was a most welcome idea.

Chairs and tables were arranged in the first-floor reading room; the rector and procurator were there, and one
or two bishops who were staying at the college. We sat
in a semicircle with Karol in the center, and he began, "I
don't want this to be just a lecture of mine to you, but a
conversation, a dialogue with questions and answers. I
know that you young men are not buried in your studies
here, but that you are *au fait* with the Council's work,
and some of you have been following it from the beginning. I don't want to tell you things you already know,
and so I'd rather answer questions."

Janusz, who had suggested the meeting, thereupon

asked point-blank, "What is the Council for?" "Some question!" I thought, as he continued, "What I mean is, up to now Councils have been called when the Church had to defend some basic truth that had been attacked, and preserve itself from schism. So, when John XXIII declared in January 1959 that he intended to summon a Council, the whole world was astonished and so, I believe, were his closest collaborators."

Wladek, another student, broke in. "The idea of the Council was something quite out of the ordinary. As Pope John said several times, its purpose is to renew the Church, bring it up to date and adapt it to the needs and problems of a changing world. Father Congar put it well in 1961 when he quoted St. Bernard's phrase about the Church looking both before and after—*retro et ante oculata*."

"But that's what I mean," objected Janusz, seeing that Wladek had not grasped his point. "Surely there's a risk of overdoing things. The Church has been going on for centuries adapting itself to various changes without trouble, in a perfectly natural way. Why did we have to have a Council with such an ill-defined object, or rather no object at all?"

Edek broke in impatiently. "Don't you see that all our habits of thought and behavior belong to the time of the Council of Trent, which was geared to the spiritual needs of people four hundred years ago? The world has been turned inside out since then, but we still use the same language and pastoral forms and religious institutions as if nothing had happened in the last four centuries."

There was a silence. I thought Janusz would return to the charge, but he said nothing—startled, perhaps, by Edek's outburst. The latter, who came from Przemyśl, was usually quiet and mild-mannered.

So far the argument had proceeded without Karol's aid, but he now took the floor.

"Perhaps I could enlarge on what Father Edek has just said. In a bull issued at Christmas 1961 Pope John spoke of the crisis affecting the whole of mankind, whether Christian or not. Among its causes was what I would call cultural deracination. Let me explain what I mean by that. The rapid development of technology has brought about a situation in which many people are living in two civilizations at once. They were born and grew up in days when there were no motorcycles, cars, airplanes, films, cameras, electric light, telephones or radio, not to speak of television. There are also the effects of urbanization. People grew up in primitive conditions, knowing nothing of modern inventions, and then came to live in towns, where they had to adjust to a different era. In the last hundred and fifty years the population of the world has trebled, but the urban population has multiplied by over twenty. Among the results of the crisis is a growing indifference to ideology, a society oriented toward consumption and blind to altruistic values. Another typical feature of our time is the worship of technology."

Teofil, who had lived in the United States, broke in at this point. "Maybe that isn't entirely so. The worship of technology may lead to disillusionment and produce a strong reaction toward metaphysics or religion. At the beginning of this century only a small percentage of the American population claimed to be religious believers, but in 1951 the Gallup poll gave a figure of ninety-three percent."

"Yes, I agree. All the same, the people who are seeking religious faith now are not the same as those who abandoned it in 1900. But let me finish what I was saying about the world crisis. Another feature of it is the demographic explosion. The population of the world in

1900 was 1,500 million, and now it's over 3,000 million. This causes grave economic and cultural difficulties, especially in the Third World. And, as John XXIII emphasized in his message of September 11, 1959, in preparation for the Council, the political face of the world has changed. One third of humanity belongs to the socialist bloc, whose leaders do not accept the Christian world view, and the question of world peace has become the most urgent problem of all."

"Yes," replied Janusz, "but I still don't think you have answered my question: why was it necessary to hold a Council?"

"Really, Janusz is giving a lot of trouble," I thought. I glanced at Edek, but he looked down and evidently did not want to be drawn into the discussion again. Wladek observed, "The Gospel has to be preached today, as Father Congar has pointed out, to a world in which one person in five is Chinese, two out of three don't get enough to eat, one out of three lives under communism, and only half the Christians are Catholics."

This, of course, did not answer Janusz's point either. Karlik (who came from Silesia) attempted to do so by saying, "The Church was in difficulties, and the Council was the best way out of them."

"That may be an overstatement," said Marian calmly—not for nothing was he intended for the Vatican school of diplomacy—"but there's some truth in it. Pope John knew that something had to be done—perhaps in his case it was more a matter of intuition or inspiration than of intellectual reflection. And he found the right answer to the Church's difficulties, or at any rate the change in its position: he appealed to the whole Church, or its representatives, in the traditional form of a general Council."

Karol took up this point and said, "No doubt Vatican II had as its starting point the awareness of a crisis situation. The Church was becoming less effectual in modern conditions, the gulf between it and the world was widening; religious faith was in conflict with science and technical progress, modern forms of behavior were in conflict with Church ethics; atheism, materialism and indifferentism were on the increase. The choice of a remedy was dictated by the Church's reflection on itself and on the world."

"But why did there have to be a Council?" Janusz persisted. Someone called out, "Give it a rest, old chap!" But Karol replied quietly:

"The Pope's decision to hold a Council had results that even the greatest optimist did not expect. In less than four years the state of the Church underwent an amazing change. Throughout the Catholic world—in cardinals' statements and bishops' pastorals, in articles by lay theologians, in answers to questionnaires by priests and laity—voices were heard again and again calling for a reinterpretation of the Gospel. An entirely new climate of rapprochement prevailed among the different Christian churches. Catholic world opinion took note of all the preparations for the Council, and realized how extremely thorough they were."

I quite agreed with this. Since I had been attending the Council I realized more and more not only how much was being done, but how much had been done beforehand. Karol continued, "The preparatory material for the First Vatican Council filled a book of over four hundred pages; the material for the Second comprises nearly ten thousand pages in fifteen volumes. There were a dozen or more preparatory commissions, composed of eminent bishops and theologians from over eighty countries, who in three years produced about seventy schemas or drafts in one hundred nineteen fascicles."

"Who on earth could read it all?" sighed someone.

"Again, thanks to Pope John's initiative there has been a sounding of world Catholic opinion in the past three years on a scale never known before. Opinions on the problems facing the Council were expressed by bishops, universities and heads of religious orders as well as a large number of lay Catholics and even non-Catholics. A tremendous part was played by such eminent theologians as Henri de Lubac, Jean Daniélou, Yves Congar, Hans Küng, R. Lombardi and Karl Rahner."

"Can you say what was Pope John's precise objective in calling the Council, or what he hoped it would do?"

"The prime objective in his mind was that of Christian unity, and we have already come a long way in that direction. The Church feels as never before that what unites Christians is stronger than what divides them. It has recognized the Christian values in other churches, and has accepted its share of blame and responsibility for our divisions."

Julek (whom we called "Giulio" because of his Italian charm) put in a word here. "Otto Dibelius of Berlin, one of the great figures of world Protestantism, has said that if the Catholic Church had presented the appearance four hundred fifty years ago that it does today, the Reformation would never have happened."

Karol continued, "The longing for Christian unity is accompanied by a longing for unity among the whole human race. The new conception of the 'people of God' has thrown fresh light on the old truth about the possibility of salvation outside the visible limits of the Church. Our relation to other religions is based on this and on recognition of the spiritual, human and Christian values contained in other religions like Islam, Buddhism or Hinduism. The Church wants to carry on a dialogue with other religions, and here Judaism has a special place. The draft declaration speaks expressly of the spiritual bond between Christianity and Judaism. Then there is an even wider scope for dialogue with unbelievers, which is especially important as atheism and unbelief today constitute a mass phenomenon as never before in history. The Church tries to discover the causes and roots of atheism, inside itself as well as outside. It realizes that the drive, under the form of atheism, to liberate man and free him from alienation may itself be part of the search for God."

"Yes," said someone, "but when John XXIII solemnly opened the Twenty-third General Council, the biggest assembly in the history of the Church, on Thursday October 11, 1962, he expected that its business would be concluded in a single session. I don't know if he was so pleased when it turned out that the first session had only scratched the surface."

"Oh, he wasn't so naïve or impatient as that. He saw what was going on and that the Council wouldn't finish its work so quickly, and he decided to call the second session in 1963."

"What did the first session achieve?"

"It is hard to point out tangible results. Of the five schemas that were discussed, none was adopted: they were all sent back to the commissions for redrafting. The Council didn't really get going until September 8, 1963, the first day of the second session."

"In that case, can one speak of any positive results achieved by the first session?"

"Certainly. It got the Council off to a good start, and did a great deal of work." Karol smiled at some memory of his own, and went on. "During its first session the Council acquired a personality and asserted the principle of pluralism; this expressed itself in the discussion on the liturgy and the demand for an increase in the authority and independence of the bishops."

"People say, rightly I suppose, that the Council is the work of Pope John XXIII, who not only got it to assemble in a short time but directed its labors and gave it the imprint of his own ideas—isn't that so?"

"Yes."

"But he also wanted the Council to finish its second and final session in 1963, the four-hundredth anniversary of the conclusion of the Council of Trent?"

"Yes, he did."

"And then he died before the second session began, at 8:45 P.M. on Whit Monday, June 3, 1963. Consequently, although the Council was his work, he didn't finish it. Can one then speak of continuity between the sessions, or are they really two separate Councils?"

"The Pope's ideas were not a private secret of his own. He left two documents: the encyclical *Mater et Magistra,* issued on the seventieth anniversary of *Rerum Novarum,* and also *Pacem in terris.* In these he expounded not only the principles of social order and peace, but also his own basic ideas. When he died, the first session had come to an end and the guidelines had been drawn for the second. Finally, it came as a surprise to no one when, on June 21, 1963, the conclave of eighty cardinals chose Giovanni Battista Montini as the new Pope. Everyone at the Vatican knew him to have been the closest collaborator of John XXIII, and he was certainly elected so that he could continue to guide the Council along the same lines."

"Incidentally," the rector put in, "you may not all know that John XXIII's last address was to a group of Polish pilgrims to the town of Piekary Slaskie." After a pause he added, "I think it's time to stop now. His Grace must have a lot more work to do. Perhaps he'll be good enough to come and talk to us again some other day."

Karol rose, and the audience reluctantly began to file

out of the library, taking the chairs they had brought with them. For my part, however, I thought that the talk had gone very well and that it was a pity to break off. I went up to Karol and said, "If you can, won't you come and have a cup of camomile tea with us? You remember, I once told you that last thing at night we always get together in somebody's room and talk about the world, the Church and Poland."

"All right. Where will it be?"

"It's my turn to be host tonight, so come along to my room when you're ready."

I hurried ahead to boil water and set out the cups and biscuits, together with some "Vecchia Romagna" in honor of the occasion. Among those who came were Alojz, Karlik, Szczepan, Edek, Prawnik (from Gdansk) and Swiec (from Lomza). Others got wind of the fact that the discussion was to be continued informally, and every minute or two someone else came in and asked if he might join the circle. Grapes and tangerines were brought, together with a bottle of grappa. There was not much space in my little room, but I seated everyone on the bed and chairs as best I could. More chairs were brought in from next door, until finally every square inch was occupied. The atmosphere was joyful and expectant. I kept on making fresh tea, and brought out all the sweets and biscuits I could find. Before long Karol came in and sat in the chair provided for him. He was surprised to see so many of us. After one or two pleasantries we reverted to the burning topic of the Council.

"Do you think there are any visible results as yet?"

"It's hard to get a full picture at this stage: it's still rather fragmentary. But, to begin with, I think there's a process of decentralization in Church institutions. The primacy of the Pope is unimpaired, and his moral authority and prestige have even increased. But the national episcopates have begun to play a bigger part; the Curia and canon law are being reformed; new central bodies are being created to meet new needs. Within the Church, there's a new relationship between the center and the periphery—between the Pope and the bishops, the bishops and their clergy; while relations between the clergy and laity are being changed by the new conception of the 'people of God,' encouraging the laity to be more mature, free and responsible."

"Which do you think are the most important documents of the Council?"

"Those on revelation, ecumenism, religious freedom and non-Christian religions are all extremely important, and also that on the Church in the modern world."

"What are the principal changes that the Council is likely to bring about?"

"Let me try to repeat in a few sentences what I said before. Firstly, the revaluation of the bishops' authority, decentralization in the Church and a return to the collegiate principle; then a review of pastoral methods and the introduction of new ones, sometimes very boldly conceived. Catholicism will be more universalized, with a different approach to the ancient cultures of non-European peoples—in other words, it must be de-Westernized. Peoples with ancient cultures of their own naturally resist Christianity if it comes to them in a Western European dress: it must be Africanized, Indianized or Japonicized by, so to speak, infusing a Christian content into those cultures. We all know that this is a slow and difficult business—I don't want to go further into it now. Then there's what Archbishop Jäger of Paderborn calls putting an end to Constantinism—the principle of a close alliance between Church and state, throne and altar, which reached its peak when the Holy Roman Empire was founded in the ninth century. This raises the important problem of working out a new relationship between Church and state and a new conception of the right to religious freedom. Then there must be an upgrading of the role of the laity in the Church, and a development of ecumenism on an unprecedented scale."

"Is the Council a place where people feel free to say what they like?"

"Yes, in fact it's quite stormy at times. The schema on the sources of revelation, for instance, was prepared by Cardinal Ottaviani, who's regarded as conservative, and was sent back to be redrafted; the vote against it was 1,368 to 822. At times, I can tell you, the Council is quite brutally frank."

"Here in Rome we hear something of what people in Poland are saying and thinking, but we don't get a full picture. What do they really think about the Council, and are they interested?"

"Let me give you an example. During the first session, from October 11 to December 8, 1962, special prayer meetings were held in parishes, monasteries and convents, a different one each day, so that continuous prayer was offered up for the Council, in that way and in many others as well. It must be the first time for many years that Polish Catholics have met together for the express purpose of praying for the interests of the whole Church. In praying for the Council, modern man is praying for something that touches him most nearly, the overcoming of historical errors and a better, more fruitful apostleship of the Church."

"Is the Church in Poland well informed about the subjects debated at the Council?"

"Extremely well. The bishops realize, of course, that it's not sufficient to know what takes place at the top, what is debated and approved and embodied in codes of liturgical or canon law. The important thing is that the ordinary man in the street should know what his representatives in Rome are aiming to do; there must be contact between him and them, and the organized prayers I spoke of are one way of maintaining such contact."

At this point I broke in. "This seems to be the right time to conclude our meeting, in accordance with the old principle: 'The elephant and the Polish question.' It's late, and we all have business to do tomorrow. I'm sorry, I know it's wrong for the host to talk like this, but I really have no choice."

Although I spoke jokingly, I was sorry to bring the meeting to an end. But it was nearly midnight, and we had to get up before six. I thanked Karol and my other guests, who were still arguing as they dispersed. I cleared up a bit, and set about returning the chairs I had borrowed. Glancing into the chapel, I saw Karol kneeling there in the dark.

20

Metropolitan of Cracow

It was not until January 18, 1964 that we in Rome heard, to our joyful surprise, that the Holy Father had appointed Bishop Karol Wojtyla to be Metropolitan Archbishop of Cracow. When I heard the mid-morning news on the radio I rushed out of my room to tell Alojz, and met him in the corridor on the way to tell me. We decided that we must do something to express our joy, and went out to the bar where we used to drink coffee in the morning. On the way we met Szczepan and persuaded him to come with us—he was from the Katowice and not the Cracow diocese, but it was all part of the metropolitan province and anyway he was a good friend of ours. We hurried to the bar, because it was simply impossible to walk slowly. It was a beautiful January day— bright sunshine, a blue sky, the oranges ripening. Discussing the event as we walked along, we decided that Karol would never have become archbishop if it had not been for the Council.

"He's so young, for one thing."

"And there were plenty of people with famous names who would have liked to be appointed."

"And Cracow isn't just any bishopric, it's the most important Polish see after Warsaw."

"Or before it, some people would say."

"Anyway, Karol's work at the Council must have played an important part. His speeches especially."

"And his contacts with bishops from all over the world, and the Curia as well."

"And the fact that he knows two or three languages, as well as Latin of course."

"His studies at the Angelicum must have played a part."

"Yes, and he saw a lot of the other Polish bishops, including the Primate."

"Then there's all his theological training, and above all his wisdom and common sense."

We ordered coffee, but decided that the day called for something special. At that moment the barman asked what we were all so cheerful about. When we told him that our vicar capitular had been made archbishop and that this was the Vatican's best appointment since Angelo Roncalli became John XXIII, he offered us drinks on the house. We accepted an apéritif with enthusiasm and, as the bar was empty, struck up the congratulatory chorus *Sto lat* ("A hundred years!"). The barman asked if it was our national anthem, saying that it sounded as solemn as "God Save the King"—a thought which had not occurred to me before.

Back at the college, we heard to our increased delight that Karol Wojtyla would also be a cardinal—Cracow being a cardinalatial see—and, moreover, the youngest in the whole Church. At lunch our rector, Father Rubin, confirmed the news with his typical warmth of language. A few days later a visitor from Cracow brought the text of the new archbishop's pastoral message, to be read throughout the province on Ash Wednesday. We listened with enthusiasm:

". . . In this letter I wish not only to inform you that I have become your pastor by the will of God and the decision of the Apostolic See, but also to discuss this event frankly with you." What an effect this must have in Cracow, I thought, and how I wish that I could see it!

"All these great and eloquent memories arouse in me a deep sense of responsibility. If this feeling does not become one of fear it is because with the aid of faith I endeavor to put my trust wholly in our Lord Christ and his Mother. . . . Together with this trust in the grace of God, which is the greatest power given to man in every walk of life and every situation, I also put my trust with all sincerity in human beings. In this place my thoughts and feelings go out to everyone in the archdiocese of Cracow, to my brother bishops, priests, brothers and sisters in religion, to fathers, mothers, children and young people, to the ill and those who are suffering in any way, to the simple and to the learned—to all those with whom I, as a bishop, am linked by the bond of Christian faith and life, and also by the natural unity that is shared by all men of good will."

We all felt that the new archbishop had acquitted himself well in his first message.

The enthronement was to take place on March 8. One of our number, Father Jerzy (George), went to Poland a few days earlier, ostensibly to deliver lectures. We suspected that his real purpose was to attend the ceremony, and we could scarcely await his return so as to hear about it at first hand. We greeted him with as much excitement as though he himself had been made archbishop.

A few of us collected in my room over homemade

coffee. We sat Jerzy in the best armchair and told him to fire away.

"Well, the ceremony began at 9:45. The cathedral was packed, of course. The archbishop was received at the foot of the steps leading up to the west door by the chief verger, who presented the casket containing the relics of St. Stanislas. The archbishop kissed it and went on up to the door, where he was met by the chapter in their ceremonial furs. Yes, furs—it's cold there, you know, not like here. The first speech of welcome was delivered by Professor Franciszek Bielak—an excellent choice, as you know; he's a Cracow man through and through."

"What did he talk about?"

"All the right things, and he said them very well. The Wawel, Cracow, the great Council that is going on now, great Councils of the past—Constance, the part played there by Polish bishops and Cracow University, Pawel Wlodkowic in particular.* When he had finished, the Dean, Bogdan Niemczewski, handed the keys to the archbishop, who entered through the main door while the organ boomed out 'Ecce sacerdos magnus qui in diebus suis placuit Deo.' He stopped and prayed at the shrine of St. Stanislas; then the procession moved on to the ambulatory, past the tomb of Queen Jadwiga† and

---

* The Council of Constance (1414–17) healed the great schism of the papacy and condemned the Hussites. Pawel Wlodkowic, rector of Cracow University, opposed the pretension of the Teutonic Knights to convert Lithuanians and other East Europeans by the sword.

† Jadwiga (Hedwig), the last of the original (Piast) dynasty of Polish monarchs, in 1386 married Jagiello, grand duke of Lithuania, who ruled Poland as King Wladyslaw II. Lithuania, which included a large part of what is now western Russia, was thus Christianized and united with Poland; the joint commonwealth (Rzeczpospolita, respublica) lasted until the eighteenth-century partitions.

the Sigismund* and Batory† chapels. The archbishop
knelt for a few moments before the Blessed Sacrament,
and revered the altar with Queen Jadwiga's crucifix. Finally, the procession got to the sanctuary; the archbishop
went up the steps to the main altar and took his seat on a
provisional throne. (Father Figlewicz told me, by the
way, that the chapter had decided to present the archbishop with the ring of Bishop Maurus, the fourth
successor of St. Stanislas, who died in 1118.) Then everyone stood up while the dean made a welcoming
speech on behalf of the chapter and clergy. Fr. Mikolaj
Kuczkowski, the chancellor of the metropolitan curia,
read out the bull of appointment from Paul VI, first in
Latin and then in Polish. I brought the text in case you
would like to hear it."

"Certainly—go ahead."

"'Paul, servant of the servants of God, to his worship-
ful brother Karol Wojtyla, hitherto bishop of Ombi, now
Archbishop elect and Metropolitan of Cracow, greeting
and apostolic benediction. There are in Poland not a few
dioceses deserving special praise, among them the metropolitan see of Cracow. Whether we consider its loyalty to
the Church, the nobility of its people, or its glorious
monuments, undertakings and achievements, this see has
always been of such importance and dignity that the
choice of an archbishop and supreme pastor has not only
required earnest thought but has been to us a source of
great joy, for it will provide the sheep of that numerous
flock with a shepherd, leader and teacher thanks to
whose wisdom they can advance in holiness. Now there-

---

* Sigismund (Zygmunt) I (1506–48) received the homage of
Albert of Bradenburg, the last Grand Master of the Teutonic
Knights, who secularized that order on becoming a Protestant.

† Stephen Batory of Transylvania, elected king of Poland
(1575–86), defeated Ivan the Terrible of Russia, also founded
Wilno (Vilnius) University.

fore, reverend brother, we appoint you Metropolitan of the archdiocese of Cracow, orphaned by the death of Archbishop Baziak of blessed memory, conferring on you all the rights and imposing the cares and duties of a bishop of your rank.' "

"Well put, don't you think?"

" '. . . Informing you, our beloved sons, of this, we adjure you not only to receive him with all honor as sons should do, but to obey and execute his commands, mindful that abundant fruits are gathered when mutual love unites the shepherd with his sheep.'

"When the bull had been read the archbishop, surrounded by his auxiliary bishops, kissed the altar stone where the saints' relics are contained, and took his seat on the throne to receive the homage of the auxiliary bishops, the chapter, seminary professors, deans and rectors, superiors of monasteries and convents, and lastly the seminarists, whom he received with a smile and with evident emotion. Then the archbishop preached a sermon. I've got the text—it was tape-recorded, but I asked him for a copy."

"Fancy bothering him with such matters!"

"Well, it's a historic document. Listen to the last few sentences, for instance:

" 'We all know that it is impossible to enter this cathedral without emotion. More than that: one cannot enter it without fear and awe, because, more than most cathedrals in the world, it is full of grandeur and speaks to us of our whole history, the whole of our nation's past. It does so by its monuments, tombs, altars and sculptures, and by the great names that dwell here and spell out a thousand years of Polish history.'

"You can see how Father Figlewicz taught him to love the cathedral—and he himself was a man who loved it more than anyone.

"'When I stood here today in front of the cathedral, and now as I kiss the altar and take my seat on the throne of the archbishops of Cracow, I feel above all the sense of something being born. I wish now to humble myself before the highest and deepest mystery of birth which is in God himself. I wish to pay the deepest worship of which man is capable, of which I myself am capable, to the Eternal Word, the Son born eternally of the Father.'"

As Jerzy continued reading I thought of Archbishop Baziak as I had seen him enthroned in the cathedral, and tried to imagine Karol in his place. I found it difficult to do so—the memories of a quite recent past were too strong. Karol during the Occupation, working at the stone quarry and at Solvay, Karol as a seminarist and a young priest, a seminary and university lecturer, then a young auxiliary bishop—all this was such a very short time ago. When he became a bishop I had of course been impressed; it seemed to remove him onto another plane, but I could get used to the change because it seemed to me that he was only secondarily a bishop and was still first and foremost a lecturer on ethics. But Karol as an archbishop and Metropolitan of Cracow, a man responsible for the archdiocese and the whole province—that was something else again. Of course I knew him to be intelligent and conscientious, but was he a good enough organizer? I knew he could run his own life, but could he run a diocese? Somehow I could not imagine him giving orders, rewarding and reprimanding, creating an administrative structure. I knew him better than most people, but I did not know whether he had such qualities.

Jerzy read on. The speech was a long one—I took in occasional passages, sometimes only sentences or words. I felt as I listened that Karol must be aware of all the problems that awaited him, or at least realize that he did not yet know what was in store. One thing was clear: it was his deep faith in God and in human beings that enabled him to bear the strain of an uncertain future.

"'. . . The life which God's Son has given us, which at the human level reflects his own eternal sonship within the Holy Trinity—that life he has also bestowed upon our mother the Church. He, the heavenly Bridegroom and Son of God, has bestowed on her the power to give birth—that is why we call her Mother Church, because she has given birth to each one of us. I speak here of the whole Church of Christ, but in particular the church of Cracow, which has borne me as a mother bears her son. And I look on this solemnity of my enthronement today as a new birthday in God, in Christ and in the Church . . . Peter, in the person of Paul VI, has said to me, "Feed my sheep," and has shown me in which part of the Church I am to do so. These words have tremendous authority; they draw strength from the words of Christ himself, when he said "Feed my sheep" to St. Peter, Paul's predecessor. So, my dear ones, I now stand on the threshold of that great reality which is expressed by the word "pastor." And I know that I stand there as of right, that I am not entering by any other way than through the Door of the sheepfold whom Christ himself has appointed, that is to say through Peter.'"

I interrupted Jerzy to blurt out the question: "Do you think Bishop Wojtyla will be good at running a diocese?"

After a brief silence Szczepan said:

"Well, he's been vicar capitular for about a year and a half—surely you ought to know by now."

"Not altogether," I replied. "For most of that time I was in Lublin or else here in Rome. And anyway, being a vicar capitular is a provisional job—it can come to an end at any time. In his case it was a year and a half, but the fact remains that you can't introduce any long-term plans, make changes in organization or pastoral methods. You have to confine yourself to short-term measures and not prejudice the task of the ordinary, who may take over at any minute."

"Well, we shall see," replied Szczepan. "But let's hear the rest of the letter, or Jerzy will never finish."

" 'And therefore I see the task that lies before me, that lies before us, as a difficult but a glorious one. . . . What I see most clearly is that my office of pastor is something we must build together. To be a pastor, it seems to me, one must know how to take what one's flock have to offer: in order to take, one must know how to give; one must coordinate and integrate everyone's gifts into a single common good. . . . My dear ones, if anyone wishes to call this a program they may do so. There is nothing original in it—it is simple and eternal. The things of eternity, the things of God are the simplest and deepest, there is no need for new programs. What we must do is to show increased zeal and increased readiness in carrying out the eternal program of God and Christ and adapting it to the needs of our own day.' "

I had not even noticed that Jerzy had finished reading when one of the others said, "Did the Mass come immediately after that?"

"No, not quite. He had to vest first of all, and it is interesting to notice what he wore. There cannot be many ordinaries in the world with such treasures at their disposal. A cloth-of-gold chasuble given by Anna Jagiello,* and the miter of the seventeenth-century bishop Andrzej Lipski. The crosier of Bishop Jan Malachowski, dating

---

* Anna Jagiello (1523–96), daughter of Sigismund I and Bona Sforza of Milan, and wife of Stephen Batory.

from Jan Sobieski's reign,* and a chalice used by Bishop Samuel Maciejowski in the reign of Sigismund I. And, the greatest rarity of all, the jewel of the cathedral, a rationale† presented by Queen Jadwiga."

"Splendor indeed," remarked Szczepan. "As to whether he makes a good ordinary, we shall see. Meanwhile, what did you think of the speech?"

"I didn't hear it all," I replied, "but the most characteristic part was at the end. May I borrow it for a minute?" I took it from Jerzy and read once more: "There is no need for new programs. What we must do is to show increased zeal and increased readiness in carrying out the eternal program of God and Christ and adapting it to the needs of our own day."

* Jan (John) III Sobieski, elected king of Poland, 1674–96; defeated the Turkish siege of Vienna, 1683.

† "An episcopal ornament, approximating to the *pallium,* worn formerly by a number of bishops of the [Holy Roman] Empire . . . in the form of a flat collar with metal appendages back and front." (*The Catholic Encyclopaedic Dictionary,* ed. Donald Attwater, London, 1949.)

21

The Pope at Work

I had no time to attend the Pope's first general audience, as the college is some distance from the Vatican, and I was leaving for Cracow next day, so I turned on the radio at 11:30 to hear about it. The audience had begun at eleven and was for pilgrims from the Dutch- and German-speaking countries. As the reporter observed, one might not have expected these Northerners to show much emotion, but they received the Pope's speech with enthusiasm and interrupted it with several bursts of applause. The Sala Nervi was crammed: it was supposed to hold 7,000, but no fewer than 10,000 turned up and were seated in the hall or filled the adjacent corridors. On the dais were 100 bishops and over a dozen cardinals from various countries. The Pope was accompanied by a small group including Fr. Juliusz Paetz and Fr. Stanislaw Dziwisz, personal secretary to His Holiness. His address ran as follows:

"Today John Paul II presents himself to you for the first time, four weeks after the general audience of John Paul I. I wish to welcome you and talk with you."

He spoke in his usual incisive voice, full of conviction, strength and courage, as the Italian press had already begun to recognize.

"I wish to continue the theme which John Paul I broached with you, concerning the three theological virtues: faith, hope and charity." The Pope explained that it had also been his predecessor's intention to speak of the "cardinal virtues" of prudence, justice, fortitude and temperance. "Today I wish to speak briefly of the virtue of prudence. This means conducting our lives at all time in accordance with a true, healthy conscience and moral principles. A prudent man is not one who, like so many, sets out to make life comfortable for himself and to get as much out of it as he can, but one who measures his life by the yardstick of moral values and the voice of true conscience. So prudence is the key to the accomplishment of the basic task that God has imposed on each one of us, namely the perfection of man himself. But a Christian has the right and the duty to consider the virtue of prudence in another dimension also. It is, as it were, the image and likeness of the providence of God himself in the dimension of actual human beings. For man—as we know from the Book of Genesis—was created in the image and likeness of God, and God carries out his plan in the history of creation, and above all in the history of mankind.

". . . Let each one of you consider his own life. Am I prudent? Do I live consistently and responsibly? Does the program I am realizing serve the real good? Does it serve the salvation that Christ and the Church want for us? I the Pope, who am speaking to you, must also consider what I must do in order to live prudently."

Listening to the speech, I thought how like Karol it was. Anyone who expected a speech full of rhetoric and a new, exciting program would have been sadly disappointed. It was more like a sermon in which the Pope addressed himself in a very personal manner to each member of his audience, urging them to apply the truths they heard and to draw practical conclusions for their own lives.

After the speech, further groups of pilgrims were presented. They were of French, English and Spanish speech, and to each group the Pope summarized his remarks in their own language. Finally he spoke in Polish to a group of fellow countrymen, asking them to come and see him often and to remember him in their daily prayers. One could tell that there was no affectation in his words—he would have been incapable of that—but that they were as authentic as everything else that he did and said.

Everyone rose as the Pope said the Our Father together with all present, after which he and the cardinals and bishops on the dais pronounced an apostolic blessing. That should have been the end of the audience, but instead the Pope went up to a group of invalids, greeting and talking to them, smiling and shaking hands. He surveyed the hall with its thousands of pilgrims and suddenly, breaking with age-old custom, he began to move from one group to another, amid shouts of joy and a torrent of applause. I could well imagine the scene—it must have been like the Polish audience on Monday, but this time there were Italians too. The outburst of joy was indescribable, and the radio reporter was at a loss for words, used as he must have been to demonstrations of all kinds. Men were shouting, women weeping, forests of hands were thrust out—everyone wanted to touch the Pope and be noticed by him, if only for a second. People held out their children so that the Pope could stroke them or lay his hand on their heads.

As the broadcast continued I felt furious with myself for not having gone to the Vatican after all. The Pope continued to walk up and down the hall, shaking hands, patting children's heads, answering questions, making the sign of the cross. At last he returned to the dais and said in Italian, "I see that one Pope is not enough to embrace everybody. I don't know how to make more of him, but luckily Christ had twelve apostles—we shall act in the same spirit of collegiality. Praised be Jesus Christ." With these words he disappeared amid a fresh outbreak of applause.

Bishop Rubin, formerly our rector at the Polish College, had asked me to lunch at the Polish center in the via delle Botteghe Oscure. His assistants (some of whom I had known at the college) and I sat at a large horseshoe table. The atmosphere was relaxed, friendly and cheerful, just as it had been in former years. I asked our host whether he thought Cardinal Wojtyla's membership of the Synod of Bishops had anything to do with his election to the papacy.

"Yes, I am sure that was an absolutely basic factor," he replied. "Of course, the Council was important too in that respect, especially the cardinal's work on Schema XIII between the third and fourth sessions. But the synod is far more important—it is a small group, not one of two thousand bishops like the Council, and there is much more opportunity for its members to get to know one another. Contacts are not casual or accidental, people speak more than once, and the synod meets regularly every two years."

"Besides," put in Fr. Juliusz Paetz, "the synod is, so to speak, the cream of the episcopate, which sends delegates from every country. Many of them become cardinals within quite a short time, and they would have helped to elect Wojtyla."

"He did not take part in the first synod in 1967, did he?"

"No, he refused to attend that, as a protest against the Polish authorities' action in not allowing Cardinal Wyszynski to go to Rome. He came to the second synod in 1969, which discussed cooperation between the Apostolic See and the bishops' conferences in different countries. The theme in 1971 was the priesthood and the problem of justice in the world. Cardinal Wojtyla spoke several times, and made a great impression. After that he became a member of the secretarial council of the synod, and was made a reporter for the next session, in 1974. The theme was evangelization in the modern world, and he presented a first-class report with the fluency and simplicity that are typical of him. After the debate it was his task to sum up, and he was even more brilliant at that than in his original statement."

After lunch Bishop Szczepan Wesoly invited me to his room for coffee. I asked him what he thought of the Pope from the standpoint of his own special responsibility for Poles living abroad.

"Well, I can tell you what I saw at first hand, on his journeys for instance. I may be wrong, but I think they too played a part in bringing about his election."

"How do you mean?"

"Well, no Pope before this one had traveled so much before he was elected. Of course his main purpose was to meet Poles in other countries and continents, but he also got to know the countries themselves, and they had a broadening effect on his mind and personality. He got to know how people in other continents live, how they think and react, what interests them—and this is of great importance in his present work. Secondly, he got to meet bishops throughout the world on their home ground, which is quite different from only seeing them in Rome, and in the same way they got to know him—so did the cardinals who were to take part in the conclave."

"I believe his first trip outside Europe was to North America?"

"Yes, to Canada and then the United States. Before that he'd paid many visits to France and Belgium, but Canada was his first encounter with a really new world. I was with him on that trip, from September to November 1969."

"How did the New World strike him?"

"He found it a bit strange at first—for instance, he couldn't get used to being offered a drink immediately after Mass. But he soon realized that if you stand with a glass in your hand you don't need to drink, and people won't pester you."

"What else did he find hard to get used to?"

"Big dinners organized in his honor—but he eventually came to the conclusion that they were a good idea, because in Poland there would have been two hours of speeches and then a reception lasting another two hours, so that really the dinners only took half as long."

"Did you go with him to Australia too?"

"Yes, for the Eucharistic Congress."

At that point we turned on the radio to hear the account of the Pope's visit to Castel Gandolfo. He rode standing in an open car, cheered by tumultuous crowds. At Castel Gandolfo he was welcomed on the square in front of the palace by Bishop Bonicelli of Albano and practically the whole local population, two thousand strong. He blessed the crowd and shook hundreds of hands. Some children presented a cage with two white doves and another of canaries, thus forming the papal colors. In his address he said, "I have now become your fellow townsman. Our first meeting has been enthusiastic and noisy, but I hope also a religious one. I greet you all and I hope that your new fellow townsman will prove himself a worthy citizen."

The Pope prayed for a long time in the chapel adjoining the room in which Paul VI died. Over the chapel altar is a large picture of Our Lady of Czestochowa.

In a drawing room of the palace the Pope received members of the local clergy, the municipal authorities and members of his own staff. He behaved with his usual unforced cordiality and disregard for traditional etiquette. As a Roman journalist remarked, "John Paul II must be a sore trial to those responsible for Vatican protocol." From Castel Gandolfo the Pope drove along the Via Appia to the little church of Domine Quo Vadis.* Here a service was being conducted and a sermon preached by the Polish Primate. Crowds were standing outside the church as well as in, and the Pope paused for a minute to bless them.

Turning off the radio, Szczepan remarked, "You see, everyone is astonished to find how simple and unconstrained the Pope is, in situations of every kind. And I am convinced that this easy manner of his owes a great deal to his travels and contacts with all sorts of people in different countries."

At that moment the telephone rang. It was Edek Nowak, who had been at lunch, inviting me to go round and see his new apartment. On the way there we continued our discussion of the reasons why Cardinal Wojtyla was elected Pope.

* The legend of St. Peter and Christ meeting at this spot is the theme of *Quo Vadis*, by the Polish historical novelist Henryk Sienkiewicz.

"Another point," I remarked, "is that the College of Cardinals nowadays is truly international, thanks to Paul VI's nominations; only thirty-eight of the one hundred and eleven are Italians."

"Yes, I was going to say the same. As you know, for some years I have been working at the Congregation for Seminaries and Universities as well as for Bishop Rubin. You've been in my office and seen how cosmopolitan it is, and in that respect it's a model of the whole Curia. This too is the work of Paul VI—people have rather stopped talking about him, but he did a tremendous lot. Of course he had his shortcomings, he didn't achieve everything, but he did internationalize the Curia and the Sacred College.

"In short, if it had not been for Paul VI the conclave would probably have been quite different and we wouldn't have John Paul II. If a majority of cardinals had been Italians they would have elected an Italian Pope."

As we were going along the via delle Botteghe Oscure in the direction from the Piazza Venezia to the Vatican, Edek said: "Have you seen the place where Aldo Moro's killers left the car containing his body? It was in that little lane, the first on the left. You remember, they left it a few hundred yards from the Christian Democrats' headquarters, so as to mock and humiliate them to the utmost."

We walked to the spot, now covered with wreaths including one with a Polish inscription. We stood and prayed. Every minute or two, passers-by came to pray or stand in silence. Occasionally a car stopped for a moment.

"There isn't much traffic now," said Edek, "but before they left the car containing the body, another car must have occupied one of the parking spaces—then it drove away at a prearranged time."

"But why did they want to kill him? I simply don't understand it."

"He was the last man the Italians believed in. All the other politicians were hopelessly compromised, mostly for financial irregularities—he was the only one with clean hands."

"Yes, I remember he was minister of foreign affairs when I was at the college, from 1963 to 1965. He had a rather shy smile and a streak of white in his black hair. He wasn't a tremendous figure, but—"

"But he was honest, right to the end, and the people trusted him. So the last authority they believed in was destroyed. And now see what is happening with the Pope. In a mere ten days he has conquered the hearts of all the Italians, especially the Romans, and in a sense the whole world as well. I have lived here for a dozen years or more, and I know the people long for an authority they can look up to, a *personaggio*. I say that of the Italians, but every nation needs a someone it can trust. So I ask myself now: is it just a passing enthusiasm for somebody new and different like the Pope, or is it a lasting attachment that will grow deeper and deeper as time passes and as they discover what a great personality our Pope really is?"

I walked around Cracow feeling like a stranger, as though I had been away for many years. Had the past few days in Rome changed me so much, or was it Cracow that was different? Probably both. Cracow was different, certainly: on the surface life was normal enough, but there was an undercurrent of excitement, a kind of holiday feeling. One soon realized that it was because nobody could forget for very long that the new

Pope was none other than Karol Wojtyla, Cardinal Archbishop of Cracow.

I had brought with me some postcard photographs of
John Paul II which I distributed more or less at random,
sometimes just to see what reaction they would produce.
Nearly always the recipient—whether it was a newspaper
seller, a dairywoman, a barber, a shopgirl or a garage
hand—spoke of some personal link: "I met him once in
the street"; "I saw him in church"; "I heard him preach";
"Oh, we knew him well, he was a curate at St.
Florian's"; "He came to this garage once, with his
chauffeur, to have a wheel fixed." They would quote
something he had said, or describe a conversation with
him. They cherished the memory like a treasure: it made
him theirs, one of them, part of their lives.

I had promised a "story" to *Tygodnik Powszechny*, but
I still felt reluctant to talk about what I had seen. On the
way to their office I met Adam Bujak, who, to my relief,
did not ask me any questions; his assignment was to take
photographs of places associated with the new Pope, and
I went with him to the archbishop's palace. The whole
of the top floor was closed to the public. The gate was
the same as in former times, though repaired after war
damage: the bullet marks near the lock and the larger
holes caused by gunfire from a tank were no longer to be
seen. We entered the huge, wide hall. On the left was
the entrance to the Curia, on the right to the cloisters.
The broad stone stairway leading to the first floor was
worn by the footsteps of countless visitors. The portrait of
Cardinal Olesnicki still looked down fiercely.* Upstairs,
the chapel door was straight in front and the archbishop's
apartments on the left. On the other side, facing the

* Zbigniew Olesnicki (1389–1455), Bishop of Cracow, states-
man and first Polish cardinal; opponent of the Hussites.

street, were the rooms in which we students had lived during the Occupation. I stood on the landing, with its tall pillars, and looked about me. Through the windows on one side could be seen the Franciscan church, next to which the German police had kept their stores; on the other side was the courtyard in which we had so often walked during recreation time. In another moment I expected a little, dark green Mercedes to drive out and stand waiting. The door of the prince archbishop's drawing room would open and out he would come with his chaplain, Fr. Julian Groblicki. He would pass the time of day with me and walk down to the car; Piasecki, the driver, would slam the door and off they would go on a parish visitation. . . .

"Come on," said Adam. We knocked at the door leading to our old quarters, which proved to be full of nuns and filing cabinets—this was now the secretariat. I described to Adam what it had been like in our day.

"Here on the right, where the cupboards are, used to be a place for jugs and washbasins. There was a curtain in front of the door, and the cardinal once nearly got his face daubed with shoe polish, by mistake for one of the students who was having a practical joke played on him. That conference hall is where our dormitory used to be. Karol slept here, on one of the iron beds. That was in 1944–45."

"Oh, that's too long ago, and anyway it's all changed now. No one would be interested."

Yes, it had all changed, but my head was full of memories of the old days. I felt as if I belonged to the world of thirty-five years ago and not the present day, yet I also knew that my world was lost beyond recall: it was no more than a historical curiosity, a biographical detail. They might ask me for dates and names, what had become of our fellow students of those days: were they now important figures in the church, had they any interesting misdeeds to account for? But for my part I could only remember the chubby face of Staszek Koscielny or the stammering voice of Karol Targos; I could see Wladek Majda with his thick glasses, or Janek Sidelko with his sleek black hair and the heavy military boots he wore under his cassock.

"Can we take some pictures of where the Pope slept and worked when he was archbishop?"

"I expect so." I rang at the door of the private apartments, and a figure in work clothes appeared: it was old Franciszek with his wise smile, a tangible link with bygone days. He said we would need the chancellor's permission to take photographs, but meanwhile he invited us in. The rooms were as I remembered them, but empty and dead. Only the large dining table had disappeared and had been replaced by a smaller one. The main drawing room and bedroom were locked. Franciszek explained that when reporters and other strangers were allowed in, things had begun to disappear: nothing of special value, but shaving brushes and such small objects.

"I shall soon be disappearing too," he added unexpectedly. "I'm retiring."

I could not imagine the palace without Franciszek. "You used to say," I reminded him, "that you had outlived so many archbishops."

"Well, I don't want to outlive any more of them."

Franciszek's eyes, usually so merry, seemed to dim with tears. He turned and led us, with tottering steps, back through the empty apartments. We parted without further conversation.

"Where to now?" said Adam.

"Let's look at the chapel. The archbishop used to spend an hour or two every day there, if not longer."

We got a key from one of the nuns and went in.

"Look at the coffered ceiling," I said; "that's how the whole chapel used to look. It was all in dark colors—red, green and blue. A few years ago someone decided it was too gloomy, so they covered the walls with ivory-colored stucco and put in these baroque chandeliers."

"But it's been like this for some time now?"

"Yes." Once again I realized that I was confusing one period with another: what Adam wanted to know was how the place had looked in the last few years, not in the 1940s.

"Where did the Pope used to pray?"

"Here, on this prie-dieu, on the left near the altar. So did the cardinal prince, but he used a different kneeler."

Adam paid no attention; I was not sure if he even knew whom I meant by the "cardinal prince."

"And what's that table?"

"The archbishop used to write at it. You see, it has a flap to make it larger. As for the vase of flowers, the nuns must have put it there."

"I shan't take any pictures today—I'll come back another time with all my equipment. But can we please get permission to photograph the study and bedroom and reception room?"

We went downstairs to see the chancellor, Father Marszowski. "When you get back to Rome," he said to me, "will you please ask Staszek Dziwisz to see if the Pope will send me a signed photograph?"

"Of course."

Goodness, I thought, how wonderful it all is and how things have changed. Father Marszowski must have seen the archbishop a dozen times a day on one matter or another, and now here he is asking for a signed photograph.

On the way from the palace to my own church I met Anna, Jerzy Turowicz's wife, in the Planty Gardens. I conveyed greetings from her husband, with whom I had been drinking coffee only the previous day on the via della Conciliazione, and asked what things had been like in Cracow since the conclave.

"We had an absolute invasion of journalists from all over the world—French, British, American, German, Italian, Spanish. Very few of them spoke Polish, of course, and with Jerzy away we had to do our best in whatever languages we could, so I spoke French, Magdalena German, Adam English, while Elzbieta—she's so pretty— even appeared on Italian television. We had to talk all day long, day after day, remembering everything we could, every single detail. We'll see what sense they made of it all when their papers start coming out. We've already seen one which said that in Stalin's time the Pope had to celebrate Mass in the woods because church ceremonies were forbidden."

"They must be crazy."

"No—we had told the reporter that Karol Wojtyla used to say Mass out of doors when he took young people on hiking expeditions, but he got it slightly wrong and made a sensational story out of it."

"Why didn't you come to Rome for the inauguration?"

"I'm very glad I didn't—here in Cracow it was absolutely unforgettable. Crowds singing and shouting in the streets, Mass at the Wawel at eight that evening, at St. Anne's at midnight, and again next evening at the Wawel, with a congregation of thousands. Then the crowds in the Market Square and at the Mickiewicz monument, and again at the archbishop's palace."

I asked Anna to tell me more about the Mass at the Wawel.

"On Tuesday the seventeenth they set up a field altar

in the courtyard in front of the Waza chapel;* to one side was a portrait of the Pope with his arms, a cross with the letter M in one corner. The white-and-yellow papal flag flew from the Silver Bells Tower, and the white-and-red Polish colors from the tower opposite. On a dais were the cathedral chapter, rectors of seminaries and superiors of religious orders. Mass was celebrated by Bishop Albin Malysiak. On the altar was a reliquary containing the head of Bishop St. Stanislas. The homily, an excellent one, was preached by Bishop Stanislaw Smolenski. There was a huge crowd, and a tremendous feeling of reverence. After Mass everyone went to the palace on Franciszkanska Street, where a portrait of the Pope was displayed in the window, and there was an astounding demonstration. As the papers put it, 'The manifestation was prolonged and joyful, accompanied by cheering and by church hymns and patriotic songs.' It was really indescribable—there can't have been anything like it in Cracow ever before, even the rejoicing when the war came to an end."

"Did the television show any of the Roman ceremonies?"

"Oh, yes. I saw Cardinal Felici announce the result of the conclave, and I saw our Pope come onto the balcony for the first time."

"What did you feel like then?"

"To tell the truth, on that first day I hardly recognized him—he seemed tense and nervous, and his voice was different, especially at the beginning. And then, on the second day, he was exactly as we always knew him—bold, free, unconstrained—but with all the qualities we used to admire raised, as it were, to a higher plane. One

* The Waza kings of Poland—Sigismund III (1587–1632) and Wladyslaw IV (1632–48)—were related to the Vasa dynasty of Sweden.

feels he has shaken off any inhibitions he may have had, and now he fears no one but God alone."

I looked in on some friends including Adam's sister Zocha, who said, "Adam was in town when the inaugural Mass was broadcast, and went to his club to see it on television. He said there were quite a lot of others watching, including some he had never thought of as being pious, but they took part in the Mass like everyone else."

"How do you mean 'took part'?"

"Why, in the usual way—they stood for the Gospel, knelt at the Elevation and so on."

"What, in the clubroom?"

"Yes, of course," broke in another friend. "So did everyone in Poland who watched the Mass on television: we stood for the Gospel, crossed ourselves, struck our breasts at the Agnus Dei and so forth. It's true I went to Mass again that evening, to be on the safe side. But you can't imagine how moved everybody was. When I went to work in the morning people on the bus were crying, and total strangers were embracing one another."

When I got to my own church the nuns were full of stories.

"You know, Father, on that Sunday the streets were absolutely empty. A bus driver told me that for three hours not a single passenger had boarded his bus. At the Church on the Hill there's one Mass that is usually particularly crowded, and on that day they had a congregation of one. And all the church bells all over town were ringing the whole time."

One of the nuns invited me to the parlor, as the Mother Superior wanted to see me. I sat on one side of the grille; a moment later a veil of some dark material was drawn aside, and I saw the Mother Superior with a younger nun. I started to tell them something of events in Rome, but soon found they knew more about them than I did—they had listened to every broadcast from Radio Vatican, which I never had time to do.

"You weren't in Rome, were you, on October 29, when the Pope flew to Mentorella?"

"No, I left three days earlier."

"Would you like to hear the radio account of the visit? We have a tape recording of it."

"Very much."

The young sister went off to fetch the recording, as the Mother Superior continued:

"Have you ever been in Mentorella, Father?"

"Yes, I went with the cardinal several times. He nearly always spent at least a few hours there whenever he was in Rome, and sometimes he stayed the night. He was there with three Polish priests on October 7, a week before the conclave began. He drove to Capranica Prenestina and then, as usual, walked the remaining eight miles uphill."

"I don't know much about Mentorella—can you tell me its history?"

"Yes, it is about the oldest Marian shrine in Italy. It is twenty-five miles or so from Rome, in the Monti Prenestini, at the summit of the Guadagnolo, which is about 1,218 meters high. The legend is that in Trajan's reign, about the year one hundred, a pagan official named Placidus was hunting a stag there, and just as he was about to kill it he saw Christ in a halo between its horns. He and his family became Christians; he took the name Eustace, and was martyred during the persecutions. Apparently the emperor Constantine in the fourth century had a church built at the spot where the vision occurred."

"Is anything left of that church?"

"Only very slight remains. St. Benedict is said to have

stayed two years at Mentorella before going to Subiaco; there is a rocky cave below the present church that is supposed to have been his hermitage. Some tenth-century documents say that the Benedictines founded an abbey there; it existed until the fifteenth century and was probably visited by St. Francis of Assisi. After the Benedictines left, the sanctuary fell into ruins. It was restored in the seventeenth century, and at that time a wooden statue of Our Lady was discovered, dating from the twelfth century."

"What does it look like?"

"Our Lady is sitting on a throne, with the Child Jesus on her lap. The sanctuary came to life again in 1857, when it was taken in charge by the Resurrectionists, a community founded by two Polish priests, H. Kajsiewicz and P. Semenenko. Three priests and two lay brothers live there now, in a little monastery beside the church."

"Oh, so that's why the cardinal went there regularly?"

"Yes, but I think he also liked the quiet and isolation of the place. It's very secluded: it has only had electric light for a dozen years or so, and the asphalt road was only completed ten years ago, when the last section was blessed by Bishop Wladyslaw Rubin. Cardinal Wyszynski used to go to Mentorella too, but our Pope was especially fond of it."

Meanwhile the young sister had returned with the tape recorder. As I watched the nuns getting it ready I was struck by the contrast between the four-hundred-year-old institution of the enclosed Visitandine nuns and the newest technical inventions. The two seemed to suit each other admirably.

We listened to the recording. On Sunday October 29, the reporter explained, the Pope, in accordance with tradition, had appeared at the window of his palace and recited the Angelus together with the crowd of 150,000 who filled the Piazza di San Pietro. This was said to be the biggest crowd ever seen there. In his address he recalled that he had said Mass on the previous day in the Vatican Grottoes, thirty days after the death of John Paul I and on the twentieth anniversary of the election of John XXIII. In conclusion he said to those present, "*Voi Romani,* can you tell me how to get to the Marian sanctuary of Mentorella?" This caused general merriment, as the crowd knew that the Pope was going there that afternoon and that he already knew the sanctuary well.

He went, in fact, by helicopter. The crowd of 40,000 that made its way to Mentorella surpassed all expectation; of these, about 7,000 got to the church or near it, while the others got stuck on the narrow mountain road. On the Pope's arrival Mass was celebrated by Bishop Giaquinta of Tivoli together with the Polish fathers. When the "sign of peace" was reached, the Pope shook hands with those around him. Afterward he spoke of his own links with Mentorella.

"We read in St. Luke's gospel," he said, "that after the Annunciation Our Lady went into the hill country to visit her kinswoman Elizabeth, and it was there that she uttered the famous hymn, the Magnificat." Speaking of Mentorella, he went on, "This is a place in which man opens himself to God in a special way—a place where, far from everything yet close to nature, man can talk intimately with God and feel in his inmost self what God requires of him."

I listened intently. The recording was full of scratches and background noise, crackling and fading, and at times it was hard to follow the Pope's words.

"Man is bound to glorify God, his creator and savior. He should, in a sense, be the mouthpiece of all created things, proclaiming the Magnificat in their name. He should declare the wonderful works of God, and at the same time show forth his own relationship with God."

As he spoke I remembered more and more clearly the little church amid pines and cypresses, with its simple façade dating from twelve centuries ago, situated on a rocky spur from which mountain slopes were visible as far as the eye could see. The sky was blue, there was a sea of greenery round about, and the only sound was that of the wind, which was pleasantly cool.

"Whenever I have been in Rome this place has helped me to pray, and that is why I wished to come here this afternoon. Prayer, which in so many ways expresses our relationship to the living God, is the Pope's first duty and his first message, the first condition of his service to the Church and the world. The Mother of Christ went into the hill country to proclaim the Magnificat. May the Father, the Son and the Holy Spirit accept the Pope's prayer in this sanctuary and bestow the gifts of the Holy Spirit on all who pray here."

After thus ending his speech the Pope entered the monastery for a moment to take his leave, and boarded the white helicopter. He gave a final wave of greeting as the machine took off. By his own wish, no doubt, and to the crowd's delight, it circled the mountain three times before making straight for Rome.

The nuns switched off the recording. "Whenever the Pope visits anywhere," I said to them, "he leaves people feeling that he has not been there long enough, that they cannot bear to part with him, that they want to see and hear him again, talking, laughing or praying."

"How much he must love people," said the young nun softly.

That evening Anna telephoned to say, "Mietek, before

you publish your book, do please let me read the manuscript."

"Certainly, I was going to ask you to anyway. But why?"

"Well, you said something about writing a book called *My Friend the Pope.*"

"Of course that's only a working title; but what's wrong with it?"

"It might upset all the people who think they too are friends of the Pope."

I felt a little injured. "If they want to, there's nothing to stop any of them writing a book called *My Friend Pope John Paul II.* The more the merrier."

But I suddenly realized, in all seriousness, what a marvelous thing it was that this man had so many friends, that to so many people he was an indispensable part of their lives, that he had become an integral part of so many human destinies.

I paid another visit to the palace—to the secretariat, now housed in a former reception room. Sister Jadwiga, whom I had known for years and who had been in charge of the secretariat under Cardinal Wojtyla, got up from her desk, took off her spectacles with a gesture I remembered well, and asked what she could do for me.

"Can you tell me anything about working for the Holy Father?" I asked on the spur of the moment.

"One couldn't imagine a better person to work for. He never fussed or got angry."

"What was his daily routine?"

"He said Mass at seven, had breakfast and went back to the chapel, where he used to pray and write till eleven. He gave audiences from then onwards, leaving letters and other simple matters to the afternoon. Practically anyone could see him even without an appointment, and certainly without having to write and explain their business beforehand."

I knew all this as well as Sister Jadwiga, but I was pleased to see that she still appreciated the archbishop's virtues—as the years go by, people tend to take such things for granted.

"You've been here a long time, Sister, haven't you?"

"Yes, I worked for Archbishop Baziak and Bishop Jop, then Archbishop Baziak again when he came back after 1956, and Cardinal Wojtyla during the whole of his time here, first as vicar capitular and then as ordinary."

Sister Jadwiga offered to show me the manuscript of the cardinal's book *Love and Responsibility*. It was in a worn brown folder tied together with tape. I looked at the neat, familiar handwriting and saw at the top of each page a pious invocation such as "Totus tuus ego sum," "Adoro te devote" or "Magnificat anima mea Dominum."

"When did he write this?"

"I don't know; it must have been the late fifties or early sixties. If you're interested in his pastoral work, perhaps you would like to look at his diary of appointments; he kept it very carefully, and I used to make a fair copy."

The diary, in Sister Jadwiga's calligraphic hand, filled four large exercise books. Dates and places were indicated in a left-hand column, and on the right was a record of the cardinal's activities.

"I used to make it fuller, but he told me there was no need. Here is his own calendar, from which I copied the information."

I looked at Karol's notes in his own hand. They were full of abbreviations, but no doubt legible enough for one accustomed to them. Sister Jadwiga also showed me one of several religious pictures the cardinal had given her. It bore the inscription: "To dear Sister Jadwiga, who helps me so much in the Curia and takes so much trouble to divine my thoughts, I offer my thanks and wish every blessing from the newborn Jesus. 5.1.1971."

Sister Jadwiga told me that on days when the cardinal did not say Mass in the morning—for instance, if he was to do so in the afternoon—he would go to the Franciscan church across the street. He also used to make the Stations of the Cross there, in the chapel of the Passion.

"Did you know," she went on, "that the Pope mentioned this church in a sermon he preached last Sunday, the fifth of November, outside the basilica of St. Francis at Assisi? That was when he made a pilgrimage to the shrines of the two patrons of Italy, St. Francis and St. Catherine of Siena."

Sister Jadwiga brought out another file and showed me the text of the sermon. I read:

"The Franciscan order spread far beyond the borders of Italy and soon reached my own country of Poland, where it flourishes no less than in other countries and continents. When I was bishop of Cracow I lived near a very old Franciscan church where I used to pray and make the Stations of the Cross and visit the chapel of Our Lady of Sorrows. It is a place I shall never forget, and we must remember too that the Blessed Maximilian Kolbe,* a special patron of our troubled times, was an offspring of that noble branch of Franciscan spirituality."

Sister Jadwiga reminded me that before going to Assisi the Pope had spoken at the midday Angelus in Rome, where he said:

"After the election but before the conclave was over, I wondered what I would say to the Romans when I presented myself to them as their bishop, a man from Cracow in the distant land of Poland. Then I thought of St. Peter, and remembered that nearly two thousand years

* Fr. Maximilian Kolbe (1894–1941) voluntarily accepted death to save the life of a fellow prisoner at Auschwitz.

ago your ancestors had welcomed another man from a strange land, as I hoped you would welcome me. . . . I thank God and all of you for the generosity with which you have received me from the very beginning, and today I wish to respond to that generosity in a special way by visiting your own patron saints. I am going to Assisi, the city of St. Francis, and to the tomb of St. Catherine of Siena, which, as you know, is in the Roman basilica of Santa Maria sopra Minerva."

The Pope went to Assisi by helicopter, said Mass at 2:10 P.M. and visited the crypt with the relics of St. Francis, after which he addressed the crowd. Sister Jadwiga showed me this text also, with its moving conclusion:

"St. Francis of Assisi, help us to bring Christ closer to the Church and the modern world! You who bore in your heart the changing fortunes of the people of your own day, help us in the spirit of our Redeemer to confront the problems of modern man, the social, economic and political issues of our culture and civilization, with all its sufferings, tensions, complexes and discontents. Help us to translate all this into the simple, fruitful language of the Gospel. Help us to unlock all these problems with the key of the Gospel, so that Christ may become the Way, the Truth and the Life for men and women of our time. Holy son of the Church and son of Italy, the man who begs this of you is Pope John Paul II, a son of Poland. He is confident that you will not reject his plea but will help him, for you are always good and have always hastened to help those who sought your aid."

We talked about the Pope's visit to the tomb of St. Catherine. "She was a patron of yours," I remarked to Sister Jadwiga.

"How do you mean, Father?"

"Well, she was a nun, and she used to write, just as you do."

"You're joking. St. Catherine was a political and literary genius. She persuaded Pope Gregory XI to return from Avignon to Rome. She visited prisoners and looked after the sick and injured, and all I do is to sit here and run a secretariat. Besides, she died of emaciation at the age of thirty-three, and I'm still alive. Anyway, here's a copy of what the Holy Father said at Mass in the basilica." I read the words:

"We are approaching the end of the day which I wished to devote in a special way to the patron saints of Italy. . . . This country was always close to my heart, it is now to be my second homeland, and today I wish to give expression to the link which binds me to it. I wish to have a share in it, in all the wealth of its history and its present-day reality. The saints of every great country are a special witness to that country and its people. . . . Here, beside the relics of St. Catherine of Siena, I wish once again to thank the Divine Wisdom for having made use of the heart of that woman, simple yet of profound character, to point the way in times of uncertainty to the Church and especially to the successor of St. Peter. What love, what courage, what magnificent simplicity, and at the same time what spiritual depth! A soul aware of its mission and open to every breath of Divine inspiration. St. Catherine has been recognized as a visible sign of women's mission in the Church. I would like to say a great deal on this subject, but today time is too short. The Church of Jesus Christ and the Apostles is also a Mother and a Bride. These biblical titles show how profoundly the mission of women is inscribed in the mystery of the Church. O that we may discover together the manifold significance of that mission, drawing strength from the qualities which the Creator from the beginning placed in the hearts of women and the wonderful wisdom with which, centuries ago, he endowed St. Catherine of Siena. As in those days she was the teacher and leader of Popes who were far from Rome, so may she be today the inspiration of a Pope who has come to Rome. May she bring closer to him not only her own country but all countries of the world in the unity of the Universal Church. Wishing thus, I bless you all from my whole heart."

As I finished reading, Monsignor Dowsilas came into the secretariat. I knew that Karol had been fond of taking him on special visits and journeys, and I had met him in Rome when Karol was made a cardinal. He was a man of great tact and *savoir-faire*, with a strong sense of humor.

"I used to tell the archbishop jokes to cheer him up," he said to me.

"For instance?"

"Well, there was a story about a woman whose husband has just died, and she comes to the priest to arrange about the funeral. The priest is fond of money, and he says, 'Shall we come to your home to fetch the body?'—'Yes, please.'—'Right, that'll be a hundred zlotys. And shall we sing the funeral service there?'—'Yes, you'd better do that.'—'Another hundred zlotys.' And so it goes on until the figure is eight hundred zlotys, and the priest says, 'Well, we've got him as far as the church.' The cardinal thought this so funny that it became a sort of catch phrase with him. Indeed, it nearly caused his death on one occasion."

"How so?"

"We were driving from Warsaw to Cracow and stopped to get a bottle of mineral water out of the trunk of the car. Suddenly a little dog turned up from nowhere and jumped into the trunk, and I said, 'Well, we've got him as far as the church.' The cardinal, who was just drinking, laughed so much that he almost choked. After he became Pope I made the same joke to him at a small private audience, and he laughed again."

"When was the last time he went on a pastoral visitation?"

"At the end of September this year, to a settlement called Zlote Lany [Golden Meadows] at Bielsko-Biala; but I wasn't with him at that time."

I asked Sister Jadwiga to show me the cardinal's record of the visit. It was headed "Totus tuus ego sum" and read:

"Friday 29 September, feast of the Guardian Angels. Bishop Stanislaw Smolenski and I arrived at 6 P.M. at the parish church of the Divine Providence at Bielsko-Biala. Bishop Stanislaw had been inspecting the parish for the past week, so I confined my visitation to Zlote Lany. This is a new housing estate, largely connected with the local car factory; it is growing rapidly and needs separate pastoral arrangements, also a church of its own.

"On Saturday 30 September I went to the chapel of the Sisters of Divine Mercy, who are looking after Zlote Lany for the time being, and heard confessions before Mass. I said Mass at 8 A.M., addressing my sermon especially to the sisters and their Caritas organization and to some sick parishioners who were present. After breakfast, accompanied by Mgr. Walancik of the Cracow chapter and Fr. Szeypta, I visited other sick people in their homes and said a decade of the rosary with each. There are lay people who help the clergy to look after them. Some of the invalids had been at the 'diocesan holiday home' at Miedzybrodzie Bielski. After these visits I went to see the priests, who have all luckily managed to find living space on the estate. Fr. Sokolowski lives in his parents' house, and they have a room set apart for religious classes. In spring of this year the house was threatened, but they managed to save it. I specially thanked Fr. Sokolowski and the old couple for what they have done in the way of pastoral care and facilities for religious instruction."

Reading Karol's account, I had a vivid impression of his personality: working hard, praying for hours on end, and keenly aware of the importance of pastoral work. He delighted in the activity of every parish working on traditional lines, and he threw the whole weight of his energy and authority into the scales when new communities had to fight for permission to build a church or enlarge a pastoral center—a chapel, for instance, that would hold a dozen or so people, when hundreds or even thousands had to congregate outside. In Cracow itself there were parishes of this sort—Bienczyce, Mistrzejowice, Krowodrza, Azory, Debnicki—each of which could tell a tale of heroic efforts and sacrifices, sleepless nights and interminable interviews, deputations and petitions to the authorities for permission to build adequate churches and, if that was granted, for the procurement of the necessary materials. In each of these parishes the faithful had attended hundreds of Masses and other services out of doors in all seasons, in wind and rain, mud and snow, sometimes for years on end, while children had been instructed for thousands of hours in cramped conditions in various private homes. Karol used all his authority to defend the right of these people to possess adequate places of worship and premises where children could be taught their faith with a minimum of discomfort. He did all he could to help priests who were prevented from living together in presbyteries and had to subsist as best they could in hole-and-corner conditions, sometimes even without residence permits. . . . I continued reading:

"The catechism center set up in 1973 in the home of a

couple named Glondys is the earliest of its kind at Zlote
Lany. It has managed to resist attack thanks to their
firmness and that of the whole Catholic community at
Biala."

As I was reflecting on what a useful thing it was that
the Church obliged bishops to keep a diary of this sort,
Sister Jadwiga remarked, "The cardinal nearly always
gave me his notes on the very same day when he returned from a parish visitation." This surprised me: I
would not have thought that Karol would be so punctil-
ious, as I knew he attached little weight to mere formali-
ties, but no doubt the overriding factor was his loyalty to
the wishes of the Apostolic See.

Showing me the book once again, Sister Jadwiga
pointed out what a large number of visits the cardinal
paid to various institutions and groups for the purpose of
sharing the Christmas *oplatek* [the wafer-breaking
ceremony] with them. In January 1978, for instance, although he was traveling about a good deal and was ill toward the end of the month, his diary recorded the following visits:

Jan. 7: Society of Lay Catechists
Jan. 8: scientists
Jan. 9: gardeners
Jan. 13: St. Salvator's college
Jan. 14: doctors
Jan. 15: Maternity Institute
Jan. 16: lawyers
Jan. 17: ex-service men
Jan. 21: Catholic Intellectuals' Club, Catechetical In-
          stitute, disabled ex-soldiers
Jan. 22: teachers, nurses
Jan. 23: priests ordained in 1974
Jan. 24: priests ordained in 1977

Jan. 26: Borek Falecki and workmates
Jan. 27: bishops of Cracow province
Jan. 31: priests ordained in 1972
Feb. 1: priests ordained in 1973

"Did you know that the cardinal used to meet his former workmates at Solvay regularly once a year? All these Christmas gatherings were quite a strain," said Sister Jadwiga quietly. So indeed they were, but I knew how fond Karol was of all the carol singing and Christmas greetings. Those who arranged the gatherings generally put on a show of some kind, often of high artistic quality; but from his point of view they were first and foremost an expression of pastoral activity, into which he threw himself heart and soul.

"Look, the cardinal sent me these notes of his very last engagements in Rome." Sister Jadwiga proudly produced three of four yellow foolscap sheets from a loose-leaf exercise book, ruled in three columns. At the end of the last sheet I read:

Oct. 16: 7 A.M. Concelebration.
St. Jadwiga of Silesia. Conclave.
5:15 P.M. (approx.) John Paul II.

I thanked Sister Jadwiga and took my leave. I did not feel like looking at anything further or talking to anyone —that brief record had impressed me too much. I wanted somehow to keep the impression to myself, not let it be dissipated or overlaid by other experiences. As I walked downstairs my one hope was that I would not meet anyone I knew. I crossed the large entrance hall, reached the main gate and turned into the street.

22

Foundations of Renewal

Fr. Marian Jaworski, whom I have known for many
years and who is now dean of the Theological Department at Cracow, talked to me about Cardinal Wojtyla's
The Acting Person, which he edited when it was published in Polish in 1969, and *Love and Responsibility*
(Cracow, 1962; Italian translation 1968). He remarked
that these books were not the work of a detached scholar
but of a man who was an original thinker with practical
experience. I asked if their language was not somewhat
traditional and involved.

"He did use traditional language," Jaworski replied,
"but he gave it a fresh content of his own. This applies
to such terms as 'consciousness' or 'the philosophy of the
subject.' His ideas form a sort of counterpoint to those
of Sartre, when for instance he says that man is not
merely consciousness but fulfills himself in action. He
lays strong emphasis on personality, and this came out in
the papers he drafted for Vatican II. He thought it was
time to work out a Christian anthropology, a philosophy
of man, and that modern philosophers were ahead of us
in this field. The Church should make use of their

findings just as it used Aristotle in the Middle Ages. Salvation should not mean alienation, but the preservation of human identity, of man's commitment to the world and responsibility for it.

"When I was last in Rome," Jaworski went on, "I saw a symbolic picture: on one side the Pope in skiing costume, on the other in papal vestments. This is a Pope who is not afraid of the world and can meet it on its own ground, whether of scholarship or everyday experience.

"Some people used to say about him that an archbishop should not have time to be a professor as well, but he never neglected his pastoral duties. The titles of his books show how concerned he is with action and responsibility, but he stays on the religious plane and does not meddle with politics or economics. I think people realize this in the West as well as here, and that it enhances his authority."

I returned home and reread the preface to *Love and Responsibility*, in which the author thanked those whose experience had contributed to the book, consciously or otherwise, and pointed out that a priest, like a doctor, by the nature of his calling acquired much experience, albeit indirect, of the matters it dealt with. The book was, he said, the result of a "confrontation" of such knowledge with the truths of the Gospel and church doctrine. As to *The Acting Person*, the preface declared that it owed its origin to the climate of Vatican II and especially the Constitution on the Church in the Modern World. It was also in a sense a continuation of the earlier book, with the same emphasis on exploring the human personality.

I looked at a third book of the cardinal's: *Foundations of Renewal* (Cracow, 1972), which was written for the benefit of synodal assemblies in Poland as a guide to the implementation of Vatican II. Again the preface emphasized that it was written not as a theological commentary but as a practical guide to action in the spirit of the Council.

All three books laid stress on the importance of human experience, both sensory and intellectual, and of the subject's responsibility for his actions; also a positive relationship to the humanity of others, and a sense of community as opposed to alienation. No individual must be treated as simply a means to an end. The essential feature of the experience of love was "belonging," of giving oneself entirely to the beloved. In Wojtyla's philosophy one recognized echoes of Gabriel Marcel's *Être et avoir*, Heidegger's *Sein und Sendung*, Jaspers, Sartre and Max Scheler—but all these are integrated in terms of Thomist philosophy, not in an eclectic fashion but so as to form a highly personal outlook of his own.

A few days later I met Father Jaworski again. He had been in Rome and told me that the Pope was talking Spanish daily in preparation for his Mexican journey. He had also been drafting his first encyclical, in Polish; the Latin translators had had trouble with its up-to-date language.

At the end of May 1967, when I was living at Münster, my friend Monsignor Lubowiecki telephoned in excitement from Frankfurt to tell me that our archbishop had been made a cardinal. He himself would be in Rome during the consistory, and offered to take me in his car. We drove via Munich, Innsbruck, the Brenner and Florence, exchanging reminiscences of the archbishop as we had known him at different times and discussing the institution of the cardinalate in modern times. After Vatican II some had argued that it was an anachronism: the cardinals were no longer genuinely the parish priests of Rome; they had no real function except to elect the Pope, and this could more suitably be done by the chairmen of the national episcopal conferences. Monsignor Lubowiecki disagreed, however: the cardinals had enormous influence and prestige, and were thought of by the faithful as representing the Church's interests in a quite special way.

We stayed at the Polish College, and met Karol at the station on the day after our arrival. He was relaxed and cheerful, looking forward to a stay in Rome during which, for once, he would have no special duties. He soon found, however, that he had a formidable program of visits to Vatican officials, especially the heads of congregations. Andrzej Deskur, who had lived in Rome for many years, was extremely helpful in arranging these.

On June 26 we went to the Vatican, where the consistory was being held. The Auditorio Pio XII was crowded with over three thousand people including diplomats, reporters, cardinals' relatives and delegations from all parts of the world. At ten o'clock Cardinal Cicognani, the Secretary of State, appeared on the platform where the new cardinals were assembled, read out their names and handed the *biglietto* to each; his speech of welcome was replied to by the oldest of the new cardinals, Archbishop Fasolino of Santa Fe in Argentina, after which the public crowded onto the dais to offer congratulations. A group of Poles appeared from nowhere, greeting Cardinal Wojtyla and offering him flowers.

The second part of the ceremony, the "semipublic" consistory, was held on June 28. At 6 P.M. Cardinal Wojtyla went to the Sala dei Paramenti to put on his robes and proceed to the Sistine Chapel, where we were waiting. Beside the altar, under Michelangelo's *Last Judgment*, the cardinals assembled on either side of the papal throne—the old ones on the right, the new ones on the left. Pope Paul VI placed a red biretta on the head of each, reminded them in the traditional formula that they must be ready to shed their blood for the Faith, and assigned to each a titular church in Rome. Karol's was San Cesareo in Palatino, a beautiful old church near the Polish College and next to the Baths of Caracalla at the beginning of the Via Appia.

Finally, on June 29—the feast of Saints Peter and Paul —the public consistory took place, out of doors for the first time in history, and over 100,000 people attended the Mass concelebrated by the Pope and the new cardinals. It was a blazing hot day. The Pope spoke in eight languages, including Polish, after which the new cardinals advanced to the papal throne to receive their rings.

On July 3 Cardinal Wojtyla had a private audience with Paul VI. It lasted about twenty minutes, after which some Polish priests, including myself, were presented to the Holy Father. He was perspiring and looked tired, but full of kindness and humility. Afterward the Pope received a group of two hundred Poles in the Sala Clementina.

Karol remained in Rome for a few days and then flew to Venice, whence he drove with us to Ossiach and Mariazell in Austria. In the car he asked me my impressions of the Church in Western Europe and North America, since at Münster I had been in contact with lay and clerical students from all countries and had also made trips to France and Britain. I replied that I was distressed by the number of clergy, both young and old, who were resigning their orders, in Europe and especially America. I did not think celibacy was the main cause of this, but that it was rather due to a general flight from Christian values and to the revolution caused by the Council. The Council itself was necessary—otherwise there would have been stagnation—but the Church was not ready for the upheaval it created. This was largely because of the new role played by the mass media, with their direct impact on people of all kinds and their tendency to look for sensations. Moreover, the invitation to rethink every aspect of the Church's activity had produced an avalanche of criticism, a chain reaction which the Council was not strong enough to control. As in all revolutions, the extremists gained the upper hand. One of the results was to downgrade the institutional aspect of the Church, secondary devotions and so on, and ultimately to call in question the whole ecclesiastical dimension and the need for sacraments. For instance, it was impressive that so many people received Communion in Western churches, but less so when you found that they did not trouble to go to confession first. On the other hand, the Polish episcopate had done an excellent job in making their flock aware of the Council, organizing special prayers and so forth, and the Polish people had responded to this on an impressive scale. I assured Karol—who, as he did with everyone, encouraged me to state my views at length—that I was not saying this merely to flatter him!

Mariazell is a place of solemn pilgrimage linked with the name of Louis the Great, king of Hungary and Poland and father of our Queen Jadwiga, who is said also to have come here. We drove thence to Kahlenberg on the outskirts of Vienna, where there is a church on the site of Jan Sobieski's victory in 1683; it was from here that the Polish hussars charged the troops of Kara Mustapha. We reflected how ironical it was that, a hundred years later, Poland was partitioned by Austria, Prussia and Russia, while the sultans of Turkey refused, then and later, to recognize this act of international piracy.

Karol said Mass in the little church, and we drove him to the station where he took the train for Cracow.

Karol's first important journey as cardinal was to Canada and the United States in August–September 1969. The Polish community in Canada was holding a congress to celebrate its twenty-fifth anniversary; the chairman, Z. Jarmicki, invited Cardinal Wyszynski to attend, but as he could not, Karol went in his stead. He was accompanied by Bishop Szczepan Wesoly and by the present archbishop of Cracow, Franciszek Macharski, whom I knew from our student days and who gave me an account of the trip.

"The main point which struck me," said Franciszek, "was that the cardinal remained himself the whole time. You know, when Europeans visit America they are very apt to imitate the local style—priests wearing ordinary clothes instead of a cassock, everybody being extroverted and hearty and so on. Well, the cardinal refused to change his style of dress or his usual, rather thoughtful manner, and at one of the banquets I heard someone say about him, 'This will never do.' Just then the Mayor of Toronto, to whom the cardinal was talking, mentioned that his son was on his honeymoon in Florida with a Polish-Canadian girl. Thereupon the cardinal asked to be put through to the young couple on the telephone and had a long, friendly conversation . . . the mayor, of course, was delighted.

"There were several other incidents like that. We had a great reception at Calgary from the local Poles and also some Croats. They were so hospitable that we arrived three hours late at Edmonton and the reception committee, headed by the archbishop, had all gone home. Dinner began rather stiffly after that, and the cardinal didn't apologize very profusely, but before long he had completely broken the ice. He must have been a bit of a trial to sticklers for order and punctuality, but everyone else was delighted with him. It was an exhausting trip on all sorts of levels—religious, official, social and cultural—but he never lost his inner poise. He kept a diary the whole time, and refused evening engagements.

"The main events were a reception at Toronto on September 13 and a Mass next day attended by eight thousand in the Coliseum, when he spoke of the Poles who had come to Canada to save their religion and culture from Prussian persecution before the first world war. In his last address to the Polish Canadians he told them that he had left part of his soul with them and would do all he could to bring them closer to the Church in Poland and vice versa."

"And how about the United States?"

"On the sixteenth we crossed to Buffalo, where there are three hundred thousand Poles. We visited all the principal sees—Detroit, Boston, Washington, Baltimore, St. Louis, Chicago, Philadelphia and New York—and also Hartford-New Britain, Cleveland, Pittsburgh, Orchard Park, Doylestown, Brooklyn and Lodi. We met six cardinals and several dozen bishops. Then we flew back to Rome for the second Synod of Bishops. (You remember that Cardinal Wojtyla refused to attend the first one because the Polish government wouldn't allow Cardinal Wyszynski to go.) The theme was collegiality in the Church; our cardinal spoke several times about the diversity of cultures, bearing in mind his experiences in North America, and he helped to draft the final declaration on the need for cooperation between the Pope and the bishops' conferences, and also among the latter.

"You also asked me to tell you about my consecration as archbishop by John Paul II. This was on January 6, 1979, the feast of the Epiphany. The year, as he pointed out in his sermon, is the nine-hundredth anniversary of the martyrdom of St. Stanislas. One of the most moving moments after the ceremony was when he took off his pectoral cross, which had once belonged to Prince Sapieha, and placed it on me. He tried to make a joke of it, saying he was giving it to me because it was a little worn. He also made a joke when he came into the Sala Clementina: we all applauded and he said, 'I see how pleased you are that we are going to part.' I replied at once that it was not a parting but a new way of being together."

In 1971, when I was staying in Germany, the priest of the local Polish parish invited me to join a group he was taking to Rome to witness the beatification of Fr. Maximilian Kolbe on October 17. I was at first reluctant to go —I had vivid memories of the Occupation and all its horrors, and one postwar visit to Auschwitz had been enough for me. Yet, somehow or other I found myself in the aircraft bound for Rome. . . . I found the Polish community cheerful, as though about to enjoy some kind of holiday—and indeed they were right, for the blessed martyr now had all his sufferings behind him.

The seventeenth was a cold, sunny day. About fifteen hundred of my countrymen had come from Poland on charter flights. I myself had come separately, so I did not have to act as a leader to the group from Germany. An hour before the ceremony St. Peter's was full of Polish groups singing hymns, and I also heard German pilgrims singing. It was an odd sensation: here were the Poles, of whom six million had been done to death by the Germans, and here were the representatives of the nation that had slaughtered them . . . I did my best to shake off the memories that beset me.

Mass began at 9:30; it was the first time in history that

a Mass of beatification was being celebrated by the Pope himself. Concelebrators were Cardinals Wyszynski and Wojtyla, Bishop Zaremba, Cardinal Krol from Philadelphia, Archbishop Shirayanagi of Tokyo, and Father Heisse, the General of the Franciscan Order to which Father Kolbe had belonged. The readings were in Polish and Italian, the Gospel in Latin. After the Creed, the Prayer of the Faithful was recited in six languages including Polish and German. From where I sat I could see Franciszek Gajowniczek, the man for whom Kolbe gave his life, taking part in the offertory. Candles were carried by two Franciscans from the monastery at Niepokalanow (built in 1927 by Father Kolbe and his fellow Franciscans) and two highlanders from Zakopane, while white and red flowers—the Polish colors—were presented by two girls, one in Cracow costume and the other a Japanese. This was in memory of the fact that Kolbe had also set up a monastery in Japan and printed his Marian newspaper there. . . . I imagined how Gajowniczek must be remembering the day when Father Kolbe, in the bunker at Auschwitz, stepped forward and said, "I wish to go instead of this man." Palitsch, the clerk, noted the change of name and, the regulation being thus satisfied, Kolbe went with nine others to the death cell while Gajowniczek was saved.

Three days before the ceremony, Cardinal Wojtyla gave a press conference in which he pointed out that Father Kolbe not only saved one man out of ten, but showed the other nine how to die. In an article in *Tygodnik Powszechny* he recalled that Kolbe's sacrifice was made on August 14, 1941, the vigil of the Assumption; he was put to death by a phenol injection and cremated in the oven on the following day. The article pointed out that Kolbe's act of heroism had made human life more human in a place of supreme inhumanity, and that it was highly relevant to the cause of justice and the role of the priesthood, both of which were principal themes of the synod then in session.

The beatification was followed by a triduum, with three days of special prayer by the Poles, Germans and other nationalities. On Monday the Poles attended Mass in the Vatican gardens and were received by the Pope in the Sala Nervi. On Tuesday Cardinal Döpfner of Berlin held a German service in the church of the Twelve Apostles; Bishop Majdanski concelebrated and spoke in German. Cardinal Döpfner in his sermon called Kolbe the "martyr of reconciliation." Cardinal Wojtyla celebrated Mass with several hundred priests living at the Domus Papis, and gave a reception at the Polish Institute for one hundred visitors from Cracow and other Poles from all over the world.

After the solemnities were over I asked my friends how the synod was going. They told me that it had begun on a pessimistic note: in the preceding seven years no fewer than 25,000 priests, or 7 percent of the total, had left the priesthood. Many bishops had painted the situation in gloomy colors, and had argued for a relaxation of the rule of celibacy. Cardinal Wojtyla, as always, had poured oil on troubled waters. He stressed the aspect of a personal vocation to the priesthood, and the value of celibacy as a visible sign of it. In his view the crisis was not an institutional but a human one. He refused to panic, and he warned against the temptation to laicize the priestly calling. As to the other main theme, that of justice, he emphasized that as well as combating poverty and underdevelopment there was a need to defend freedom of conscience and of religion.

The synod closed on November 6 after appointing a permanent secretariat of fifteen members, three nominated by the Pope and twelve chosen by the synod on the basis of three each for Europe, Asia, Africa and the Americas. The three Europeans were Cardinal Wojtyla, Cardinal Hoefner of Cologne and Cardinal Tarancón of Toledo.

I was excited and somewhat perturbed by the news that Pope John Paul II was to visit Mexico. The journey would of course be primarily of a religious nature, but he would certainly not confine himself to saying rosaries and reciting his litany. In his sermons, would he come down on the side of the military governments or the liberation movements, both of which had members of the clergy in their ranks? Mexico, moreover, was an anticlerical country which had no relations with the Vatican, and if the Church managed to function there at all it was only because the laws were not fully enforced. When John Paul II let it be known that he intended to visit Puebla, the Mexican Government had announced that they would not be in the capital to receive him. I felt full of misgiving, but could only offer up my prayers and those of my congregations.

The Pope's plane took off at 8 A.M. on Thursday January 25. It was divided into three compartments: one for the Pope himself, another for twenty-five members of his suite and another for about one hundred forty people, half of whom were reporters and cameramen. Shortly after takeoff the Pope gave the journalists an interview of an hour and twenty minutes. Asked if his conversation with Gromyko, the Soviet foreign minister, had been about peace, he replied, "Certainly—that is always the main subject when I talk to statesmen."

At 1:30 P.M. local time the plane touched down in the Dominican Republic. Alighting, the Pope knelt and kissed the ground. To the cheers of a huge crowd he proceeded in an open car to the cathedral, where the bishops of the Republic and neighboring countries were waiting, and concelebrated Mass in Independence Square before thirty thousand people. He declared that he had come to America as a "pilgrim of peace and hope." He stressed the need for political, economic and social justice, and said that the Gospel had the power to give men freedom because it was the manifestation of God's love for each and every man.

On Friday at 1 P.M. the Pope landed at Mexico City in a plane of the Mexican airline. It took forty minutes for him to get from the plane to the car that drove him to the cathedral, a journey of five miles which itself took an hour to accomplish. The streets were lined by over a million Mexicans from all parts of the country. Three hundred thousand were assembled on Constitution Square in front of the cathedral to take part in the pontifical Mass. In his homily the Pope urged them to make their lives conform to their allegiance to the Church, to become a spiritual leaven that would make the world more human and more brotherly.

After a visit to the Apostolic Delegation the Pope had a private interview of an hour and ten minutes with the Mexican President, which we prayed might help to normalize relations between the Church and the state. On Saturday he addressed the local Polish community, pointing out that recent events had emphasized Poland's place in the universal Church and that it was all the more incumbent on Poles to be loyal to it.

The Pope then went to the shrine of Our Lady of Guadalupe twenty miles outside Mexico City, the drive taking nearly two hours, and invoked a blessing on the Third Conference of Latin American bishops which was about to begin at Puebla. On Sunday he opened the conference, the theme of which was the evangelization of the continent today and tomorrow. The ninety-mile drive from Mexico City took nearly six hours. On the way he blessed crowds who had spent the night by the roadside in the open or under primitive tents. Altogether it is calculated that there were about ten million of them. The Pope stopped three times at villages where he talked to the Indian population. At Puebla he said Mass and preached to fifty thousand people, and in the afternoon he spoke for an hour at the conference, to which he was welcomed by Cardinal Baggio, chairman of the Committee of Latin-American Bishops.

The Pope began by saying that it was a mistake to equate political, economic or social liberation with the salvation brought by Christ. The first duty of pastors was to teach the truth—not human or rational truth, but the truth of God on which true human freedom was based.

At this point I feared, as did some of my congregation, that the Pope's words might be interpreted as reactionary. However, he went on to say, "In our time much attention is given to man, yet these are times of the greatest uncertainty for any man who reflects on his own personality and future. The Church, thanks to the Gospel, knows the truth about man and is constantly deepening that knowledge. It is the Church's right and duty to proclaim the truth, especially when different social systems see mankind only in an economic, biological or psychological light. . . . Man is not subordinate to economic or political processes, but they are subservient and subordinate to him." In conclusion he said, "Unity among bishops does not come from human calculations and machinations but from serving one Lord, from the inspiration of the Holy Spirit and the love of the one Church. . . . Unity among bishops builds up and strengthens unity with priests, religious and the whole People of God."

On January 29 the Pope visited a children's hospital in

Mexico City, after which he flew in the President's plane to Oaxaca, three hundred miles away, where about half a million Indians were waiting in rapturous excitement. The Indian population of Mexico is about ten million, most of whom are Catholics. Listening to the radio, for the first time in my life I heard Polish highland music played by Indians. In reply to a speech of greeting the Pope proclaimed his solidarity with the Indian cause and his desire to put an end to the era of exploitation and wrong. "The Pope speaks for those who cannot speak, and embraces their cause."

On Tuesday January 30 the Pope flew to Guadalajara airport and thence by helicopter to the slum district of Santa Cecilia. He expressed sympathy with the inhabitants and urged all who regarded themselves as Christians to share out their wealth in the interests of justice and human dignity, so that all might have food and clothing, a chance to work and a roof over their heads. At 1 P.M. he met the local workers, after which he went to the local prison; he greeted the twenty-four hundred inmates by loudspeaker and said the Hail Mary with them. Later he visited Our Lady's basilica at the neighboring town of Zapopan, where he was greeted with songs in Polish, Spanish and Italian.

In the grounds of the basilica of Our Lady of Guadalupe the Pope addressed some two hundred thousand students, urging them to work hard and cooperate with all who sought to bring about justice in the world. He was serenaded from five in the morning, or even earlier, by groups who assembled outside the house in which he was staying.

The industrial city of Monterrey was added to the Pope's itinerary at the last moment. About a million workers flocked there, and all the factories stopped work. Here the Pope said, "We cannot shut our eyes to the situation of millions of people who, in search of work, have left their native land and often their families, only to encounter new difficulties in what are not always pleasant conditions." He rebuked those who exploit immigrant workers, and urged governments and industrialists to safeguard the workers' right to a just wage, social security and the opportunity to improve their lot. "The Church has and will continue to have the courage to reprove those who exploit workers and despise human dignity."

On February 1 at 4:57 P.M. the Mexican plane carrying the Pope on his return journey touched down at Fiumicino airport. John Paul II had acquitted himself triumphantly in the most important trial of his pontificate up to this date.

I made an appointment with Jerzy Turowicz, the editor of *Tygodnik Powszechny*, to discuss the Pope's former contributions to his paper and also the Mexican journey. It was no good trying to talk at Jerzy's office, which has always been like a railway station with people dashing in and out on any excuse or none, and was naturally still more hectic at the present time. Even at his home in the evening it is hard to find Jerzy alone, without visitors, and he himself is constantly traveling all over Poland as well as to Western Europe and America. He lives on a third floor, in two rooms so crammed with books and papers that it looks as if the floor would collapse at any moment. His voluminous files are most methodically kept, and he works till late every evening. At last, toward midnight, we were able to have a quiet talk.

Karol's writings for *Tygodnik Powszechny* were of four main kinds. There were sequences of articles on doctrine and ethics, personal memoirs of people he had known and admired (such as Tyranowski, or Jerzy Ciesielski of whom more later), letters to the editor, with a distinctive style and purport of their own, and finally poems and articles about the drama. These were written under a pseudonym: Andrzej Jawien, or sometimes Piotr Jasien. (Some poems about the Vatican Council [1962–5] also appeared in *Znak* under the pseudonym Stanislaw Andrzej Gruda.) In addition there were special articles about the Vatican Council, the millenary celebration in 1965 of Poland's conversion to Christianity, and so on. All these articles were written before their author became archbishop, after which he confined himself to letters. These sometimes struck a critical note, but bore witness to the importance he attached to the paper.

Jerzy said that Italian critics to whom he had spoken agreed that the Pope's poems were of high literary quality, and that a semidramatic work entitled *The Jeweler's Window* was exciting much attention in Italy. Karol's prose writings in *Tygodnik Powszechny* went back to at least 1948, when he wrote an article on his return from abroad entitled "Mission France." Other subjects were "Elements of Ethics" and "Thoughts on the Laity." The style, Jerzy told me, was at first rather abstruse but got simpler as time went on. Apart from *Tygodnik* and *Znak*, Karol also wrote in specialized journals. He had shown his interest in the Catholic press by setting up a special commission on which the Cracow clergy and the two journals were represented and which met regularly to discuss their affairs. I myself was the secretary of this commission, and occasionally, at my suggestion, Karol attended its meetings, which were both friendly and animated: at an early stage the Curia was somewhat perturbed by *Tygodnik*'s hospitality to new trends of a Western European type, liturgical and theological.

As to the Pope's visit to Mexico, Jerzy remarked that the church in that country was split between a conservative and a revolutionary wing and the Pope was concerned to restore unity. "A point which some people miss is that he not only talks about collegiality but he practices it. The bishops are on the spot, and he does not want to take their decisions for them. The Puebla speech was taken out of its context as a one-sided plea for conservatism. In other addresses, especially to the press, the Pope emphasized human rights, and what he said must be taken as a whole. Some of the radical theologians out there took a more favorable view of his remarks than the European press did. Some who were apparently left-wingers were not admitted to the Puebla conference, but the bishops drew up a document condemning the military regimes and exploitation by international concerns; the regimes used this as a stick to beat the Church with, but in any case it shows that the bishops understood what was in the Pope's mind.

In April 1972 a letter from the archbishop was read in all churches of the diocese recalling that Stanislas of Szczepanow became Bishop of Cracow in 1072 and was martyred by King Boleslaw the Bold in 1079; canonized in 1253, he became the chief patron of the Polish Church. Poland was originally evangelized by St. Wojciech (Adalbert) of Prague; our archbishop compared his role and that of St. Stanislas to the sacraments of baptism and confirmation respectively. At the same time it was announced that a synod of the archdiocese would be held to ensure that the lessons of Vatican II were duly transmitted and assimilated by clergy and laity. The cardinal also published *Foundations of Renewal*, which bore the subtitle *Studies concerning the Realization of Vatican II*; it was basically an arrangement of Council texts for pastoral purposes, with extensive comments in his still rather difficult style. Study groups sprang up all over the diocese to discuss the message of Vatican II, and *Foundations* was a valuable aid to their work.

The cardinal took as much part as he could in the daily life of the diocese but was obliged to travel more and more, both to Rome and to remoter destinations. One of these was Australia, where he attended the Eucharistic Congress in February 1973, accompanied by his chaplain, S. Dziwisz, and by Bishop Szczepan Wesoly. With the latter's help I refreshed my memory by consulting the cardinal's diary of the Australian journey, comprising thirty-seven closely typed pages. The first stopover was at Manila in the Philippines, where the cardinal was deeply impressed by the devotion of many of the faithful who advanced up the nave of the Redemptorist church on their knees. The party visited New Guinea where many of the Divine Word missionaries are Poles. The Mass at a mission station was in Latin and a local language, into which the cardinal's Polish homily was translated, and the native choir gave a fine performance. Schools and farm buildings completed the picture of missionary activity; there were also Polish nuns from the congregation of Handmaids of the Holy Spirit.

At Brisbane a reception was given by the flourishing Polish Club, and besides songs and speeches the children gave spirited performances of Polish dancing—the polka, polonaise and *krakowiak*. The cardinal noted that Polish spirit in these and other communities abroad is kept alive by "Saturday schools," youth organizations, scout troops, and so on.

From Brisbane the cardinal flew via Sydney to Wellington, New Zealand, where he spoke at the Polish Club and visited World War II veterans in the hospital. Returning to Sydney on February 14, he was welcomed by Archbishop Freeman, shortly to be made a cardinal, and visited Polish centers in the suburbs of Cabramatta,

Bankstown and Ashfield. Two days later he flew to Canberra, and on the next afternoon to Melbourne, where the Congress opened on Sunday February 18. Next day he visited the Polish community in Hobart, Tasmania, and on the evening of the 20th concelebrated Mass with the cardinal legate on the Melbourne cricket ground, where there was a vast crowd of immigrants and others from all over the world: the languages of the Mass were Italian, Polish, Dutch, French, Croatian and Maltese, while the Prayer of the Faithful was heard in Chinese, German, Syriac, Arabic, Lithuanian, Latvian, Czech, Russian, Slovak, Slovene, Ukrainian, Hungarian, Irish, Spanish and Portuguese.

Ceremonies continued through the week, and on the Saturday the cardinal consecrated a shrine of Our Lady, Queen of Poland at Essendon, Melbourne. On the following Tuesday and Wednesday he visited Adelaide and Perth, where there are also flourishing Polish communities, and then flew back to Rome via Singapore, Kuala Lumpur and Bahrain.

The cardinal's notes were mainly factual, but I got an idea of the atmosphere of the visit from Bishop Wesoly, who described the terrific heat and humidity, occasionally broken by heavy showers, and the need to remain cheerful and alert at every moment of the day. It was the first time a Polish cardinal had been to Australia, and thousands wanted to shake him by the hand and exchange a precious word or two, in addition to innumerable public ceremonies and official contacts that filled every day of the Congress.

The fourth Synod of Bishops in Rome, which opened in September 1974, was devoted to the theme of "Evangelization in the Modern World." The Polish representatives were Cardinal Wyszynski and Wojtyla and

Bishop Ablewicz, together with the Pope's nominee Bishop Andrzej Deskur, chairman of the Papal Commission on the Mass Media. The secretary-general of the synod was Polish, Bishop Rubin. Cardinal Wojtyla was entrusted by the Pope with the task of reporting on the theological problems of evangelization. He emphasized that faith was a matter of orthodoxy and orthopraxis, of true belief and right action; in proclaiming the Gospel the Church was proclaiming itself as well, though it was an instrument of evangelization and not its final purpose. Evangelization meant preparing human beings not only for eternal life but for life in this world, and that involved their economic and social liberation. The Church must defend justice and peace by recognizing the true liberty and dignity of the human person. The Gospel must be preached differently to different people: in the old Christian lands, in mission territories, to the separated brethren, to non-Christians and to unbelievers.

Karol's paper was commented on in debate by seventy-six bishops, while thirty-three more gave their views in writing. This was perhaps the first synod at which the Third World bishops, especially those of Asia and Africa, spoke out frankly and freely. Summing up the discussion, Cardinal Wojtyla said that Latin America had brought to the fore the problem of human liberation, Africa that of the indigenization of the Church, Asia that of relations with the great non-Christian religions, while Europe and North America bore witness to the role of Christianity in a world that was becoming more and more secular. The declaration in its final form was drafted by a commission under Cardinal Wojtyla's chairmanship. The synod then elected twelve members of the Permanent Council of the Secretariat, the Europeans being Cardinal Wojtyla, Cardinal Döpfner and the Archbishop of Marseilles, Monsignor Etchegaray.

I visited Stanislaw and his wife Danuta, who had been students in the days when Father Wojtyla first started to take young people on country excursions. "One day in April 1952," Danuta said, "when we had known him for about a year, someone happened to say that the crocuses were in bloom at Zakopane. It turned out that a lot of us had never seen crocuses, and Father Wojtyla hadn't either, so we agreed to make a party and go and look at them. Five of us girls turned up at the station on Saturday night—some boys were to have come too, but they were prevented by exams. Father Wojtyla agreed to take us just the same, though at that time it was almost unheard-of for a priest in lay clothes (he always wore knickerbockers on those occasions) to be taking a party of girls on an overnight excursion. However, off we went. It was on that trip that we decided, with his permission, to call him 'Uncle' in public, as it would have caused a sensation if we had addressed him as a priest. Anyway, we saw the crocuses, and here's a photograph of our group. The sun was shining, but there was still snow on the ground.

"After that we went on day trips to all sorts of other places round about. Once I got everyone to come to Bielsko, where my parents lived. The boys spent the night at Kozy, where the parish priest was Franciszek Macharski, the present Archbishop of Cracow, and the girls stayed at our home in Bielsko. We all met for Mass at six in the morning and then set out to climb Mount Magurka. Here on this photograph you can see 'Uncle' in a typical attitude, standing apart from us and gazing into the distance as he did from time to time, while we chatted about our affairs—was he thinking or praying? I don't know.

"One day in 1952 we came to see you, Father Malinski, at Rabka—do you remember? We used to call you

'Uncle Ha-ha,' because of the way you laughed—just as you're doing now. Here's a picture of our group in front of the convent of the Sisters of Nazareth, where we girls slept on that occasion." I remembered, but very dimly—it all seemed so long ago, and as if I had been a different person then.

"Then in April 1953 the first of our people got married —Jadzia and Stach—and we all went to Starachowice for the wedding and then to Czestochowa. We went there again every year—Uncle cycled with us on two occasions, though it's a good 150 miles. What's more, we were planning to go there with him last September, when he came back from Rome after the election of John Paul I, but he never managed it on account of the second conclave.

"Do you remember Jurek Ciesielski, who came with us for the first time in July 1953? It was he who kept persuading us to go on canoe trips."

"Of course I do—I used to call him 'the bodyguard.' " I looked at photographs of a tall, strong young man with close-cropped black hair.

"And here's a picture of yourself—do you remember it?"

I remembered the sensation of hiking in the mountains—the hot sun, the heavy knapsack, the taste of water in a mess tin, the welcome rest and the laughter of my companions—but I could not recall any particular time or place. I had even forgotten that anyone took pictures of me.

"That's strange," said Danuta. "We thought it must have been you who gave some pictures of the group to *Newsweek*."

"No, I didn't even know they had published any."

"Then, also in 1953, we went for a fortnight to the Bieszczady Mountains. One night we were caught in a downpour and had to ask the border guards for shelter.

They put up in a kind of attic and we slept with all the girls on one side and the boys on the other. It rained solidly for two days and we never left the place. We even had Mass said up there—the soldiers of course didn't know, or pretended not to.

"The packs we carried on those tours were quite heavy —the girls' weighing about thirty pounds, the boys' more, of course. But often there was no chance to buy anything, so we had to take all our provisions with us.

"Our canoeing trips started in 1954—we were on the Brda River in the Bydgoszcz area in September of that year, and in 1955 on the Czarna Hancza near Augustow [northeast Poland]. Generally we went for a fortnight and covered about two hundred miles. Uncle was particularly fond of the lakes in the Koszalin province [inland from Pomerania]."

"What was the daily program?"

"Uncle would have an early swim while we were still asleep, and went canoeing by himself at about six o'clock. He said Mass every morning at an altar consisting of two boats turned upside down, with two paddles lashed together to form a cross. Then we had breakfast and spent the rest of the day afloat, with a short break for lunch and a main meal in the evening."

"Did Uncle have any special privileges?"

"He had a canoe to himself, at least after he became a bishop, and slept in his own tent—that was all. In the evening we sat round a campfire and sang—he was fond of singing, and sometimes made up words for us. Then there would be prayers and hymns to finish off with.

"At first we had no inflatable mattresses or sleeping bags—we used to blow up bicycle tubes, put them in sacks and sleep on those. Uncle insisted on our sleeping for nine hours—he didn't himself, of course."

"How were the groups organized? I believe there were 'captains' and 'crews'?"

"Yes, the 'captain' of a boat would be the more experienced one and would sit astern and steer, while the 'crew,' usually a girl, would sit in the bow, paddling."

"How many were there of you?"

"Groups of about ten at first; afterward they got bigger. From about 1970 families with children would also come and make excursions from a central point.

"Our last trip with Uncle was in September 1978, and here's the last picture of him canoeing. He was still wonderfully fit—the lake you see there is nearly nine hundred yards across, but he could swim to the other side and back without stopping.

"Back in Cracow, after each of our trips he used to give a tea party at which we discussed the next one. The last party was set for January 1979, and he didn't forget it—he wrote from Rome saying how sorry he was not to be there.

"Here's a page in the album about Jerzy (Jurek) Ciesielski. You remember, he went for two years to Khartoum in the Sudan as a visiting professor of engineering, and he and his two young children were drowned in an accident on the Nile in December 1970. He was buried in Cracow, and there's a memorial tablet in St. Anne's church. Here's the article that Uncle wrote about him in *Tygodnik Powszechny*."

I opened the paper and read the article half to myself. It spoke of Jurek's piety and love of nature (he had taught Karol skiing and canoeing) and of conversations on the theme of marriage which, Karol had said, had helped to inspire *Love and Responsibility* and his contribution to the Roman synod on the theme of "the Church in the modern world." Remembering Karol's other young companions, I thought to myself that his description

might very well fit all of them—thanks to his example
and precept, they all had the same devotion to the sacraments and liturgy and the same resolve to express it in
their daily lives.

Marek Skwarnicki, who went to Mexico with the
Pope as correspondent for *Tygodnik Powszechny*, gave
me some more sidelights on the journey.

"You know, what surprised everybody was that the
Pope neither praised nor condemned anyone. After the
Puebla speech the press got the idea that he was against
any kind of political commitment by the Church, but
then at Oaxaca, addressing the Indians, he spoke sharply
about the exploitation of the poor by the big landowners,
and he talked on similar lines to the workers at Guadalajara. By that time people began to realize that each of the
Pope's speeches in Mexico was supplementary to the one
before, and that they must be taken as a single whole.
Wherever he went you saw him, bronzed by the sun,
blessing the crowds who were sitting or standing on
roofs, balconies and trees, on the tops of cars and buses
and anything else they could find to stand on; he blessed
the Indians who stood by the roadside, took their grimy
children into his arms and embraced them. When he got
into the plane on the homeward journey I saw the Mexicans of the police bodyguard kissing his hands. There
were banners in Polish all over the place, made by Mexicans as well as Poles. One of them showed Our Lady of
Guadalupe welcoming Our Lady of Czestochowa. There
were bands, choirs, flags with the Papal, Polish and Mexican colors, balloons, confetti—old people and children,
Indians and half-breeds, rich and poor, all equally excited, moved to tears and deliriously happy. An American journalist told me he had never seen such crowds except in Argentina for the World Cup, and the difference
was that there it was soccer but here it was human

beings. Some people said that the crowds turned out on such a scale because they don't think much of their own clergy or find them spiritual enough; if so, it would seem to show that the People of God have a better idea than they of what the Church should be like.

After some hesitation, I decided to attend the Eucharistic Congress at Philadelphia in August 1976. For years past, ex-students of mine who had emigrated to the United States had been inviting me to go and see them. I did not approve of their emigrating—it was a drain on Poland's natural resources, and I believe people should live and die in their homeland—but I did not want to lose touch with my young friends. I had been in the U.S. during my doctoral studies, and on a holiday from Rome at the invitation of Cardinal Krol, whose acquaintance I made during the Council; besides staying with him at Philadelphia I worked for three months at a Polish parish church in Brooklyn, as a replacement for priests on vacation. But my friends kept urging me to go back and see them, and so I asked Cardinal Krol, with Karol's agreement, if he could arrange for me to attend the Congress, which he very kindly did.

A large delegation of eighteen Polish bishops, headed by Cardinal Wojtyla, attended the Congress, after which they were to visit Polish centers throughout the United States. I spent the first two days after our arrival visiting my young friends Lucy and Andrew, who lived in a suburb of New York and felt thoroughly at home in the new country. In Philadelphia I stayed at the Seminary of St. Charles Borromeo together with Jerzy Turowicz, who was representing his newspaper. I saw Karol almost at once, and we often ate at the same table in the cafeteria.

The Congress consisted of religious ceremonies, more or less popular lectures and conferences, and artistic performances, including a performance of *Godspell* and songs by Ella Fitzgerald. Most of the functions took place at the Civic Center and Convention Hall; the three main stadia held respectively twenty thousand, sixty thousand and one hundred thousand people. The proceedings were organized with an eye to the spectacular and with many "stars" such as Mother Teresa of Calcutta and Dom Helder Camara of Brazil. I was deeply impressed by the latter's eloquence. A short, slim figure with a charming smile, a brown complexion and a face wrinkled like an old slipper, he ended his speech— devoted to the problem of famine and economic inequality—with a Brazilian proverb: "One man's dream is only a dream, but if many dream it may become a reality."

The famous Mother Teresa, of Yugoslav origin—a slight figure in a white sari and veil edged with three violet bands—spoke in a quite different style: quietly, almost in a whisper. She told a story of a mother with several children, one of whom was deformed. "I offered to relieve her burden by taking it, but she replied, 'That is the one I love most.'" Another story was of a child who brought her a lump of sugar to give to those who never had any. When she had finished, Dom Helder Camara took the floor a second time to open the discussion, but first he went up to Mother Teresa, placed his cheek against hers and kissed her hand. She nestled up against him, to the delight and applause of the audience.

At one point in the session somebody came up to me with a large piece of bread and asked with a smile if I would share it with him. I did so, and saw that all around the room complete strangers were doing the same. After some hesitation I myself took a piece of bread, about half a loaf, from a table outside the hall, and went round offering it likewise. The atmosphere was friendly and natural, and in a short time the whole building was full of the smell of fresh bread.

The theme of the Congress, chosen by Paul VI, was hunger of all kinds, both physical and spiritual. Karol spoke in English at the Veterans' Stadium on "The Eucharist and hunger for freedom and justice," mentioning especially religious freedom. Next day the West German TV correspondents asked for an interview and wanted to know why he had chosen that particular subject. Karol had prepared a reply beforehand which he asked me to translate into German and which he read out to them. In it he said that the experiences of the Polish nation had given it a keen sense of freedom and justice, which it had shown for instance in its resistance to the Teutonic Knights and in Pawel Wlodkowic's plea to the Council of Constance against the principle of forced conversion. "Today," the Cardinal added, "we may broaden the argument and say that no one should be compelled to embrace either Christianity or atheism, or compelled in any other way."

Along with forty thousand others I attended a "charismatic" Mass in the Veterans' Stadium, conducted by Cardinal Suenens. No doubt many, like me, were present simply from curiosity. But there was nothing very unusual except applause, hands raised aloft from time to time, and a swaying of the body to the rhythm of songs with catching tunes and simple words like "Christ is Lord, Christ is Lord, Christ is Lord." These were sung alternately by a choir of several hundred and by the whole congregation. Jerzy also attended a "Black Community Mass" at the Spectrum Stadium, which he described to me. "The music was splendid. There were about fifteen thousand present, whites and blacks, a choir of five hundred and a band with African drums. Cardinal Otunga, the archbishop of Nairobi, presided in a red, yellow and black robe symbolizing blood, the soil and the Negroes. The opening song was from a little hunched-up Negro with a tremendous voice. The tom-toms never stopped beating. The lesson—it was more like an incantation—was read beautifully by a tough-looking old Negress. Everything was done to the rhythm of drums and Negro melodies, with everyone swaying rhythmically the whole time, and the whole thing completely authentic and genuine, all absolutely *theirs*."

Later, Jerzy and I discussed our impressions with Cardinal Wojtyla over a meal at the seminary. European Christianity, we felt, had become overintellectualized and regimented, paying too much attention to the mind and not enough to feelings. We should learn from the Negroes and charismatics, not of course imitating them directly or abandoning our own values, but becoming more natural and simple in our own fashion.

One day of the Congress was devoted to an ecumenical discussion attended by Anglican, Lutheran and other dignitaries, with Archbishop Sheen representing the Catholic clergy. It was not a theological discussion, rather an exchange of cordialities in American style. One speaker gave an example of a "Polish joke": the union of all Christians, it was usually said, would not come about till the end of the world, but the Poles maintained it would be a few days later.

At an ecumenical service held that evening under the presidency of Cardinal Knox, the papal legate and twelve cardinals including our own Wojtyla washed the feet of twelve representatives of non-Catholic churches, a ceremony which I found extremely moving.

On the last day but one of the Congress twenty-six Masses were celebrated at different centers for various U.S. ethnic groups including the Poles: fifteen thousand Polish-Americans attended Mass at the Veterans' Stadium, concelebrated by Cardinal Wojtyla and Cardinal Krol with a sermon by Bishop Ablewicz. Afterward Cardinal Wojtyla presented to Cardinal Krol an urn containing Polish soil from Warka near Warsaw, birthplace of Casimir Pulaski, the Polish nobleman and American national hero who fought and died in Washington's army.

The final Mass of the Congress, known traditionally as *statio orbis,* was held on Sunday August 8 at the Kennedy Stadium, with a congregation of over 100,000; it was preceded by a parade and an address was given by President Ford. A message from Paul VI to the assembled faithful was transmitted by satellite from Bolsena, not far from Rome.

It would be wrong if my account of the Congress gave the impression that it was a mere spectacle. Certainly it was American in style, but it served serious purposes as well. For instance, during the preparatory period an operation known as "Rice Bowl" collected five million dollars, with which a cargo of two thousand tons of rice was sent to relieve famine in Bangladesh. Also in connection with the Congress, young American Catholics gave twenty million hours of work for the benefit of old people, children and invalids.

After the Congress, Cardinal Wojtyla and the other Polish bishops spent a month visiting Polish communities in the United States and also the American clergy. The country's population of 220 million comprises over 50 million Catholics, and there are probably about 9 million Americans of Polish origin. From Philadelphia we went to Washington to visit Archbishop Bernardin, chairman of the Congregation of the American Episcopate, and then flew to Orchard Lake near Detroit—a beautiful spot on a lake, comprising a Polish-American seminary, high school and college—where there was a three-day conference on Polish-American problems. I then visited friends in Chicago while Karol went to, among other places, Stevens Point in Wisconsin, San Francisco, Los Angeles and Cincinnati. There followed a few days' relaxation back at Orchard Lake, where we also talked about a lecture Karol had given at Harvard on July 27 entitled "Alienation or Participation?"; Stanislaw Dziwisz showed me a photograph from the front page of the university magazine with a caption ending with the words: "A probable successor to Paul VI." Karol also lectured to the Catholic University of America at Washington on July 29 on "Problems of the Autoteleology of Man."

At Orchard Lake, Karol received a telephone call proposing an audience with President Ford. He declined, however, on the ground that the visit might be given a political interpretation, especially after the Polish bishops had been traveling all over the United States.

We flew from Orchard Lake to New York, whence Karol returned to Rome and I to Poland.

Cardinal Wojtyla's two chief assistants in running the diocese were his chancellors, Mgr. Mikolaj Kuczkowski and Mgr. Stefan Marszowski.

I talked first to Stefan Marszowski, who described how he used to report to the cardinal every afternoon on the events of the previous day. He emphasized the cardinal's calm and self-command and said that in a dozen years or so he had only once heard him express impatience: this was when a priest at a meeting said he had to leave early because he had work to do, and the cardinal replied, "We are working too, you know." He would listen to reports attentively and, in case of need, take time to reflect on his decision—he was not one of those who pretend to have an instant answer to everything. He showed great trust in people, and when they proved to be deceitful or hostile would say, "Never mind, perhaps God will bring it to some good."

I found Mgr. Kuczkowski in his office in front of a model of the church being built at Nowa Huta—Mistrzejowice, to which he had been appointed parish priest. I reminded him that when we were both students he had complained that he had not become a priest in order to do office work. He laughed and agreed; he had in fact been employed at the Curia since 1948, becoming chancellor to Archbishop Baziak in 1952. He would not say much about the cardinal's methods of work, but spoke mostly of the remoter past. *A propos* of the Pope's first encyclical, he remarked that its author had always had the gift of being able to say the same thing in either simple or complicated language.

Mgr. Kuczkowski recalled that when Karol was at St. Florian's there was a priest in Cracow who organized lectures on various scientific subjects for the benefit of young priests who wanted to improve their knowledge. Karol later took over this activity, but gave it a more literary slant. "Once," Mgr. Kuczkowski recalled, "he organized a 'dialogue' at St. Florian's between himself and a Benedictine on the subject of pastoral work." After he had said his say the discussion fell flat, and I said to him, "Listen, Karol, you have been talking with the tongue of an angel; now say it again in human speech so that we can understand you." He did, and there was a lively discussion. It's the same thing nowadays: when he concentrates on a problem he writes in difficult language, for instance in *The Acting Person,* but he can also make things intelligible to children if he puts his mind to it. He never minds being teased or criticized, for instance when friends who knew about his poetry writing complained that the poems were obscure.

"I remember being taken to meet him at Tyniecka

Street during the Occupation—it must have been in 1942. Somebody had said, 'There's an interesting young man from Wadowice, you ought to meet him.' I went there a few times, and a relative of his who didn't approve of his underground theater activities said, 'I'll eat my hat if he ever becomes a priest—he's far too keen on the theater: he's not a priest, he's an artist.'

"Actually we must have met in Wadowice, though there were a good many years between us. Wadowice was a small place, but it was quite active before the war —an infantry regiment was stationed there, it had a district court, a state school and a teachers' college. What is more, it had two theaters, at one of which Mieczyslaw Kotlarczyk's father used to produce plays, and at the end of the thirties they built a Catholic center which also put on performances: so the cardinal's interest really dated from then."

I went back once more to Sister Jadwiga, this time to borrow an album presented to the cardinal in 1966—on the occasion of the millenary celebrations—by his former workmates at the Solvay factory, with photographs and reminiscences. Here are some of them:

Franciszek Labus, shot-firer: "When he first came he was so young I didn't think he'd be any use, but he was—he used to help with stringing up fuses and carrying explosives."

Jan Zyla: "When the students were assigned to work for us Krauze, the foreman, said we should go easy and not give them too much work at first. Karol Wojtyla did his job well, but whenever he had any free time in the afternoon he would stick his nose in a book. He always carried books around. I once said to

Krauze, 'I wonder what it's all for,' but Krauze said, 'Well, let him go on studying, if he's got time.'"

Leon Hojda, stoker: "At the beginning of the shift it was Wojtyla's job to carry four buckets of lime that was used to purify boiler water, and after that two buckets of reagent. On the night shift or in the afternoons he used to talk a lot to Pokuta, who was interested in scripture."

Franciszek Pokuta, electrician: "I once asked him what a student like him was doing at Solvay. He said his college had been closed down and he had to take a job or else be deported to Germany. He was a wonderful chap, full of spirituality and sympathy for others."

Wladyslaw Cieluch: "On the night shift, at about twelve o'clock he would kneel on the factory floor and say his prayers. Not all the other workers took kindly to this—some of them used to tease him by throwing things, bits of tow and so on."

Jan Wilk, stoker: "He wore coarse, shabby clothes and wooden clogs. I used to see him kneeling and praying by himself during the night shift. He once asked me for permission to go to a church service during the day, and I agreed to finish off his work for him."

Jozef Pchacz, assistant machinist: "Once at noon, an angelus bell rang, and he at once put down the buckets he was carrying, crossed himself and prayed; then he went on with his work, not embarrassed in the least."

Jozef Krasuski: "We didn't know in those days that he was going to be a priest, and we once tried to introduce him to a girl, but he wasn't having any. He didn't make a fuss, just ignored the subject. I guessed after a bit and asked him if he did mean to be a priest, but he wouldn't admit to that either."

Jozef Trela, loader: "He wore a waterproof jacket, short drill trousers and clogs over his bare feet. I often used to walk back to town with him after work, but he never talked much. He sometimes used to read at a desk, kneeling."

Finally the album contained a note signed by the cardinal himself: "I began work at the Zakrzowek quarry in September 1940. In summer 1941 I was transferred to the boiler room in the water purification department, and in spring 1944, after my accident, I was transferred again. I left the factory at the beginning of August 1944 and entered the metropolitan seminary, starting the course at the third year. As regards my priestly vocation I owe a great deal to Jan Tyranowski, R.I.P., of whom I have written in *Tygodnik Powszechny.*"

I closed the album full of photographs of simple workers, many of them taken at the factory, and remembered Karol as he had been in the days of the Occupation. Calling to mind what he had said to the Mexican workers and peasants, I said to myself that there would not have been a Pope John Paul II if he had not had the experiences he had. He knew what human dignity was, he knew fascism at first hand, he had seen the exploitation of man by man and by the state. He knew all these things, not from books but from his own life.

I took up the encyclical *Redemptor Hominis.* After all the Pope had done and said in Mexico, no one would be surprised by its text: it said the same things and even said them in the same language, though more systematically. Even the title was significant: not "the Savior of the world" or "of men," but "of man." It was typical of Karol that the encyclical used the pronoun "I" instead of "we," and that it was addressed to "all men of good will."

Typical, above all, was what it said about the human person—to quote only a short extract:

"Man in the full truth of his existence, of his personal being and also of his community and social being—in the sphere of his own family, in the sphere of society and very diverse contexts, in the sphere of his own nation or people (perhaps still only that of his own clan or tribe), and in the sphere of the whole of mankind, this man is the primary route along which the Church must travel in order to fulfill her mission: he is the primary and fundamental way for the Church, the way traced out by Christ himself, the way that leads invariably through the mystery of the Incarnation and the Redemption."

When Paul VI died in August 1978, none of the editors of *Tygodnik Powszechny* was able to go to Rome for the ensuing conclave, and I therefore offered to act as the paper's correspondent. Arriving on the eighteenth, I found the City parched and deserted on account of the mid-August holiday. I stayed at the Polish College and went next day with Karol to the Vatican, where the cardinals were holding discussions about the conclave and church affairs in their respective countries. The Swiss guards were in mourning, with dark blue uniforms and berets. I joined the crowd in St. Peter's filing past the tombs of John XXIII and Paul VI, and visited the photographic archives of the *Osservatore Romano*.

On Sunday the twentieth I went to the seaside with Bishop Andrzej Deskur, who had served Paul IV for twenty-seven years. He talked to me of the late Pope's interest in cultural affairs and his recent reorganization of the gallery of modern art in the Vatican.

Next day, on St. Peter's Square, I ran into Fr. Edward Nowak, who showed me his office in the Congregation dealing with Catholic universities and theological faculties throughout the world. He emphasized how Paul VI had internationalized the Vatican bureaucracy by placing non-Italians in key posts, which greatly improved efficiency and enabled prelates from foreign countries to get their bearings and feel at home during their visits to the city.

During the next few days I was in constant touch with Karol and naturally discussed the forthcoming election with him—sometimes seriously, at other times in a more bantering mood. I argued that the new Pope should be a man of the center or right of center, with pastoral experience; he need not be an Italian, but must be strong enough to consolidate the Church after the upheaval caused by the Council and its aftermath. One evening at supper, when Karol and two or three others were present, I voiced a prediction that if the Italian cardinals were at all divided in their choice, the election might well fall on Karol himself. Karol laughingly told me not to be foolish, but I stuck to my guns. I pointed out that, apart from meeting the above criteria, he had been repeatedly chosen as one of the three European members of the secretariat of the Synod of Bishops. Poland, not being a great power, would be acceptable as the country of origin of the new Pope, and it would be especially suitable as the Polish episcopate had done so much to make Vatican II an occasion of renewal instead of disintegration, as well as battling for religious education in spite of material and political difficulties.

On Thursday the twenty-fourth, the day before the conclave, Karol said early Mass at the college and I was one of the concelebrants. The Prayers of the Faithful were recited by one of the nuns, and when she had finished I put in my own petition: "We beseech thee, O Lord, by the intercession of St. Bartholomew, whose feast

we are celebrating, to bring it about that Cardinal Wojtyla is elected Pope." After a moment's pause the response duly came: "Lord, graciously hear us." I was
standing close beside Karol, and looked at him out of the
corner of my eye. He stood silent, his clasped hands
pressed to his lips. There was a further pause; the Offertory should have begun, but Karol made no move toward
the altar. To ease the situation the rector put in a further
petition—for the sick, or for holiday makers; this was responded to, and still Karol made no move. Suddenly he
lowered his hands and prayed aloud: "We beseech thee,
almighty God, that if a man is chosen as Pope who does
not believe himself capable of bearing the heavy responsibility of being the vicar of thy Son, thou wilt give him
the courage to say as St. Peter did: 'Depart from me, for
I am a sinful man, O Lord.' But if he should accept the
burden, we beg thee to grant him enough faith, hope
and love to bear the cross thou layest upon him." We
replied with one voice: "Lord, graciously hear us." The
Mass continued, and I thought to myself that for the first
time Karol had taken seriously the idea that he might be
elected Pope.

At breakfast I said jokingly, "You were very careful to
explain to God how my petition ought to be interpreted."
Later, when the subject was discussed again, Karol said
the main requirement was to choose a deeply religious
man; he also thought that the Bishop of Rome should be
an Italian. He expected the conclave to take about a
week; I was glad at this, as it fitted in with my hope that
the Italian vote would be split and that Karol would be
elected. He himself fended off my predictions and arguments, as he had done the other evening, with a half-in-
dulgent, half-mocking smile.

Next day, after driving with Karol to the Vatican, I attended the cardinals' Mass at St. Peter's and returned

alone to the college. On Saturday afternoon, unable to bear the suspense, I made my way to the Piazza di San Pietro and joined the crowd which, an hour or two later, heard Cardinal Felici's announcement: "*Annuntio vobis gaudium magnum: habemus papam, Eminentissimum ac Reverendissimum Dominum, Dominum Albinum.*" So it was not Karol after all! I waited for the new Pope to appear on the balcony ("He seems a nice fellow," I thought, "perhaps even very nice") and went home to the college, where my friends laughed at me for backing the wrong horse, as they put it.

Next morning John Paul I said Mass for the cardinals and delivered his first message to them. Karol emerged some time after eleven, and we waited in the piazza until twelve for the angelus and the Pope's first address to the people, in which he rapidly gained their hearts. Karol remarked that the conclave had lasted barely eight hours. Albino Luciani had scarcely been named in the various speculations beforehand; our Lord, said Karol, had mercifully sheltered him from all the fuss and electioneering. But he thought the new Pope an ideal choice on account of his humility and piety, and was evidently much relieved that he himself had not been elected.

23

Mrs. Kotlarczyk Remembers

Early in 1979 I visited Mrs. Kotlarczyk, widow of the director of the wartime "rhapsodic theater" in which Karol had worked as a young man. Her husband Mieczyslaw had died in the previous spring, and Karol had preached at the funeral. The theater had closed in 1952, the year before Stalin's death, and reopened in 1957, during the "thaw" after Gomulka came to power in Poland. Karol, under the pseudonym Andrzej Jawien, had published articles in *Tygodnik Powszechny* paying tribute to Kotlarczyk's organizing talent and his power to discern the dramatic potential of great novels, poems etc. During the German occupation, from 1941 to 1945, numerous Polish patriotic and classical works were given clandestinely, often by celebrated actors in private homes all over Cracow: altogether there were twenty-two performances of seven or eight different works, and over one hundred rehearsals. One day, however, Karol, who was one of the most talented of the younger actors, came to Kotlarczyk and said, "Please don't cast me anymore, I'm going to be a priest."

"After that," Mrs. Kotlarczyk went on, "he didn't

come to any rehearsals or performances but spent all his time studying. He used to pray a tremendous lot, and he was extremely hardy, I used to find him sleeping on bare floors. Every week he would go to visit his father's grave at the Rakowicki cemetery, and after he became a bishop he had the remains of his mother and his brother Edmund brought to Cracow and reburied there.

"As for girls, he always kept aloof from them. There was a relative of ours who stayed in the house for some time; he said once, 'She keeps on eyeing me, I wish you'd say something to her, it makes me feel awkward.' That was before he spoke to my husband, but I already had a presentiment that he wanted to be a priest. Of course he was good-looking and good company, and there were girls from time to time who took a fancy to him, but he never paid attention."

"How was it that you and your husband came to live in Karol's flat?"

"Karol didn't like being there after his father died, and at first he went to live with the Kydrynskis, but not for very long, perhaps partly because Mrs. Lewaj was also staying there—she used to teach him French before the war. When we moved into Karol's flat he came back there with us. That was when we started organizing the theater. We had to leave Wadowice in the first place because it was annexed to Germany and my husband was on the 'wanted' list for what they called anti-Nazi propaganda, so we came to Cracow and Karol invited us to share his place; he kept a small room for himself and gave us the bigger one.

"Karol is seven or eight years younger than I am, but my university studies were delayed by illness, and he and I went to some of the same lectures. He often used to turn up late in those days, and sometimes arrived in a disheveled state. In spite of the difference in our ages we knew each other fairly well in Wadowice—it only had four thousand people in those days, and we were close neighbors. We sometimes went to early Mass together before school, in Advent for instance. Karol would serve Mass, but not just one Mass at a time—as they reached different stages he would dodge from one altar to another.

"His brother Edmund was a medical student then. He used to take Karol to football matches, carrying him on his shoulders so that he could see better.

"Even as a boy Karol was interested in the theater, and he often used to visit the house where my parents and the Kotlarczyks lived—we met there hundreds of times. I remember once he came dashing into a room where a design for some scenery was lying on the floor, and dirtied it with his boots. He was terribly upset, and took off his boots and started cleaning it up at once.

"Do you know what I long to do?—to go to Rome just once and see Karol again. I'm sure he doesn't know how much we all think about him here, but he must miss Poland a little."

The day after my conversation with Mrs. Kotlarczyk it was announced that the Pope would be coming to Poland in June. The secretariat of the Polish episcopate issued a communiqué stating that Cardinal Wyszynski had sent an official letter on February 22 thanking the Pope for his willingness to visit Poland and expressing the hope that he would do so at an early date. A few days later the text of the Pope's letter to the Chairman of the Polish Council of State was released: "With my sincere thanks for your letter of March 2, I write to express my joy that I shall be able to come to Poland, my home country, from June 2 to 10, and shall be able during that time to perform the important duties that arise from my pastoral office in the Church."

24

Past and Present

1978–79

In September 1978 a delegation of the Polish episcopate
consisting of the Primate, Cardinal Wojtyla, Bishop
Wladyslaw Rubin and Bishop Stroba paid a five-day visit
to the Federal Republic of Germany. This was a further
step in the process of postwar reconciliation which the
Polish bishops inaugurated by a memorable appeal to
their German brethren in December 1965, at the conclusion of Vatican II. The presence of Cardinal Wyszynski,
famous for his stand against political pressure, aroused
keen interest in West Germany, to which it was his first
official visit. Cardinal Wojtyla, for his part, received com-
paratively little notice from the media, and he made no
attempt to steal the limelight.

At Fulda the whole German episcopate, headed by
Cardinal Höffner, assembled to meet the delegation in
front of the ancient Carolingian cathedral. In a sermon
next day Cardinal Wyszynski invoked the memory of St.
Boniface, the Anglo-Saxon evangelist of Germany whose
tomb is revered in the cathedral, and prayed that the visit

might help to heal the wounds of former times and of the recent past. In Cologne, which they next visited, the Polish bishops met representatives of Catholic social and charitable organizations including the Pater Maximilian Kolbe-Werk. An evening service in the cathedral attracted crowds such as had not been seen since President Kennedy's visit or Adenauer's funeral.

The next destination was Neviges, a small town near Wuppertal with a Marian shrine which has been venerated by generations of Polish miners and other workers in the Ruhr district and Westphalia. Pilgrimages continued even during the war until the Nazis stopped them in 1944, and resumed as early as 1946. The enormous church, built a few years earlier, was hardly big enough for the crowds of Poles that assembled on this occasion from all over North Germany and the Benelux countries, including the priests of over thirty Polish parishes. At Munich, where the enthusiasm was no less than at Cologne, the delegation visited the grave of Cardinal Döpfner to pay tribute to his work for the reconciliation of the German and Polish churches. Some of the bishops also went to Dachau, where in a chapel dedicated to the Agony of Christ a memorial tablet states that between 1939 and 1945 there were 35,600 Polish inmates of the camp including 1,777 priests; of these over 10,000, including more than 850 priests, lost their lives. Cardinal Wojtyla, celebrating Mass in the Frauenkirche at Munich, recalled the martyrdom at Auschwitz of Fr. Maximilian Kolbe and the German Carmelite nun Edith Stein, a philosopher and a convert from Judaism.

At Mainz the delegation paid homage to Bishop Wilhelm von Ketteler (1811-77), an early champion of workers' rights and the position of Catholics in the German state. Here Cardinal Wyszynski gave his only newspaper interview, declaring that Europe must beome a new Bethlehem and a cradle of peace instead of an arms factory. He said that the bishops' visit had shown that a new language of mutual understanding could be found, and had led to agreement on some controversial points. One of these was the position of priests coming from Poland to exercise their ministry in ordinary German parishes, thus relieving the shortage of priests in the Federal Republic. Another question was whether the Polish priests who had for many years been ministering to Poles in West Germany should be subject to the authority of the local German bishop or to the Polish hierarchy, represented in this case by Bishop Rubin in Rome.

Although the visit was treated as a purely religious occasion and received no official notice from German federal or local authorities, it was extensively reported by television and the press, and many individual politicians expressed enthusiasm at its results.

After his return from Germany, Karol spent a week or two in the Bieszczady Mountains and on the rivers of northwestern Poland. He celebrated the twentieth anniversary of his appointment as Bishop of Cracow on September 28, the feast day of St. Waclaw (Wenceslas of Bohemia), patron of the diocese, and spent the preceding day in meditation at Our Lady's shrine at Kalwaria Zebrzydowska, a famous place of pilgrimage not far from Cracow. He little knew that he would never again be free to visit this well-loved sanctuary as he pleased, or to enjoy carefree holidays in his native land.

Early in 1979 I went to Karol's birthplace of Wadowice—a little town of some 10,000 inhabitants with a typical onion-domed church, its interior resplendent with white walls and gilded baroque altars. The central nave is barrel-vaulted, and on the left is a chapel dedicated to Our Lady of Perpetual Help.

The Catholic center across the street was full of children attending religious classes. I entered the presbytery next door and asked for the parish priest, Mgr. Edward Zacher. While waiting I picked up a guidebook and read a few pages about the town. It was already *"oppidum"* in 1327, when it belonged to the dukes of Silesia, and fell to the Polish Crown in 1494. It was a center of crafts in the eighteenth century and of industry in the nineteenth. Under Austrian rule it became the capital of a rural district in 1867. Among its citizens were Marcin Wadowity, rector of the Cracow Academy and born here in 1567, and also Emil Zegadlowicz (1888–1941), a writer of the period between the two world wars who had left-wing sympathies. The high school, which in Karol's day bore Wadowity's name, had been renamed after Zegadlowicz, who founded a group of poets known as *Czartak* ("Watchtower") and wrote novels that were considered daring in their time. A monument was put up to him a few years ago, and there is a museum of his life and work in the neighboring village of Gorzen Gorny. The guidebook also informed me that the earliest part of the church dated from the fifteenth century and that on the outskirts of the town was an early nineteenth-century mansion in classical style, built by the local sheriff, Mikolaj Komorowski.

Soon Monsignor Zacher was free to receive me and to relate his reminiscences of Karol.

"Although Karol went to live in Cracow in 1938, he always kept in touch with us. He came here to celebrate his first Mass as a priest, and also as a bishop; on that occasion he pointed to the Sacred Heart altar and said, 'That is where my father and I used to pray.' He also came here especially to say Mass when he became archbishop and afterward cardinal. There was scarcely any year when he didn't come at least once. In 1970, on his fiftieth birthday, he consecrated a peal of new bells that I had ordered; I christened one of them Charles Borromeo, after the cardinal's patron saint. In 1977, on the fiftieth anniversary of my ordination, he came and preached at Mass and put a laurel wreath on my head.

"When the journalists descended on Wadowice after he became Pope they were agog to see if there was any kind of sensation or minor scandal to be discovered. I kept telling them that I had known him through and through, and that he was above reproach of any kind. I taught him from 1932, when I first came to Wadowice, until 1938. It's a small town, everybody knows everyone else's business, and if there had been anything out of the way I would have heard about it. Besides, for three years he was in charge of the college sodality, and I saw a lot of him that way.

"I remember Prince Sapieha once came to the school, and Karol made a welcoming speech which he had shown me beforehand. Afterward the cardinal said to me, 'Does that boy intend to become a priest?' I replied, 'Not as far as I know. He has a passion for the theater, and he's fascinated just now by Dr. Kotlarczyk.' 'That's a pity,' the cardinal replied."

We spoke about the transfer of the remains of Karol's mother from Wadowice to the Rakowicki military cemetery at Cracow, where members of her family (the Kaczorowskis) and the Wojtylas are buried in the eastern section, in Block VI. I had seen the graves on the previous All Saints' Day, when crowds of visitors had decked them with flowers and lighted candles. The inscription to Karol's brother Edmund, with his dates of birth and death (1906–32), recorded that he had been assistant resident physician at the municipal hospital at Bielsko and had sacrificed his life to the victims of an acute epidemic of scarlet fever.

I said I had always thought of Karol's father as an old man. "No," said Monsignor Zacher, "I remember clearly: he was born in 1879 and died in 1941. But he was in poor health and had to retire at an early age. He had been through the first war, and served in the Legions.* Karol's mother was only five years younger; she was about thirty-five when Karol was born."

Monsignor Zacher asked me to stay to lunch, after which we were joined by Mrs. Kotlarczyk's brother, a former schoolmate of Karol's (though older than he) named Opidowicz. The latter told me that his parents and the Kotlarczyk family had lived in the same apartment house; Mieczyslaw Kotlarczyk used to design theater sets at home, and Karol often came to see him there. "Later, in 1938, when my sister was studying Polish philology in Cracow, Mieczyslaw lived at Sosnowiec and used to visit Karol and his father in Tyniecka Street. He and Karol would often sit up talking until the small hours."

Monsignor Zacher showed me a long and affectionate message that he had received from the Pope in reply to congratulations from the Wadowice parish on his name day, November 4. I went around to have a look at the high school—a typical turn-of-the-century building, with large windows but rather small classrooms—and what had been Karol's primary school but was now a municipal office. After that I went to No. 2 Koscielna Street, alongside the church, which had been the Wojtylas' home until 1938 and now bore the proud inscription, "The Pope lived here." Apart from this it was unimpressive enough: a small gate, a dark and poky yard full of rather smelly dustbins, and inside the front door a steep, crooked flight of stone steps with an iron handrail, lead-

* The volunteer force raised by Pilsudski in Austrian Poland in 1914 as the nucleus of a future independent Polish army.

ing to the first floor. Here, off a long narrow balcony, was
the entrance to the Wojtylas' former home. It contained
one large room with several windows, three facing the
church and one overlooking the street, also a kitchen and
bathroom. The owner of the house, Mrs. Maria Putyrowa, explained to me that in the Wojtylas' day the
lavatory belonging to each flat had been located separately, off the main corridor; only afterward had the
rooms been repartitioned so that the flat was self-con-
tained. She and her husband had lived in it for some
time, though not immediately after the Wojtylas. Mrs.
Putyrowa, it turned out, was a semiretired teacher who
had lived at Wadowice for many years and had studied
Polish literature at the Catholic University of Lublin.
She showed me a visitors' book she had started to keep
shortly after the house became famous, with appreciative
comments in all languages, especially Italian. She had
been particularly impressed by a group from Naples; having left them alone for a few minutes in the large room,
she returned to find them on their knees in prayer.

I called on Boguslaw Banas—another schoolmate of
Karol's, two years younger than he—who formerly
worked at a power station and is now in the Highways
Department. His health was undermined by the Occupation; he was deported to forced labor in Germany, and
his father died at Auschwitz. Before the war his parents
kept a dairy and café, and he and Karol had been close
friends from an early age.

"Karol's father," he told me, "used to let down a milk
can from their window on a string, and I would fill it
with milk, so as not to have to climb up the stairs.
Where we lived there was a well on a hillside, and our
two mothers would sit there talking while we boys

played around it, or we would kick a football about the street."

I asked about Karol's school days, but he seemed preoccupied. Suddenly he interrupted a question of mine and said, "I must tell you one of my most frightful memories. As I told you, my parents kept a small bar, and there was a policeman who used to come in for a drink or two after duty. When he thought he had had too much, he would take off his revolver and leave it with my parents for safekeeping. They put it in the till, and it stayed there until he came for it next day. Once, when I was about thirteen, and Karol fifteen, I opened the till and saw it there. It was nothing new to me, I'd seen it a dozen times and never touched it, but that day for some reason I took it out. Karol was sitting on a bench opposite, with my brother beside him. I don't know what got into me, but I pointed the revolver at Karol and said, 'Hands up, or I'll shoot.' He was only about five or six yards away. I was joking, of course, but before I knew it I'd pulled the trigger and the gun went off. It was pointing straight at Karol, and it's a marvel I didn't kill him. The bullet missed him by a hair's breadth and broke a window. It woke my father from his afternoon sleep, and he came dashing in. I was standing there, green with terror, and Karol and my brother were frightened too. My father said nothing—he didn't beat me, just took the revolver without a word and put it away again. Even now, when I visualize the scene I get gooseflesh and think to myself, 'My God, I might have killed the Pope.'

"As for Karol, he said nothing about it either—he was like that. I knew he would be a priest, even in those days, in spite of the theater and all his other interests. And it wasn't just because he played at saying Mass, because small boys often do that."

"What form did the game take?"

"His mother had made him a sort of worsted cape, and over it he put a kind of alb or cotta and 'said Mass' at a homemade altar consisting of a table with a holy picture and two candles, with me and my younger brother as servers."

I called on Helena Szczepanska, who had been a friend and neighbor of Karol's mother. She told me proudly that at the age of eighty-eight she had become a film star, as TV crews had made a program in which she answered questions about the Pope.

"Karol's father was an official in the recruiting office, and his mother used to eke out his pay by sewing. She died in 1929, when she was forty-five and Karol nine; his elder brother Edmund died three years later. When I told him how sorry I was he answered, 'It was God's will.' He said it with such conviction that I was startled and impressed, even though I was thirty years older than he. When he was a baby in his carriage his brother Edmund, who was about fourteen, used to have to run errands all the time up and down those awful stairs—I kept hearing his mother telling him to fetch this, that and the other. Even in those days she used to say, 'This baby will be a great man someday.' Of course all mothers think that about their sons, but she said it with a kind of intensity I've never heard from anyone else. And I remembered her the other day, when I walked into the street and saw some Italians kneeling in the snow and praying in front of the house where the Pope had lived as a small boy."

I went into the church. Evening Mass was over; beside the font was a visitors' book with comments of all kinds, long and short, simple and profound. One, in a childish hand, read: "How happy I am to have been baptized in the font at which John Paul II became a member of the Roman Church." On the adjacent wall is a brass plate with a relief of St. John the Baptist and the words: "At this font there took place on June 20, 1920, the baptism of Karol Wojtyla, Cardinal of the Holy Roman Church, Archbishop and Metropolitan of Cracow, born at Wadowice on May 18, 1920, who, together with the faithful people of God, renewed the covenant of Holy Baptism and thanked God for the grace of faith on the occasion of a parish ceremony on November 27, 1966, in the jubilee year of the one thousandth anniversary of Christianity in Poland."

I visited Wadowice once again after reading in the press that the Pope had cordially welcomed the priest of his old parish at a Wednesday audience on March 14, 1979. Monsignor Zacher told me that the Pope had written inviting him to come and had insisted on his sitting on the dais, in the front row. He showed me the passage of the Pope's address welcoming the group of priests from Wadowice and expressing his joy at the prospect of visiting Poland in spring "at the time agreed upon by the state authorities and the Polish Episcopate." Referring to his Lenten address on prayer, the Pope continued, "Through prayer we are linked in a marvelous manner with our heavenly country and our Father, but also with our earthly country: for we always pray in our native tongue, and even if we are outside our country it is in prayer that our native speech endures the longest." Monsignor Zacher showed me with pride a golden medallion with Karol's likeness on one side and on the other, the Papal arms with his motto: *Totus tuus*. He went on to say that he had had the upper floor of the presbytery repainted and intended to put it at the Pope's disposal. Karol had promised to come to Wadowice and to say Mass on the market square in front of the church.

I asked if it was true that the Pope also intended to go to Auschwitz.

"Yes, I'm quite sure he will. Those who were murdered there surely deserve to have him come to them, more than anyone else."

On October 2, 1978, the day on which Karol left Cracow to attend the funeral of John Paul I, I went to ask his permission to spend a week at Münster preparing a book of mine for publication. He agreed, but added, "Why don't you come to Rome for the conclave?"

I replied, "I would be glad to, but I haven't really got an excuse. Jerzy Turowicz will be there for *Tygodnik Powszechny*. Of course, if you give an order . . ."

"No, it isn't an order, but it would be nice to be able to talk to you there."

"I should like it, of course. Especially as this time there's every chance . . ."

He smiled, gave me a mocking glance and disappeared.

We met next day at Cracow airport, whence we both flew to Warsaw. Karol was leaving for Rome on the fourth; Cardinal Wyszynski was to follow two days later, after a conference of the Polish episcopate.

At Münster I stayed, as usual, with the Franciscan nuns. I kept feeling, however, that I ought to be in Rome. As the day of the conclave approached, speculations in the press and radio were on similar lines to those in August, but there was also a feeling that the new Pope should be familiar with the Roman Curia and should be physically fit enough to stand the strain of his position. One heard some names of archbishops who were not cardinals, such as Bellestrero of Turin, and of non-Italian cardinals such as Pironio of the Argentine, Basil Hume and Wojtyla.

The last session of the Congregation of Cardinals was held on Friday October 13. Next day, in St. Peter's, Cardinal Villot celebrated Mass *"pro eligendo Pontifice."* The conclave on Sunday the fifteenth was inconclusive, as was that on the Monday morning. Finally, late on Monday afternoon the chimney over the Sistine Chapel began to pour out white smoke . . .

Index